GUIDE TO
WHITETAIL
STRATEGIES

Shooter's Bible

GUIDE TO
WHITETAIL
STRATEGIES

DEER HUNTING SKILLS, TACTICS, AND TECHNIQUES

PETER FIDUCCIA

SKYHORSE PUBLISHING

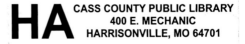

Skyhorse Publishing books may be purchased in bulk at special discounts for sales promotion, corporate gifts, fund-raising, or educational purposes. Special editions can also be created to specifications. For details, contact the Special Sales Department, Skyhorse Publishing, 307 West 36th Street, 11th Floor, New York, NY 10018 or info@skyhorsepublishing.com.

Skyhorse® and Skyhorse Publishing® are registered trademarks of Skyhorse Publishing, Inc.®, a Delaware corporation.

www.skyhorsepublishing.com

10 9 8 7 6 5 4 3 2 1

Library of Congress Cataloging-in-Publication Data is available on file.
ISBN: 978-1-61608-358-8

Printed in China

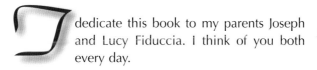 dedicate this book to my parents Joseph and Lucy Fiduccia. I think of you both every day.

CONTENTS

INTRODUCTION

*I*f you've never been to a sportsmen's show or outdoor exposition, you don't know what you've been missing. Typically held in a huge hall or event center, these shows usually take place in January, February, and March, when most of us are getting serious cases of cabin fever. These shows help us make it through to Spring.

At a recent expo in Suffern, New York, I wandered up and down the aisles, jostling my way through the crowds as I checked out all the outfitter booths. With representatives from Canada, South America, Africa, Alaska, and the lower 48, these booths—with promises of trophy fish, game, and adventure—give you a serious case of the daydreams. Maybe I could save my money and actually hunt for kudu this year in Botswana. Maybe this is the year to sign up for that salmon trip to Russia that I've wanted to take. Or, maybe I'll try that bowhunting lodge in Illinois that always produces Pope & Young whitetails.

After going by all those booths, after inspecting all the new gear that everyone is coming out with this year (it's better than last year's!), I found myself at the Peter Fiduccia–The Deer Doctor's booth, near the hall's entranceway. And there, as he has been for 26 years, was Peter Fiduccia. The inevitable line was also there, with guys wanting to talk with Peter about deer hunting. One guy hadn't gotten a buck in five years, and wanted to know what he'd been doing wrong. Another hunter shot a huge 10-pointer last season, and wanted to tell Peter all about it. Still another hunter had his 14-year-old son with him. He wanted to ask Peter if his son could take a photo with him and of course, Peter smiled widely and said "It would be my pleasure."

Peter, as always, was fielding every question, giving advice when he could, listening to success stories because he was genuinely interested, and telling his own stories when people asked how his hunting was last year.

Also in the booth were his son, Cody, who's an honors student entering his senior year at Hartwick College in Oneonta, New York, and Peter's wife, Kate, an accomplished author and video producer. While Peter was talking to people, Cody (who got a nice 10-pointer last season) and Kate were helping customers buy what they needed at their booth . . . some

of Peter's hunting books or Kate's game cookbooks, DVDs on calling and rattling, grunt calls, deer drags, rattling antlers, hunting knives, a plethora of stuff we all can't be without in hunting season.

At 2 o'clock, Kate nudged Peter and whispered into his ear, "You're almost late for your whitetail strategies seminar," she said. "You'd better get moving." And he did, telling the remaining folks in line that he had to go give his seminar, and why didn't they come along? Many did. Peter's been giving deer hunting seminars at this show (and others throughout the Northeast) for years, and he always packs the house. I know, because I've had trouble finding an empty seat in the past. The same happened this year, but I did find some standing room along a side wall. Peter entered the room.

"Hey fellas, who got a deer last season?" he asked, looking around the audience. Hands went up here and there. "Well, you guys better give this seminar, because I didn't get a buck, so you're probably more qualified to talk about hunting than I am."

"Yeah, right," someone answered back, as friendly laughter emanated from the crowd. But then Peter launched into his seminar. No, he didn't get a deer last year. Why? Because he was after one specific buck, and that deer didn't cross his path. "I was out checking his core area last week, though, and I jumped him," Peter said. "He had dropped his antlers, of course, but I'd recognize that huge body anywhere. It's nice to know he made it through the season. He could be a 145-class buck when the next season comes.

"And that's the point," he said. "I don't shoot the first buck that crosses my path . . . unless, of course, he's a keeper . . . but because I'm at our farm almost every weekend, by hunting season I know which specific buck I'm after, I know where he lives, I know what he does, and when, all before the season starts. Scouting . . . it's the beginning of what could be your most successful season . . ."

I listened as he went on, describing how a hunter needs to create an illusion through the use of scents, antler rattling, using deer calls, and unusual decoys to make deer react. "You want that buck to react instinctively; you want to make him so interested that he'll come in with his guard down and looking to find whatever illusion you have created for him."

He also talked about being innovative, about using such things as deer tails on strings to catch the attention of passing bucks. Or how about plastic scented apples? Put them down and hang a few on branches and they'll attract deers' curiosity even in areas where apples do not grow. Peter discoursed on one smart hunting idea after another, with the crowd riveted to his every word.

The hour flew by, and before I knew it the seminar was over. It went so fast because Peter is always animated, walking back and forth, conversing with the audience, demonstrating calls, grunting, snorting, answering one question after another, posing his own to members of the audience. When Peter stepped down from the stage, a crowd of people followed him to his booth for more of the same.

There are a lot of so-called deer hunting experts in this country. Some of them are full of hot air, some are the real deal. Peter is the latter. Throughout the Northeast, in particular, he is a well-known commodity, someone who knows whitetail deer hunting, someone who has a passion for it and studies it, dissects it, thinks about it, and then devises new and better theories on how to hunt. The best part is that he is willing to convey his knowledge to anyone who wants to know.

Now he has come up with "The Shooters Bible Guide to Whitetail Strategies." I've read his other books and frankly, I didn't really think there was anything else he could write about. Hasn't he already covered it all? The answer is an emphatic no.

In this "Shooters Bible" guide, Peter takes whitetail hunting to an even higher level.

Here, you'll see that he has come up with never-before-published theories on the rut. From his exhaustive research, Peter has figured out that some ruts are vastly different than others. It's all based on his theory about Perihelion and Aphelion, a phenomenon in which the earth moves toward the sun, and back, over an 11-year period. How close or far the earth is from the sun will directly affect how active the rut will be. Don't believe that? Check out chapter 5, and you will. And you'll also learn how to hunt the different ruts, depending on where the earth is in relation to the sun.

Want tips that are relevant now, in the 21st century? There are thousands of them in these pages. Thinking about planting a food plot? Peter has planted many of them in his farm in upstate New York, and he'll not only tell you exactly what types of crops to plant, but how to plant them, and where. Want sound advice on deer management? Peter covers that too. Want to buy some hunting land? Peter gives tips and advice on how to find and purchase the best land for deer (and other wildlife), how to get it at a fair price, and how to manage it once it's yours–all through his own trial and error.

Tactics, gear, scouting, field dressing, cooking tips and recipes–they're all here, presented in a format that's easy to read and understand. And if you've got a question, e-mail Peter at peter@fiduccia.com. He answers every email he receives, because that's what he does. He wouldn't do it any other way.

Jay Cassell
Senior Editor
Skyhorse Publishing
New York, New York
May 2011

PREFACE

What It's All About

All too often we are lead to believe that deer, especially mature bucks, have the ability to think and reason. How foolish is that? Deer do not possess the power of thought and reason. They survive entirely on their instinctive behaviors.

A mature buck isn't a wise and scholarly animal as so many writers like to make him out to be. These writers unintentionally mislead hunters into thinking that the odds of taking such a stealthy creature with consistent success are very low. Friends–nothing, and I mean nothing–about deer hunting can be further from the truth.

Deer are only creatures of habit. They live their lives and survive by either avoiding danger or making a fatal mistake and walking into it.

Big, mature bucks do not grow old from brain power. Nor do they become trophy-class bucks by being foolhardy. Actually, they get to be wall-hangers by simply being nervous wrecks! I strongly believe that some buck fawns are born with a gene that makes them more scared of everything around them than other fawns.

As fawns, these "nervous wreck" bucks are frightened out of their hooves by the snap of a twig. When a crow cries out a warning they heed it instantly and run off. If a doe makes an alarm-distress snort, this type of

What it's all about . . . Here my son Cody poses with his first 8-point buck taken on our farm. It's all about family, friends, and fun. Isn't it?

fawn buck doesn't wait to respond. Instead, on the first sound he is heading at warp 9.9 into the closest available secure cover. This reaction to an alarm-distress snort remains with him the rest of his natural life.

As he gets older, this condition only intensifies. Now he doesn't second guess anything. Every little sound, odor, or noise he encounters from moment to moment is taken seriously. He lives his life worrying about predators. Because of this he becomes a loner and–by accident–a survivor. By no means is this from brain power–but by a finely tuned instinctive behavior that makes him more sensitive to danger and his surroundings than other bucks that were not blessed with this over-sensitive gene.

As a 2½ year old, if he smells danger, he doesn't run–he's too scared. Instead, he holds tight hoping the danger will not detect him and pass him by. If he hears a noise, he freezes and remains motionless until he decides to either run or hide. If he sees danger approaching, he slips away quietly with his tail tucked between his legs into the thickest of cover. His nerves only fray more and more as he gets older making him less apt to be seen as other bucks are. In reality, he is nothing more than what we would term a scaredy-cat. He certainly doesn't possess the power or reason or intellect to be anything but that.

My point is that hunters have to believe that we are capable of taking deer no matter what size their antlers are or how old the deer is. If not, we're half way on our way to failure as consistently successful deer hunters.

In this book, I will address the type of tactics that hunters can use to increase their chances of taking a trophy buck. Now let's be clear here. A trophy buck can be a buck that has eight points, a 16-inch wide rack, and is 3½ years old. This is especially true in New England and the Northeast where hunters stalk the most pressured bucks in the country.

All too often you are led to believe by many pros (who own and hunt their own 1,000 private acre pieces of land) that you are doing something wrong in the deer woods and that is why you are not taking the type of trophies they are. Hog wash. They are hunting un-pressured areas and so their deer get older and have better racks. They're also hunting in areas where the soil is highly conducive to developing trophy-size bucks.

I challenge any of them to come to New York, Pennsylvania, New Jersey, Connecticut, Massachusetts, New Hampshire and Vermont, and take the type of trophy-class bucks you see them bag on television and on their DVDs. I'll bet bucks to donuts that they will not be able to produce any better than you do my friends.

The number one factor in taking big bucks consistently isn't anything else and I include a hunter's skills, tactics, woodsmanship aptitude, or any other element– it is only the ability to hunt areas that have little to no pressure. Don't let anyone else tell you anything differently. Big bucks are just as likely to be killed as small bucks are as long as they are not dealing with heavy hunting pressure.

With that in mind, now use your seasoned, heavy hunting pressured experience, and take it to the next level by applying plain old common sense to your deer hunting strategies. The end result is going to be seeing and bagging more bucks.

And remember, any buck or doe is a trophy as long as it is a trophy in your mind. It doesn't matter what I think, or your hunting buddies think, or what you think you have to live up to regarding deer hunting. If you're happy with the hunt and the animal, you'll have a memory for a lifetime and a successful hunt. By keeping the fun in deer hunting–it will become less stressful and more enjoyable. Another benefit here is that the more fun it is, the more likely your wife or children will want to join you. Now there's some food for thought.

This buck will not roam too far from his core area, especially early in the fall. Later on, when the rut is in full swing, he will be tempted to search for does out of the comfort of his core area. (credit: Ted Rose)

Section I

ADVANCED TACTICS

ADVANCED TACTICS

1. Buck Core Areas

*I*f you started reading this book without reading the preface, please don't. What I wrote in the preface is *the* most relevant information in the book. I strongly suggest you read it *before* you read anything else.

There has always been a lot of confusion about the term "core area." Basically, a core area is where a deer beds, feeds, and waters throughout most of the year. A mature buck uses this area throughout most of his life. A core area should not be confused with the term "home range." Home range is everywhere a deer goes throughout the year. For a buck, that includes areas he visits on a transient basis during the rut. During this period he may leave the security of his core area and venture greater distances to locate receptive does. Although a buck may leave his core area during the

rut, studies have proven that it is rare that he will venture from his home range even to locate hot does.

One of the only elements that may make a buck leave his home range is when a younger buck's home range includes a mature buck's home range as well. When an older buck consistently has run-ins with a subordinate buck, the younger buck realizes the only way he will get an opportunity to breed an estrus doe is to leave his home range or leave that older buck's core area. That's when a hunter may get to see really big bucks in sections of land where they've never been seen before.

Over the years, my success with taking mature bucks (remember that in some areas, like New York, a mature buck may only be a 120- to 125-class buck) can be directly linked to having a basic understanding of a

▼ Mature bucks like this fellow will remain in their core area as much as possible. They only venture from it to find receptive does, food or if they are continually disturbed.
(credit: Ted Rose)

ADVANCED TACTICS

◀ A core area provides comfort, security, food, water, and thick cover that offer an ideal place to bed out of harm's way. (credit: Ted Rose)

buck's core area. Any hunter who consistently takes mature bucks understands the importance of locating and hunting buck core areas. The more you learn about buck core areas the more success you will have in taking older deer.

While most hunters who consider themselves trophy hunters and have heard the term "core area" many times, there are a lot of hunters who are not familiar with the term. So, let's clarify the difference between "core area" and "home range."

Defining a Core Area to the Nth Degree

Core areas are places occupied by whitetail bucks outside of the rut. This is when they are not seeking out receptive does or struggling with predators, deep snow, lack of food, etc. A buck will spend the majority of his time feeding, watering, bedding, and traveling within

▼ Core areas come in all sizes depending on the buck that chooses the location. A primary consideration for the buck selecting a core area is that it offers thick cover. (credit: Ted Rose)

the boundaries of his core area. This is the best way I know to describe a core area. Some might add slightly more to that explanation–but the truth is a core area is nothing more than what I described above.

I'm often asked, "Just how big is a core area?" That is a loaded question as no two core areas will ever be the same size. There are just too many elements that dictate how much deer dirt each individual buck will use as his core area. The most significant factor is whether or not the area has enough *bedding cover* in relation to available food and water.

When I have jumped mature bucks during the day, I found them to be in cover, within rock-throwing distance of a currently available primary food source where he has established a small core area. When a buck has to travel a long distance from his bedding area to his feeding area, his core area will be much larger. This is often true of bucks that live in what easterners term big woods–woods that are found in Maine and in New York's Adirondack Mountains. Deer that live near or on farmlands or in suburban areas do not fit into this category.

As most hunters know, during the summer months and into very early fall, whitetail bucks hang out in bachelor groups and stick close to home. They spend the majority of their time bedding, traveling, and feeding within their core areas and extended home range. Once the bachelor groups start breaking up, however, this changes.

Core Area Relocating

Bucks begin to test their position within the herd by sparring with other bucks. This competition is often the main reason why bachelor groups break up. This isn't a secret but there is an observable fact that is not as widely known.

Some hunters and researchers feel that when bachelor groups break up, the bucks simply move off short distances and take up residency there. While I find this true in some cases, some biologists suggest that bucks will relocate long distances from their summer areas.

Some say mature bucks in velvet have a tendency to become a lot less visible once they shed their velvet. Most believe that the bucks simply go into a more reclusive fall lifestyle. The fact is, however, the bucks have just relocated and established their core areas

away from where they had been spending their summer time. Again, this can mean that the core area is relatively close by or even miles from where they lived while they were in velvet.

You can take this to the deer bank–most of you have experienced seeing bucks during the late summer and into September and noticed how they turn into less visible bucks as fall progresses. This is is more evident if a buck happens to be a subordinate member of the bachelor group.

When a young buck of 1½ to 2½ years old starts to get intimidated by a mature buck of 3½ or 4½ years old, he begins to get the message that it is time for him to relocate. This is more evident once the playful pushing and shoving of late summer turns into more staid pushing, shoving and even fighting in the early fall. The smaller bucks within the bachelor group only take so much mistreatment by the mature bucks before they instinctively understand it is time to move off and establish their own core areas.

Core Areas Do Change

It is also important to understand that bucks do not stay within the same core area all year, especially during the big chase period of the three rut cycles. Contrary to what you have read, heard, or believe, a whitetail buck will suddenly decide to relocate during the early fall transition period and take up residency in a completely different area. Often, this is where you'll find the majority of the buck's rub lines and scrape lines.

Tom Indrebo, who has written a book for my publishing company Woods N' Water Press titled *Growing & Hunting Quality Bucks*, lives and hunts in one of the most trophy-rich areas of the county–Buffalo County, Wisconsin. Along with operating a trophy-hunting deer camp called Bluff Country Outfitters, Tom has spent thousands of hours observing, recording and video taping mature whitetail bucks. Tom is a valid deer expect who knows all aspects of deer behavior, biology and management. He is very savvy about bucks and their core areas.

In his book, Tom places great importance on the role that food, cover and water seem to play in a buck choosing his core-area location. Tom's research has showed there's often a big difference between summer core areas and pre-rut core areas of bucks.

The problem for most of us who hunt pressured areas of the east like New York, Pennsylvania, New Jersey, Connecticut, Massachusetts and the like, is that it is almost a sure bet that it will be very difficult to find a mature buck after he relocates. No matter whether you are hunting private land or public land, odds are that a big buck will relocate on property you don't have permission to hunt! We all know the reality to that scenario. The only way to find a buck that has relocated onto private land is to try to get permission to hunt the land the buck has taken up residency on.

Reasons Why Bucks Move

As I said, conflicts with older bucks are at the top of the list on why a big buck suddenly decides to take up a living area in a new location. Other elements that will make bucks seek out new core areas are changes in their preferred food sources. Loss of habitat also plays a big role in the reasons why buck relocate. But very high on the list is pressure from humans.

As any hunter who has consistently killed mature bucks understands, mature whitetail bucks will take only very little pressure from humans during the early fall and especially during the high pressure of hunting season. Simple scouting ventures are enough to

▼ We built this pond on our farm to provide a reliable water source for our deer and other wildlife. Ponds (and even small watering pot holes) are crucial to deer during the chase period of rut when bucks and does become dehydrated.

▲ This buck has clearly ventured from the safety of his core area to tend this doe. Bucks often establish more than one core area to use during different times of the year. (credit: Ted Rose)

warn any mature buck about what is to start and their immediate instinctive response it to move out of the pressured area. Sometimes they do not move far off, however, sometimes they move quite a distance away.

Just how much human presence is too much pressure for a mature buck to tolerate before he decides to relocate? I can guarantee you can take this to the deer hunting bank–not much at all, especially in heavily populated or hunted areas. This is especially true with a buck of the temperament I described earlier in the book–you know the buck I refer to as the type of buck that grew up being afraid of his own shadow. This type of buck leaves with the least amount of pressure applied to his area while a buck that doesn't inherit the "scaredy-cat" gene is more reluctant to relocate.

For the "scaredy-cat" buck, it may only take more than one or two intrusions into his home range or a single incursion into his bedding area to alert the buck to abandon his core area. A more relaxed mature buck may either tolerate several intrusions before relocating or simply adjust his travel and hiding routines and

decide not to move at all. It is the mature buck that has grown up to be spooky of everything that turns out to be the buck that will be most likely to relocate the quickest when pressure is applied to his home range or core area.

The Importance of Water

Too many hunters pay little attention to one of the most crucial elements when it comes to whitetails and their daily lives as well as their penchant on selecting a core-area location. Over the years, I've seen times, especially in dry years, when whitetails have abandoned their core areas and established other core areas, all based on the lack of wanting to be near a reliable water source.

When I first purchased my farm it was during a major two year long drought. The deer were leaving my property and taking up residence on the neighbor's 250 acre farm because he had several small watering holes, as well as a couple of large ponds. It didn't take me long to figure out that I had to give them a few reliable watering sources if I wanted them to feel comfortable enough to remain on my land. I built a good size pond that had several underground springs and also dug several pot holes with underground springs that afforded year round water even in dry years. If you have land you lease or own, this is a very important element to consider in providing your resident deer with watering options that do not require having them leave your property.

Keep in mind that it isn't always dry weather that influences bucks to relocate to find water. Several years ago, flooding wrecked havoc with several of my fields and low ground areas that were ideal bedding places for my deer. The extensive flooding forced the deer to find other areas, abandoning places where they had lived on my farm for years. It didn't take long to figure out that in this circumstance, deer will seek higher, dryer ground which helped me to pinpoint their new core areas quickly.

The Rut Keeps 'Em Moving

One of the most instinctive reasons for a buck to abruptly depart from his core area is the breeding season. The instinct to breed can not only take bucks from their home ranges for long distances—sometimes miles, but also for several days or weeks at a time as well. This usually happens in areas where the buck to doe ratio is out of whack and the bucks have to search high and wide for receptive does. In areas where the ratio is more balanced, the tendency to roam far and wide to locate hot does is much less dramatic. After the rut is finished and bucks have made it through the rigors of breeding, have safely avoided being killed and successfully dodged getting hit by cars as they cross roads in search of does, most mature bucks will return to their core areas they used during the pre-rut period unless they have found a more secure area that offers better food, water, security and less competition from other mature bucks.

However, once safely back in their familiar haunts, bucks will start traveling along the same routes they used prior to the rut. Until they get comfortable with their core area again, many times they will only move under the cover of darkness–for a few weeks anyway.

It is important to remember that it is entirely probable that some mature bucks establish separate core areas during the four seasons of the year. Why some bucks do this is an enigma not only to me, but to a lot of biologists with whom I have discussed this. I suspect it is most likely related to the availability or lack of food, water, and cover though.

If you take the time to figure out where mature bucks prefer to feed, water and bed, and the routes they use to get to and from these destinations, you will immediately improve your deer hunting success. The wise hunter learns all they can about a buck's core area. It has been one of the most overlooked and misunderstood aspects of deer hunting–hopefully after reading this I have set you on the right track about core areas.

2. Nocturnal Bucks

How many times have you heard the phrase, "He went nocturnal"? If you have been hunting deer for any length of time, you have probably heard it more than once. The term refers to a buck, that for a variety of reasons, never moves during daylight hours at all, not even during the rut. Deer that fit into this category supposedly never leave the safety and security of their bedding areas during daylight hours–not for any reason! It doesn't take much sense to figure out that these "nocturnal bucks" are therefore impossible to kill.

OK. At the risk of being controversial, let me say that is a bunch of hog-crap. You can go to the deer bank with the fact that there isn't a single buck alive that moves exclusively at night without any movement whatsoever during legal hunting hours. In believing that, you are limiting your potential not only as a deer hunter, but also as a successful deer hunter and that is a fact.

With that said, there are some bucks (usually mature deer) that live in heavily hunted areas and restrict their movements to the cover of darkness. Most of their daylight travel is limited to moving during the first few minutes of dawn and the last few moments at dusk. Or, at least that is what we are told to believe. Trust me, that simply is not the case. At least part of the time during daylight hours, even the most cautious buck will move about.

Many other whitetail experts agree that nocturnal bucks (deer that do the majority of their movement under the cover of darkness), travel during daylight hours sometimes–making them susceptible to being taken by hunters.

I've learned time and time again that there are bucks who adapt to various degrees of nocturnal behavior. I have also seen hunters suspect that a buck has gone nocturnal, when he really hasn't. The problem with believing that bucks go totally nocturnal is that it provides many hunters with an unconscious reason (notice I didn't

◀ Do a lot of mature bucks end up "going nocturnal"? Not so, says the Deer Doctor. (credit: Ted Rose)

ADVANCED TACTICS

say excuse) to give up on hunting a particular buck in a given area where they have become less visible during daylight hours. This one factor is a major reason why many hunters end up not killing a buck during the season. They are convinced they have no valid chance of taking a buck that is nocturnal in his movements. They end up missing terrific hunting opportunities for all types of bucks, including mature deer. My advice is to take the phrase "nocturnal buck" out of your deer hunting vocabulary, or at least take it with a grain of salt!

Off-Hour Movement Patterns

Several years ago while in Saskatchewan, Canada, I shot a 16-point trophy whitetail buck that ended up scoring 198 5/8 Boone and Crockett (B&C) points on a hunt. I saw the buck three times during that hunt and all three times it was between 11:30 am and 2:30 pm! Despite the fact that I was in my stand before daylight and hunted until legal light was over, I only saw the buck during off-hours, instead of the prime times of dusk and dawn.

On this hunt, I was using an estrus doe blat and I managed to call an estrus doe in all three times. Each time the doe came in, the buck was close behind her. It wasn't until the final day of the hunt–three days after I had seen the buck for the second time–that I called in another hot doe. She ran across an overgrown field that was about 200 hundred yards long. As she got to my position, she passed me and went down an embankment behind me looking for the other doe.

As soon as the doe was out of sight, the huge buck instantly broke out of the woods. On a dead run, he chased after the doe across the open field. With a loud alarm blat, I slowed him up enough to take my shot. I shot this 6½ year old, 16-point buck in the middle of the day. So much for the theory of big bucks moving only during the night.

Some researchers have discovered that mature does and bucks have three peak times they seek water and browse. Those times are 7 am, 11 am, and 6 pm While they may only move short distances for short periods of time to drink and browse, during the rut (when they get dehydrated from chasing each other) they may move to water more often and end up moving for longer periods during these times as well.

Deer remain bedded most of the day chewing cud. But they are instinctively motivated to stand up, stretch, and move short distances several times a day which is directly tied to their metabolism and cud-chewing habits. Being in the right spot during these movement times can pay off in big dividends.

Of course, many hunters fall into the trap of hunting pressured deer at the edge of fields along a planted agricultural field or a food plot (which is always a no-no). The problem here is that it only takes a mature buck or doe one bad encounter to figure out that they can't go to the field during day light hours.

If you want to ambush a deer in a heavily hunted area leading to a field, you must plan to do so from inside the woods. Post in a position that will allow the buck to reach you before darkness falls. Move your stand further back from the field by 100 yards or more into the thickest cover available to you. Many times, this means setting up just outside of a bedding area. If it is done correctly, this can be the most lethal of all ways to take a buck that is traveling during the low light of dusk and dawn. It can also be a deadly tactic to ambush a buck that is moving only during the off-hours mentioned above.

Creative Strategies for "Nocturnal" Bucks

Many times the area that a buck uses is small and difficult to approach without spooking him or other deer. When this happens, you may want to try a tactic

ADVANCED TACTICS

that has worked for me. Enter the area in the middle of the day and set up your stand. Most times you will end up spooking the deer from their beds. Then, don't hunt the stand for a few days. Return to the stand long before daylight when you decide to hunt it. Now, it all boils down to whether or not the buck returns and beds down in the same spot as it did before. If he does, you are in the perfect setup for a shot.

An alternate strategy if he doesn't return at the crack of dawn, hunt until you want to leave and then don't return to the stand for at least several days. The next time you go to it, however, arrive no earlier than 9:30 am. Still-hunt in to the stand as quietly as you can. Then hunt it until 1:30 pm. I'm going to bet that if you try this plan, you will see a good buck moving off-hours during your post.

The key factor to taking a so-called "strictly nocturnal buck" is pinpointing exactly where that deer is bedding and trying to call, rattle, decoy, or ambush him during off-hours.

A crucial element to taking a buck like this is not only to arrive at your stand without being detected, but you must also take every precaution not to leave any evidence that you've penetrated his sanctuary. Before entering, clean the soles of your boots (rubber or leather) with a non-scented soap. Wear clean clothing and spray it with an odor eliminator. Take a shower with unscented hunters soap before you leave and cover your approach ever so slowly.

Remember you only get one shot at fooling a mature buck in his core area. If you blow it, you better not plan on going back for at least several days or more. If he detects you the second time, the hunt is over. Go look for another buck in another area. This buck will really give you nightmares now.

Fellow hunter Jay Cassell rattles from a stand more than 100 yards from the nearest field. That's a good location to catch a mature buck moving toward the fields late in the afternoon.
▶

▲ I like to grunt softly rather than loudly and aggressively. By keeping my tone and volume natural sounding, I have had consistent calling success for over 40 years.

Call or Rattle During Off-Hours

Trying to kill a sly semi-nocturnal buck (that's a more practical term) can be done but it takes a little more planning. You will have to take all the same precautions I mentioned above and then some.

Now is the time to employ my favorite tactic by creating the entire illusion! If you're hunting a buck who is moving only during the start and finishing minutes of dawn and dusk or during the off-hours, he obviously isn't going to come trotting out of his bedding area with his guard down unless you make him do so! So how do you make a daylight-shy buck leave his bedding area? Create the illusion–that's how. Often that means using a decoy tail, rattling antlers or a variety of deer calls other than a grunt tube (if you have any of my other books you can read the detailed chapters on using deer calls or you can order my deer calling DVD, *"Tactics for Talking to Deer–How to Effectively Use Grunt, Blat, Bleat, and Snort Calls"* by going to my website www.deerdoctor.com).

As I mentioned, don't start by using a grunt call. Begin with a soft, guttural doe estrus blat. Make the call from several different directions. If you don't get a response, then add a soft grunt vocalization (never make an aggressive loud grunt in this situation).

You can also make a mock rub or scrape near the bedding area. Sometimes a buck will be lured out simply by the sounds of rustling leaves or a visual sighting of a fresh rub in his bedding area. To create the entire illusion here, use appropriate scents as well.

But regardless of whether you choose to use rattling antlers, grunt calls, bleat calls, or any combination thereof, your basic strategy for attempting to call in a nocturnal buck should remain the same. Always use extreme care when approaching your stand. Take every possible preventative measure to avoid spooking other deer. Also, avoid making any unnatural noises like clinking metal on metal, or coughing, talking on your walkie-talkie, etc. That last one should have been a no-brainer–yes?

Before making any deer vocalizations, let things settle down for awhile so the natural behavior of the squirrels and other wildlife has returned to normal. When you are dealing with a mature buck, it is wise to never over-call. When you're trying to call in a semi-nocturnal buck, you can bet your deer stand you will definitely lose him if you over-call.

If there's one place where calling, rattling, or decoying too frequently can be disadvantageous to your chances for success, near a bedding area is the place! If a buck is in the mood to come in, he'll respond to your first good effort or he'll ignore it.

You should also remember that you're dealing with a buck that has inherited the "nervous wreck gene." That is probably why he is mostly nocturnal to begin with. Anything you do to make him even more spooky than normal will cause him to leave the bedding area post haste. These types of bucks are inclined to move around during daylight, but they do so cautiously. But once these deer sense the least bit of human pressure, their behavior quickly changes.

Lastly, there is always a chance that a buck you think has gone into a strict nocturnal movement pattern actually really hasn't. I promise you this happens more often than most hunters care to believe. Misinformation regarding nocturnal bucks and their bedding areas often results in not filling your buck tag for the season.

Selecting a certain buck and ending up killing it whether he's nocturnal or not can prove to be a tough ordeal. I can promise you this, if you are hunting in an area where the deer is not bedding it may prove to be impossible!

If you are still not convinced that mature bucks do not go completely nocturnal consider this, if they did, how are all the Boone & Crockett bucks and other record-book bucks killed during legal hunting hours?

▲ Is there any truth to the old saying that big-antlered bucks are the only bucks that make big rubs and scrapes? Read on to find out. (credit: Ted Rose)

3. Rubs, Scrapes & Antler Size

One of the ongoing arguments and misnomers about deer hunting is the relationship between the size of a rub and a scrape to the body and antler size of the buck that made it. The old-timers (actually that's me now), but I mean the old-timers from the 1950s through the 1970s, believed and promoted that the larger the scrape and rub were–the bigger the buck was who made it. While that is certainly true to some degree, it is absolutely not always factual.

With the continuing research about whitetails and their behavior, biology, and habitat, it has been noted over the last 30 years that big bucks (mature bucks 3½ years old and older) often rub small saplings. This behavior begins early in the first stages of the pre-rut which usually starts around the 10th of October give or take several days.

It has also been documented that mature bucks often make small scrapes especially if they are the early false scrapes. False scrapes are the scrapes that appear in mid-October suddenly. One day there isn't any sign, the next day there are dozens of small circular scrapes that soon dry up and are unused. Mature bucks also make common secondary scrapes–the scrapes you find in a line in November that are found along fence rows, social areas, logging roads, and the like. Primary scrapes are much larger than the aforementioned scrapes and are usually made by mature bucks. Most hunters recognize this, so there is less confusion among hunters about what size (actually age class) buck made them.

Most of the time, a rub can provide more information about a buck's age-class, body size, and the potential size of his antlers than scrapes. When you find larger than normal false and secondary scrapes, it isn't indicative that a mature buck made them. A large scrape may only mean that several bucks attended it and pawed it into an ever-widening size. The old belief that only one buck makes a rub and scrape and only he uses it is just an absolute fairly tale. Rubs and scrapes are meant to be olfactory and visual sign posts in the deer's world. As such, they are often used by several bucks. You can take that fact to the deer hunting bank!

Most pre-rut rubbing is carried out by what many biologists and hunters refer to as dominant bucks. I would like to clarify that definition for you. There is no such animal as the "dominant" buck. Not in the true sense of the meaning of dominance in the whitetail's world anyway. True dominance is relevant for animals like wolves (canines) and lions (felines) who urine-

This buck is working the over-hanging branch above his scrape. He is depositing scent from his vomeronasal gland in the roof of his mouth, from his preorbital gland in the corner of his eye and from his forehead gland. (credit: Ted Rose) ▶

▲ The aggressive body language of this buck helps him avoid blood-shed by showing his high ranking in the pecking order through posturing. (credit: Ted Rose)

mark their territory. If the area they have stalked out as "their own turf" is trespassed on by another of their species they react immediately by physically engaging the violator–many times with enough "extreme prejudice" to kill the intruder. If the transgressor is not killed, he is severely beaten up and chased until he departs across the scent line that marks the territory of the other animal. This is a much more accurate way of describing dominance among animals.

In the world of the whitetail, there is certainly a dominant type of behavior, but it can be more accurately described as establishing and maintaining a mature buck's "pecking order" within his herd, among his peers, and with transient bucks that may egress his so-called territory as well. Bucks, even mature bucks, do not like to fight if it can be helped. They instinctively want to avoid injury. So, most of their confrontations are done via aggressive body language, posturing, eye-contact, pushing, and shoving–especially during the early part of the fall. Each buck within a given herd actually knows his place on the totem pole (so

to speak) as early as July or August and certainly by mid-October.

If down-and-out fights do break out–and they do on occasion–they are usually between transient bucks and are not intended to inflict mortal wounds as is the case of truly dominant animals. I mention this so there is no confusion about dominance among whitetails. If you don't understand it as Mother Nature intended it to be, you will be sold a bill of goods regarding products that are meant to attract the dominant buck in your area. The dominant whitetail hype is total nonsense and nothing more than a marketing ploy.

Over the 25 years I have been taping the behavior of whitetails I can tell you this–I have dozens of scenes where young bucks are breeding does directly in view of much older bucks. In a world of true dominance, this is simply not allowed to take place. The dominant animal would knock the snot out of any other male who threatened his rank and, therefore, his breeding status. Have you ever seen what happens to a poor gorilla, chimpanzee, wolf, or lion, when it tries to

◀ When you locate a scrape that is three feet by three feet or more you can bet it is a primary scrape of a mature buck. It will be worth hunting over, unlike the small false scrapes found in October (above) and the secondary scrapes found in lines along fence rows etc.

it suggests your buck population may be out of whack and contain more young bucks than mature bucks. Late rubbing indicates a lack of pre-rut social order and behavior.

The body weight, age class, and rack size of a buck usually (which means more often than not) corresponds closely to the size of the sapling or tree he rubs. But this is not written in stone. I have also video-taped many small racked bucks (in the 100 to 110 class) making large rubs on semi-large trees. Why? Because, like all teenage males, they just have to show off and this is one way they can do it without getting themselves pushed around by bucks higher in the pecking order.

I have also seen mature bucks in the 125 to 140 class rub the heck out of small trees and even saplings,

ADVANCED TACTICS

sneak getting a piece of a _ _? The dominant animal teaches him a lesson he won't soon forget! Take the word "dominance" out of your whitetail vocabulary and replace it with the more accurate term "pecking order" or "rank status."

According to researchers, when the rut begins, high ranking (note I didn't say dominant) bucks rub less and concentrate more on making and attending scrapes, licking sticks, and overhanging branches. The intensity and seasonal pattern of rubbing often reflects the age class and the degree of social pecking order among bucks of a given herd or area. Biologists also say that the amount of rubs in the early fall, for example, reveals the presence of one or more older bucks that rank high in the pecking order. Seeing and interpreting that in an area that has many rubs should not necessarily mean they were made by many different bucks.

With that said, however, when you discover that a lot more rub activity is taking place later than normal,

I watched a big racked eight-point buck make this rub on this little sapling. So much for big bucks making only big rubs! ▶

especially in early fall before the younger bucks start rubbing. If you're trying to match a rub to a mature buck with a good set of antlers, be on the lookout for rubs that are made high on trees that have trunks at least four inches in diameter. Also take notice of any deep indents high on the tree–these would come from a buck with a multi-tined rack.

More than 30 years ago I discovered a neat trick in how to find out more about what type of buck made a rub. I found a rub that had many tiny holes midway up the rub. I looked closely and determined that it was probably made by a mature buck whose antler base included a lot of burrs by the pedicles. When the buck rubbed a tree, these nubs made countless tiny marks that were lower than the deep indents made by the tips of the tines. Since then, I have been able to match them to the antlers of a mature buck that I either killed in the same area or I was able to capture the phenomenon for myself on tape. Many times, the rubbed tree's bark was frayed to smithereens (for those of you who don't know that Brooklyn word, it means frayed to ribbons). This also indicated the base of the buck's antlers were most likely heavily burred.

There are, of course, exceptions to every rule and that applies to rubs as well. Never overlook buck rubs that are made on large trees with 16- or 18-inch trunk diameters or on trunks that are the size of your wrist. Another of my best kept strategies has been to focus my attention on rubs when I want to bag a mature buck.

It should be noted that in different areas of the country (and in Canada), bucks favor different species of trees on which to rub. It may be visual or scent-related but it does occur. In some areas a buck will show a preference for white pines, while in other states they may concentrate on white cedar or aspen.

I also use the attraction of rubs to create natural decoys. I will often create a mock rub near a natural rub to encourage a mature buck into checking it out (young bucks do as well). It has been a very successful tactic for me over the years.

4. Hunt the Inside Corners

There aren't a lot of hunters (including me) who have access to large tracts of land (1,000 acres or more) that are in prime deer hunting areas. Most of us hunt a couple of good spots and a few that are not-so-good. We all have to deal with hunting within restricted borders, neighbors (if you choose to call them that) who erect tree stands within inches of your property lines, and in some cases even trespassers.

No matter how many deer are on the property it always seems the action is right on the border of someone else's land. I guess that's why some unethical sportsmen don't think twice about putting up stands that are literally within inches of your line. So, instead of getting frustrated and driving yourself crazy trying to find the hottest places to hunt on your land, spend some time finding where changing terrain features are located. These spots are called "inside corners," areas where two or more terrain features meet.

I have rarely found a piece of hunting ground that doesn't have at least one inside corner on it. One such hot spot on our land is where one of our fields dips low and meets a woodlot. Another is where an overgrown apple orchard meets a rising hillside with a big rock ledge. We also have a spot where a small woodland opening is boxed in by a creek on one side and a swamp on another side. Any spot where two or more terrain features meet are great areas to post, especially when you're hunting a piece of land for the first time.

Our best inside corner is a place called the Finger Field where the end of the field is bordered on three sides by three different types of heavy cover. There is a stand of pines on the west side, a wet thick overgrown area of second growth along the east side, and a large

▼ My favorite "inside corner" on my farm can be seen in the upper portion of the photo. Finger Field has two corners that offer a change in terrain, woods, and other foliage.

▲ This heavily-used trail is used by does and other young deer.

chunk of mature woods on the north side. Deer always feel safer when they have more than one way to enter a field. In the areas I just covered, there are heavy trails and some lighter buck trails at the corners bordered by woods, second growth, and the stand of pines leading into the field. You can always find well-used trails in the corner's peak and in select spots very close by.

I have found that the best time to take advantage of an inside corner is during the first week or two of bow season and as the big chase starts just prior to the rut. The best way, however, to hunt these inside corners is to set up a stand about 50 yards into the woods along trail intersections or near parallel trails. Mature bucks often use parallel trails and will linger there to scent-check fields before entering them. Be certain

the placement of your stand is based entirely on wind direction. I usually have more than one stand in areas like this so I can work the wind and not have it work me. Remember to keep this tactic in your deer hunting bag of tricks, as it regularly pays off in big dividends.

Seek Pinch Points to Intercept Wary Bucks

When I first started hunting, it took several years of trial and error to learn how effective it was to hunt funnels and other areas that force deer into small necks of terrain. Since then I haven't spent a lot of time scouting or using topo-maps trying to find areas that look good on a topographical map. Instead, I study the land during May when I am turkey hunting and note the exact places of funnels and pinch points that I can hunt during deer season. By doing the same, you can outwit other hunters who spend a lot of time setting up on heavy deer trails that are almost entirely used by doe groups.

Many of us are drawn to these heavily used trails that are often found along creek bottoms or in the pines and through hardwoods; they seem to almost litter the woods at times. They are inviting places to set up especially when the trees are straight and make for good climbing with a portable tree stand. These heavily used trails should not be ignored; however, they offer good opportunities only when deer are traveling without a lot of hunting pressure.

I like to look for the faint trails that lead to and through funnels and pinch-points. They are trails that are barely noticeable and usually parallel the slightly more noticeable trails of does and younger bucks. Most of the time they are the paths that bucks take through these narrow escape routes or passages.

Bucks use these areas as crossings when the hunting pressure starts. Remember this when the deer start to become less visible during the season due to hunting pressure. While does, fawns, and young bucks often use common routes of escape, older bucks typically skirt the major trails and slip out of sight by using the lesser-used routes. We have all seen bucks do this. Commonly, when a hunter spooks a group of deer that includes a buck, the does, fawns, and yearlings, the group breaks out in one direction, the buck almost always heads off in another direction. The other deer usually run off with the tails flagging while the buck runs with his tail tucked tightly between his back legs.

You don't always find these types of trails in secluded spots–sometimes they are in less hidden areas. My cousin Ralph likes to hunt pinch points that are only yards off the road where faint buck trails cross from one side of the road to the other. While they offer opportunity, I find them unattractive because they take the lure out of hunting for me. I don't get a big kick out of ambushing a buck as I watch the cars go down the road. The point is, however, pinch points are excellent places no matter where they are located as bucks will use them when the pressure is on.

One such pinch point (on my cousin Leo's land) runs from high ground along a fence line and down to his swamp. At the point where the deer cross the water, they pick up another narrow trail on the other side for just about 50 yards before breaking out into a much wider pattern of trails.

Last year, Leo set up a portable stand at the edge of the swamp and not only shot a mature doe there, but also took a couple of coyotes that were using the same run. He did see a good buck, but because of the thick cover, he wasn't able to get a shot. Ralph also hunted this spot on one occasion as well. While he was on stand, I walked along the uppermost trail that was several hundred yards up the hill from Ralph and jumped a dandy buck that headed right down the funnel toward him. Ralph said that as the buck got to the narrowest point along the trail, he turned left and took another pinch trail away from him, instead of crossing the water.

I have a few similar type of pinch points on my land. One comes from my neighbor's land and funnels from the pines through a very thick overgrown area. The stand we call "White House" overlooks a tiny opening the deer pass through as they travel this pinch point trail. It isn't often when you can post on the stand and not get to see deer, even when the pressure from the neighbor's place gets heavy.

Pinch points, funnels, narrow draws, tight gullies, small ravines, and any other areas that force deer through them are natural hot spots and will provide hunters with greater opportunities to see and bag deer. They should never be overlooked and a savvy hunter uses them to his advantage.

5. Getting Into the Rut

I'll bet dollars to doughnuts that most of you probably opened the book to this chapter first. That's understandable. For most sportsmen across the nation, what they know about the rut, has for the most part, been hunting lore and techniques passed down to them by their fathers, grandfathers, and friends. Although some of what they have learned is based on solid, hard-core knowledge and experience, some of these skills and information are also mixed with a generous portion of old wives' tales and misnomers.

The simple truth about today's hunters are that they are fortunate to have a lot more facts about deer hunting and the rut available to them through books, the web, and from articles and papers written by biologists and the hunting press than any other time in history. Today's well-versed hunter knows a deer has thirty-two teeth, knows how to manage a deer herd, understands the importance of selective buck harvesting, can decipher the body language of a deer and can not only name all the deer's external glands but knows how each functions as well!

Even with all this knowledge, for a majority of deer hunters, the most anticipated and least understood part of deer season is still the rut. I'll bet the most frequently asked question of the "deer hunting authorities" is "When is the rut?" If I had a dollar for every time a hunter asked that question at a seminar or via e-mail, I would be a rich man. And I would be spending that money deer hunting across North America during one of the three periods of the rut!

One of the most persistent old wives' tales about the breeding season is that the rut is extremely dependent on cold weather. After all, almost everything we have heard and read as a young hunter emphasizes the best buck hunting happens when cold weather brings in the rut. In fact, throughout my early hunting years, I often planned my strategy around cold weather.

I believed in this theory so much that I took my vacation each year to hunt in the northern regions of New York, where cold weather (in those days), came early and hard and stayed late. Many of these hunts took place in the small town of Childwold, New York nestled in the foothills of the Adirondack Mountains between Tupper Lake and Cranberry Lake. There, I hunted a large tract of land owned by International Paper Company that was open to hunters in the early 1960s.

I often scheduled my vacation in late November, usually around Thanksgiving, when I thought the rut was "on" because of the colder weather. It wasn't until about 1975 when, through sheer experience, I discovered there was a flaw in this philosophy. Over the years, I saw the same amount of breeding activity during that particular week whether it was warm or cold! In addition, as the years went on, it didn't matter whether I was hunting in the southern or northern part of the state. It seemed cold weather wasn't the single magical element needed to spark the rut. It was as if I

In 1997, I arrowed this buck as he chased a doe back and forth during the peak of the chase period of the rut. I stopped him with a few competitive low grunts. ▶

▲ Warm weather or cold weather, bucks like this come into the rut the same time, season after season. (credit: Ted Rose)

was hit on top of the head with a ball-peen hammer—and a light came on.

I learned during those early years of my deer hunting that although cold weather stimulates diurnal (daytime) activity during the rut, it is not responsible for the onset, or even the intensity, of the whitetail's breeding cycle. Mother Nature, perfect in her design, just can't rely solely on weather to perpetuate a species. Plain common sense would tell you that.

Where cold weather does come into play with white-tailed deer is where it encourages them to move about much more throughout their territory during the day and more in the evening. In other words, it simply generates more daytime buck/doe activity levels. Bucks are motivated by the crisp temperatures to seek out does and, in extreme cold weather conditions, extra daytime rutting movement also helps them stay warmer.

During a warm rutting period, bucks become lethargic and tend to bed down more throughout the day. They breed does mostly at night when the air becomes cooler and they feel more motivated to chase does in estrus. A good comparison is to ask yourself, when are you more motivated to participate in lovemaking? During a 75-degree day with high humidity or in the evening when the humidity is gone and the temperature has dropped 20 degrees? These weather factors are what motivate deer to move throughout the day during a cool or cold rut as opposed to staying bedded and moving to seek out does during the night and at dusk and dawn.

This factor also holds true for signs like scrapes, licking branches, and rubs left by bucks in the woods and fields. During a warm rut, bucks make fewer scrapes and rubs and leave less rutting-type sign. They simply are not as motivated to paw out as many scrape sites or rub as many trees. The plain and simple truth is they're just lazier because of the warmer temperatures.

As soon as the weather begins to turn colder, however, bucks immediately begin to move about leaving rutting type sign such as primary scrapes and rubs all over the woods. This obvious over abundance of "rut sign" is seen by more hunters and interpreted as indicating that the rut is in full swing. Hunters become more excited, hunt longer and harder and therefore see and bag more deer than they would when this type

◀ I took this unusual 13-point buck during the peak of the rut at Hidden Valley Adventures in New York. I shot the buck soon after he mounted and bred a doe.

into motion. Light, or more correctly stated, photoperiodism (except near the equator) is what Mother Nature depends upon to initiate the breeding cycle of the white-tailed deer. As fall approaches, there is a "decreasing ratio of daylight to darkness that triggers the start of the reproductive cycle in whitetails." (*Halls, White-tail Deer*). This has been documented with deer that were moved from one hemisphere to another. These test subject deer adjust[ed] their breeding cycle to the current photoperiod in which they are/[were] living! (*Marshall* 1937).

Recent tests document that other than in the most northern and southern regions of North America, where there is a significant latitude difference and the amount of available light is less or more than other regions, the breeding cycle of white-tailed deer is dictated by decreasing light, which is absorbed in a gland in the corner of a buck's eyes called the preorbital gland. This gland then sends a chemical signal to the brain that releases hormones throughout the buck's system, which then drop his testicles, and dramatically

of active sign is not as prevalent during a warmer rut period.

Unfortunately, when a hunter doesn't see a lot of rubs, scrapes, or bucks chasing does during the day, the analysis invariably leads him to an erroneous conclusion (a deduction that is too often shared and believed by too many buck hunters): the rut is late or worse yet, it's all over! Shockingly, because of this assumption, many hunters unknowingly wind up hunting either the early or the late sides of the peak of the chase of the rut. Warm fall or cold fall, the peak of the rut, as with the entire rut itself, will take place one way or the other. You can take that to the deer hunting bank and deposit it for a future withdrawal.

Mother Nature must rely on a much more dependable stimulus mechanism to set the breeding cycle

This buck chases a subordinate buck to let him know where he stands in the pecking order. This is common behavior during all phases of the false, primary, and post rut periods. (credit: Ted Rose) ▶

▲ This photo of a bachelor group of bucks was taken in late August in Indiana. They will stick together for another four to six weeks before the onset of the rut breaks them up. (credit: Ted Rose)

raises his levels of testosterone. The extra chemical raises his "maleness" making him more belligerent to other bucks and less tolerant of their social company. Now he is more inclined to become a loner and to seek out does rather than "hang" with his once bachelor group buddies.

The facts are that the breeding cycle of a white-tailed deer, from southern Canada to northern Georgia, generally lasts about three months. This means the peak of the primary rut usually takes place from about the 10th of November through the 25th of November. If you would like additional proof, search the web for a whitetail guide in Saskatchewan, Wisconsin, Maine, or New York. Ask him when he thinks you should book a hunt to coincide with the peak of the rut in his area. I bet you he will suggest coming "in mid-November."

Now as we all know, nothing, not even the rut of the white-tailed deer, is written in stone. Mother Nature has built in some safety valves that can compensate for natural disasters by pushing up, delaying, or even putting off the breeding cycle of deer altogether. The

elements to cause such a drastic action are wide and varied. They include stress from a prolonged period of a lack of food, a thick layer of ice or very deep snow on the ground over a long period of time, flooding, injury to the doe, very extreme cold or heat periods over a long time, unusual amounts of heavy predation, fire, and even severe overpopulation levels. All these elements can cause changes in the regular timing of the whitetail's breeding cycle. Other than these conditions, the rut will take place in cold or warm weather. Ask yourself this, "If the rut was put off because of warm weather, how do deer breed in Texas, Mexico and Florida?"

However, there are high and low levels of rutting behavior and activity within this three-month-long breeding period. Many variables come into play. In fact, there is documented evidence of bucks breeding does as early as September and as late as March! While the latter is rare, it can happen. The bottom line is whitetails will mate over long periods if the opportunity presents itself despite weather conditions. If a

◀ This buck spars with a small sapling. If you imitate the sounds and smells of a sapling shaking, a soft, estrus doe blat, the smell of buck urine and doe estrus, it will create the "entire illusion" to any nearby buck drawing him to you. (credit: Ted Rose)

Pre-Rut

Generally, this phase of the breeding cycle occurs mid-October. Just before this period, bucks of the same age class hang out together in small groups called bachelor herds. In addition, although they can breed soon after they shed their velvet, which occurs as early as the end of August, their primary concern in September and into early October is still food.

However, archers hunting this time of year can relate to and confirm what I am about to say. Archers are usually the first wave to take up the hunt after deer. As such, they get to witness a lot of changing deer behavior related to their demeanor, food sources, activity levels, etc. Archers are also the earliest hunters to witness the first rubs and scrapes made by bucks.

Many of you know what I am about to describe is fact. Archers and even early season black powder hunters can be hunting an area for several days that really doesn't have much sign in the way of buck rutting activity. You know what I mean. For several days you're hunting and you might see an occasional rub and perhaps a small scrape that looks old and dried up, but not much else. Then, the very next day, unexpectedly, you find not only one old dried up scrape, but several fresh scrapes that weren't there just 24 hours ago. And they look like active scrapes. They are usually small in size, pawed bare to the ground, and an occasional one may even be muddy and have a strong musky odor. What just happened? You have just observed a yearly phenomenon regarding the rut. What happens to cause this obvious intense breeding activity in bucks? Mother Nature–perfect in her design–has just initiated the first of her three stages of the rut called the pre-rut or (more sadly for the buck) the false-rut.

Here is the scenario. As a bachelor group of bucks depart from their bedding areas to feed, they aren't thinking of anything else but gathering food. They casually walk through the woods, sometimes in groups of two or more bucks, eating acorns, leaves full of sugar, or perhaps they are heading to the apple orchard. Then, out of nowhere, they're met by the estrus pheromones of a mature estrus doe. Wham-o! It's like a cold slap in the face and the next thing that happens is the beginning of a flurry of intense activity. Bucks that smell the estrus odor of a doe immediately

doe has not been bred successfully she will continually come into her estrous cycle (her period) every 28 to 32 days until she is successfully mated. As long as a buck has antlers on his head, he is ready, willing, and able to breed, albeit less enthusiastically in March than he is in December, January or even February. Like any male, he will breed a doe no matter what time of the year it is or how warm it might get. Hunters who understand this will immediately be rewarded with more success.

So far, this chapter has covered an overview on the entire breeding sequence. Now, let's closely examine the three different stages of the breeding cycle. The first stage is the most overlooked and, therefore, least capitalized on by hunters–the highly productive first rut–which is also often called the preliminary rut, false rut, or pre-rut. I like to refer to it as the pre-rut because while it isn't of high intensity, it can create a short burst of activity and draw a lot of bucks to one area and a few mature does.

forget about food and begin to make a flurry of small but numerous scrapes, hoping to attract the hot doe. They also start to make rubs with the same intention. They are all excited (you would be too if you had to wait a year for you-know-what)!

I believe they are somewhat confused and their immediate instinctive behavior to the first scent of estrus pheromone is to react with a flurry of breeding activity including running all over the woods seeking out potential hot does! Mother Nature uses the pre-rut to intentionally knock the buck over the head (so to speak) to alert him to the onset of the breeding season. From this point on, bucks think more about mating and less about food.

Unfortunately for the bucks, this false rut is only 24 to 36 hours. It is also confined to only the most mature of does in any given herd (4½ to 5½ year olds). Again, Mother Nature steps in. Counting on her older does to come into their reliable and predictable estrus periods, she has this group perform a vital and important service: getting the rut started. Contrary to popular belief, it is not the males who initiate the rut. Not by a long-shot. It is the mature doe population that determines the onset of the rut and, to some degree, its intensity.

It's just like a mature woman in her prime; her menstrual cycle is predictable and reliable. Where in younger woman, their period may be less dependable and they may even skip a cycle here and there. In older less healthy does, their periods will definitely become less calculated and this leads into menopause. You can relate what happens to female deer to this scenario. On the other hand, if you're still not convinced, relate it to what happens to a female dog. Young female dogs experience erratic estrus cycles. Mature bitches in their prime, however, come into a reliable estrus cycle twice a year. But as the female dog grows older, her cycle becomes erratic again and inevitably stops all together.

Once bucks discover estrus pheromone permeating their range, they forsake eating and everything else other than frantically searching out estrus does. This phenomenon causes the dramatic increase in scrape and rub activity that archers witness during this false rut cycle of mid-October. Occurring around October 15th to October 20th, the false rut only lasts for 24 to 36 hours. Then it is gone, over, done, and finished, leaving bucks frustrated, angry and confused–with Mother Nature smiling because that's exactly where she wants them.

Only a few lucky bucks that quickly locate these hot does will get to service them. The rest are destined to be left out in the cold. This false rut plays a role in quickly breaking up the bachelor herds. Bucks are no longer tolerant of each other and become more belligerent to each other day by day. As the month of October moves on, they often engage in immediate aggressive behavior and spar willingly, upon meeting

This is one of the first bucks that I ever rattled in. He was taken in 1987 in Georgia. ▶

any other buck. In addition, because of the building tension and continuing decrease in daylight, they also take out their anxieties on the nearest sapling or tree. This is nature's way of helping to deposit the scent from their foreheads in order to leave a chemical message to other competitive bucks and possible receptive does. Strengthening their neck muscles helps them to vent their frustrations and it also helps to get them physically and mentally prepared for the inevitable and more serious battles that are sure to come over the next several weeks.

As most archers and blackpowder enthusiasts who are in the woods during this pre-rut will attest, this stage of the rut usually takes place around October 10th or so. The next time you're hunting and there is no scrape sign one day, and the next day you find fresh scrape activity almost everywhere in the woods, write the date down! Now count 28 to 32 days forward and you will have figured out when the second stage of the rut will kick in. The most intense activity during the

three rut phases occurs during this time. It is known as the primary rut or second rut.

It is during this "false rut" period in October that hunters can incorporate a variety of different types of hunting strategies to bag a good buck. Non-aggressive rattling and using a deer call to make soft estrus doe blats are two excellent techniques this time of year. Just remember not to be over aggressive. Bucks are just not fired up enough to respond aggressively now. Creating mock scrapes, rub grunting, and gently shaking brush and saplings dramatically increases the odds of success during this first period of the rut.

Subdued rattling for bucks during these two to three days usually creates immediate response from bucks that are frustrated from not finding a willing doe to breed. I have had curious bucks respond quickly to my soft clicking of antlers thinking they found a buck protecting his hot doe from another buck. With soft rattling, bucks often think they can sneak in and sneak out with the doe long before the other two bucks notice. Just keep the rattling sequence toned down. In addition, mature does undergoing this brief estrus cycle are eager to respond to this hunting technique as well. There is no better lure than rattling in a hot doe. She will inevitably attract a horny buck.

I have kept detailed records of my encounters with bucks during the false rut. These encounters have proved how productive this early rut can be. I specifically remember making an entry about rattling in several good bucks one day during the false rut in New York State. The entry was made October 10th. I was slowly putting up my portable tree stand and now and then it hit small branches, snapping them free from the trunk of the tree. When I thought about it, I realized it could have sounded like two bucks in a pushing and shoving match. After a few minutes, I heard a deer crash down the mountainside toward me. I stopped climbing mid-tree and waited to see what was about to unfold. Within moments, I saw a large racked buck trotting toward me. I could hear him grunting very softly as he got within fifteen yards. His eyes were bulging from his head. Within seconds, he

◄ Bucks often mistake the sounds of scraping bark and snapping branches made by a portable stand ascending a tree as noises made by other bucks fighting or rubbing trees. (credit: Photo courtesy Summit Tree Stands.)

saw me. To my surprise, the buck totally ignored me and paced defiantly around the tree several times. He then walked off several yards, pawed up a small scrape and left–all the while continually grunting. My only regret is that I couldn't get to my bow that was resting at the base of my tree stand.

The buck probably thought there were two other bucks fighting over one of the few does that were in estrus at the time. Throwing caution to the wind, he came in ready and willing to meet the challenge head on. When he left, I thought my opportunity had disappeared along with him. Once I got set up, however, I rattled the determined buck back in only thirty minutes later. This time, he never got close enough for a shot. Over the next few hours, I rattled in three more bucks.

Another testimony to the success a hunter can have during the pre-rut happened on October 13, 1989. It was 1:00 pm and I had just finished my first grunting sequence when I heard a twig snap. I watched a really big buck recklessly walk through a patch of second-growth just out of range from my tree stand. Grunting and drooling from the corner of his mouth, he walked around the area several times before departing. I waited a few minutes and tried grunting him back. When he didn't respond, I became a bit depressed. As I began to feel sorry for myself, I heard the soft grunting of a deer behind me. A small six-point emerged directly under my stand and paced nervously several minutes before leaving. Again, I waited a few minutes and grunted. Within a few minutes, *another* buck responded. It was an eight-pointer this time. As I drew on the buck, he looked at me, turned inside out, and bolted away as my arrow sailed harmlessly over his back.

Not believing the intense activity of the day, I blew one more grunt, not thinking for a moment that I would attract yet another buck. I did. This time, however, it was slightly different. After grunting softly for several minutes, a doe stepped out, looked around, urinated and walked off. Moments behind her, another eight-pointer appeared and, with a purposeful walk, slowly followed the trail of the doe. He never saw me stand, draw, and release the arrow as all his attention was focused on the hot doe's trail. Reliably, as the buck ran off before surrendering to his fatal injury, two more bucks walked past my stand! This is a testament to the unimaginable success the false rut can generate for hunters who know when to expect it.

By acknowledging that the rut has three phases that last up to three months long, you can prevent yourself from falling into the routine of believing that there is only a short period to hunt the breeding season. By understanding that there are three peak periods of rutting behavior during these months, you can capitalize accordingly. The next time you are hunting in October and you discover many scrapes that seem to magically appear over night, know that you are involved with the false rut for the next 24 to 36 hours.

Primary Rut

As I mentioned earlier, if you count 28 days forward from the false or pre-rut, you will have the prime time of the "primary rut." During this phase of the three ruts (which has its peak activity for about two weeks or so), most of the does in any herd come into estrus. In most of the areas I mentioned earlier (from Saskatchewan, Wisconsin, Maine, New York to northern Georgia above) this primary rut occurs from November 10th through the 15th–give or take a few days on either side. These dates are generally regarded as the peak period of the primary rut within the areas of latitude these states and provinces lie in. In addition, the mature does that came into estrus 28 days earlier who were not bred, also come into estrus again during this period. It is worth repeating here, ask any guide worth his salt when you should come to hunt the rut and he will tell you mid-November . . . from southern Canada, to Kansas, Missouri, Pennsylvania or West Virginia–these dates take in the primary rut.

I have talked with Justin B. Henry, owner of a hunting lodge in Sherwood Park, Alberta about this several times. Henry is noted for having guided many of his clients for some of the largest-racked and heaviest whitetail bucks in North America. During one conversation, I asked Henry when he thought I should hunt at his lodge. Henry said, "I'd be a fool if I had you here any other time than the peak of the primary rut. A good time would be during the second or third week of November." In case you missed it earlier, Henry's lodge is in Alberta, Canada, where it's cold and snowy and the peak of the primary rut is the same as the peak of the primary rut in the east: mid-November!

▲ I took this Montana buck as he aggressively chased after a hot doe. Even after being shot, the buck continued to run after the doe until he fell! ▶

If you still need more convincing, a peer and friend, Gene Wensel has often told me that in his state of Montana, "Our doe deer normally come into heat about November 16th through November 18th on an annual basis. This peak lasts for a week or so at a fever pitch." That's Montana, folks. And, it's very close to the same dates I suggest are the peak of the rut throughout New England and the rest of the country for that matter.

A week to ten days before the primary rut is the peak time of aggressive activity. Bucks are really frustrated now and are more than just jousting for position as they did in the pre-rut. Now they are looking for trouble and are deadly serious about any encounter they have with another buck, especially transient bucks that they don't know at all. These encounters can range from quick and injuring fights to down-and-out life-ending encounters because they are playing for all the marbles now. Semi-aggressive types of hunting strategies bring maximum results. If you are a rattler, you can rattle a little more aggressively and have success this time of the season.

However, this is an appropriate time to say that I am not a believer in over-aggressive hunting strategies. Despite what you might have read or heard from other experts, I can assure you from the standpoint of sheer common sense and my own experience that when bucks are their most aggressive, they fail to respond to overly aggressive tactics. No buck, no matter how big or how sexually frustrated he is, wants to have a physical encounter with another buck that may wind up seriously injuring him.

A comparison of this can be made by simply remembering your high school days. Remember? Did you

▲ Full-size decoys are excellent aids when rattling or deer calling. The decoys help draw the buck's attention from the hunter. (credit: Ted Rose)

▲ I rattled and grunted this 14-point buck to me in Sarita, Texas in '87. He hung up brush and only came out when I made a soft estrus doe blat. He scored 178 2/8 B&C inches.

ever or did you know anyone whoever picked a fight with someone who was *obviously* physically stronger, taller, or heavier? The chances are overwhelming that the answer to that question is a resounding–No. Even if you were one of the toughest guys in school, odds are when you had a fight it was with someone who was of similar or lesser size, strength, and weight than you.

Mother Nature is no different. Within the male whitetail's society, the pecking order is established mostly by body language during the spring and summer months when the bucks are in velvet. By the time a buck sheds his velvet, he is aware of his rank with other bucks in the herd. He knows whom his superiors, his equals, and his subordinates are. He only tests his status with his equals or subordinates, if they should be so daring, during the mating season.

You will be a lonely hunter if you think using over-aggressive calling or rattling tactics are going to work best for you. Trust me, they won't. Most of the time,

less aggressive calling and rattling tactics work more effectively.

Making your calls or your rattling techniques sound submissive draws the attention and aggression of all size bucks–especially big so-called dominant bucks. These mature bucks realize most of the time all they have to do to scare off a submissive buck is exhibit aggressive body language. This only changes when a physically stronger buck (with a rack of equal or slightly smaller size) decides to fight with a buck with a bigger body and rack. The smaller buck may have reserved energy because he hasn't undergone as much stress as the larger buck. He may not have even had as many fights. Therefore, he is much more "fresh" than the worn out bigger buck. He may temporarily overpower the number one, larger buck with bigger antlers, exile him from his position in the hierarchy and become the leader of the herd until he, too, is ejected from power.

Post-Rut

Now, getting back to the rut. Count 28 days from the primary rut date and you have the prime time of the "late rut" which is the third phase of the white-tailed deer's breeding cycle. During the late rut, most of the year's fawns and yearling does, and any other doe that was not successfully bred or skipped a cycle during the last period, come into a potent estrus cycle and are bred during this period. It is Mother Nature's way of ensuring the perpetuation of the species. Many hunters have relayed stories to me that during the late rut, they have had a lot of success with tactics like decoying, rattling, and calling. This doesn't surprise me. Rattling and calling can be effective into January and February. That's because some does in the heart of the country are still experiencing estrus cycles in December. In southern parts of the country, many does come into heat in late January and through February.

An innovative hunter firmly believes and understands the rut can last a quarter of the year. More important, he uses this information to plan a lethal whitetail strategy. Some of these strategies include patterning bucks. Although in the heavily hunted areas of the Northeast, bucks are harder to pattern during the post-rut because they must substantially extend their territory throughout their range in order to locate late-season does that have come into estrus. Therefore, deer-hunting strategies that pay off in big dividends during this period are those that imitate bucks seeking out does in estrus. Once a buck thinks he can hear, smell or "see" another buck after a doe in estrus, he is sure to investigate it in hopes of getting the hot doe himself.

Other late-rut strategies include rattling, calling, mock scrape making, using decoys (both male and female), laying mock urine trails, and using new techniques such as "Shake, Rattle N' Roll." In addition, some traditional tactics can pay dividends. These methods include posting near well-used runways along secluded swamps and ridges, watching and waiting along agricultural field edges, and ambushing deer in social areas.

During the third phase of the rut, just a single doe in estrus can attract several bucks. Not all at once, but over several hours many bucks may pick up and follow the trail of a single hot doe. This means a hunter could get the opportunity to see a few different bucks over an extended period that are all following the trail of one estrus doe. Having patience during this last phase of the rut can yield a hunter a trophy buck. Often, I have passed up lesser bucks that were obviously on the trail of one of these hot does and bagged a bigger buck by being patient. I specifically recall one such incident while hunting on the ridge behind my home.

It was December 19th and I was hunting during the black powder season that starts the day after regular firearm season ends. Two days earlier, I had noticed a flurry of rut-type behavior activity. This was after not seeing a buck in this area for several days. Knowing that the post rut was due (keep in mind that the post rut is similar to the pre-rut in that it is relatively short

▼ This doe is young and obviously in her first estrus cycle (which would happen late in December). She is so excited–she is the one making the advances. The buck looks like he needs to rest for awhile. (credit: Ted Rose)

compared to the primary rut). I immediately surmised the activity I saw was from the bucks that had scented the pheromones left by an estrus doe or two. I decided to hunt the area for the next two days from a tree stand that overlooked a social area.

On the last day of the season, I saw four different bucks walk up the trail and continue up the mountain without ever lifting their noses from the ground. The first two bucks were small four- and six-pointers. By the time the third buck had passed, the rack size increased as he was a decent eight-pointer. I was contemplating shooting him when I spotted yet another buck about 100 yards away making his way up the same trail. As he slowly trotted past my stand with his nose firmly held to the ground, the big ten-pointer never suspected I was there as one clean shot ended his pursuit of this estrus doe.

It doesn't take a rocket scientist to learn how to identify and capitalize on methods to take good bucks during the late rut. During this time of year, throughout most of the whitetail's range, except in the south, there is usually snow cover on the ground. This is an ideal opportunity for hunters to narrow down their search of a doe in estrus. Obviously, if you can locate a "hot" doe, it won't be long before you will also locate the bucks that will be searching her out. Very often, hunters see pink or red droppings left by an estrus doe as she urinates in the snow. Because there are not many does in estrus during the post rut, it doesn't take long for the pheromones from this scent to permeate the woods and attract a lot of interested bucks from great distances. It is also the best time to pick up the track of a good buck doing some tracking of his own. His mind is so focused on the doe ahead of him that he often forgets to watch or care about his back trail. I have one thing to say to a buck who offers me that opportunity, "Track your doe, my pretty–track!"

Once I have located this type of hot doe sign, I try to figure out the route the doe is traveling. Keep in mind, as with bucks, does are also difficult to pattern, especially in highly hunted areas. They, too, have increased their overall range in search of mates. However, what is unique with does as opposed to bucks during the post rut is that there are far more bucks ready to service an estrus doe than there are during the primary rut.

During the primary rut, an estrus doe has a substantial amount of competition from many other estrus does.

During the post-rut, an estrus doe simply has to follow her normal travel routes and amorous bucks will enthusiastically seek her out. By keeping track of her travels, you will inevitably find yourself at the right place at the right time.

The late rut often offers this type of opportunity to hunters as the few does that come into estrus often attract several bucks to themselves. Unless the very first buck is the one you want to take, patience pays off by waiting to see what other buck has picked up the doe's estrus trail and makes its way by your stand. Getting to see several bucks chase after one doe is one of the most exciting aspects of hunting the post rut.

Although the false and primary ruts get much attention, the post rut continues to be a stepchild by being mostly ignored by hunters. Perhaps, as I said earlier, it is because most hunters are led to believe that the rut is long over or perhaps they grow tired by the end of the rutting season and fail to effectively interpret rutting behavior and sign and turn this information into a harvested buck. This season, if you find yourself still looking to score on a buck when the post rut arrives, chin up.

Phase #4

Finally, this is a phase of the rut many hunters are not aware of. It occurs under certain extenuating conditions usually relating to extreme weather occurring during the normal phases of the primary and post rut stages of the whitetail's breeding cycle. It normally occurs during the months of January and February. Only a few does experience this late, late phase of estrus, but the few who do quickly attract bucks to their sides. Biologists are beginning to understand this breeding phenomenon more and they should be providing interesting and exciting documentation over the next few years regarding this extra late phase of the rut.

Frenzy Period

Now that we have examined the phases of the rut, here is some additional information you probably haven't heard before. This is the meat and potatoes of hunting the three phases of the rut. While most hunters assume that the best time to try to take a buck is during the peak phase of the primary rut, and to a large degree, this is true, it is also misleading. While it is certainly true that bucks are looking for does during the peak of the primary rut, and keep the words *primary* and *peak* in mind during this paragraph, bucks that are high on the status ladder are most likely to already be hooked up with a doe in estrus. This buck is the one so often heard about whom mindlessly and, almost like a robot, follows a doe in estrus through the woods and is inevitably intercepted and shot by a hunter. While the peak of the rut certainly presents these types of opportunities, if you really want to be successful while hunting the *primary* phase of the rut, always prepare to hunt several days prior to when you think the actual peak of the breeding will take place.

By hunting just a few days prior to this peak period during the primary rut, you increase your chances of seeing many more bucks and taking a really big bruiser–tenfold. I call this the "frenzy" period of the *primary rut*. In addition, unlike the other phases of the breeding cycle that Mother Nature has designed to be shorter, this phase has a definite and obvious frenzy demeanor to it. It's when most of the does begin to come into estrus and begin to emit the estrus pheromone.

Although does are discharging an estrus pheromone, they are not ready to breed. Basically, it is foreplay by the doe to excite as many bucks as possible. As more does come into heat, the pheromone begins to

▼ For years I have recorded all my deer hunting information on my "Deer Diary" statistic cards. They have been an invaluable source of reference that has helped my success.

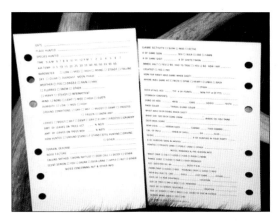

dominate the whitetail buck's world. These females unknowingly accomplish their goal to excite any and all males within their range. Now, bucks become extremely aggressive toward each other and will no longer tolerate other males' presence. While the pheromone puts the buck in an excited sexual state of mind, he is destined to stay frustrated until the estrus cycle reaches the point where the doe actually accepts the buck's advances to mount and breed her. Actual copulation is quick and can happen often over a 24- to 48-hour period.

However, before this acceptance takes place, bucks are so excited by the pheromone they will, at times (like bull elk), masturbate from frustration of not having a doe accept their advances. As the odor of the pheromone gets stronger and stronger, bucks literally go haywire. They chase every single doe they see to check their current estrus status. If they can't visually locate a doe, they run hell-bent (many of us have seen this happen) through the woods, fields, and mountainsides searching out does who are leaving these tantalizing pheromones scattered throughout their range.

For thirty years, I kept eighty different detailed statistics on my Stat Cards and, year-in and year-out, a majority of the time, I have noticed that the frenzy period falls from November 10th through November 13th. Some years, my records show it was from the 7th to the 10th and other years it was from the 12th through the 15th of November. Generally, the frenzy period lasts 48 to 96 hours and during warm falls, 48 hours or so. It is unmistakable to identify. If you are driving to work during any period from November 1st on and you happen to see a big-racked buck zigzagging through an open field, call in sick. The frenzy period is on! Other indicators that the frenzy period is on include bucks running along fence lines in the middle of the day, bucks darting from woodlines into fields and back again, and any other abnormal buck activity, especially midday. Besides this, if a buck acts atypically by being defiant, you surely can bet the frenzy is on.

Let me explain what I mean by defiant bucks. Often while calling or rattling, I have encountered bucks that, for one reason or another, make me. Most times, these bucks turn themselves inside out (a few because of their general belligerent nature stand their ground;

but, this is the exception rather than the rule this time of the year) and hightail it back into cover. However, as the primary rut gets closer and the estrus pheromones become more widespread, the general attitude of a buck certainly changes.

During the frenzy period, I have called, rattled, walked up on, and even accidentally bumped into bucks while hunting. I immediately know the frenzy period has begun when these bucks exhibit very unusual behavior in relation to man. Bucks have stared me down as if they were saying, "Yeah, What do you want?" Others, which were only a few yards from me and clearly identified me as a man, continued to casually walk past me almost as if I didn't exist. Obviously, a buck showing this type of behavior smells something so sweet that he ignores the danger nearby. Still other times, I have seen bucks with their eyes bugged out, come zigzagging past my stand and disappear into the brush as quickly as they appeared, only to have them reappear moments later and repeat the process again and again, sometimes for many minutes. This kind of behavior is a definite indication that these bucks have forsaken their normal fear of man and are preoccupied with only one thought: sex. Their behavior is understandable.

Hunting this frenzy period will be like no other type of hunting you have ever experienced. No matter where you live, every primary rut phase is preceded by this 48 to 96 hour frenzy period of sexual activity. *I recommend to hunters to plan their vacations around this period.* It is the best two to three days of hunting during the entire season. It beats hunting during the opening week of the firearms season.

No matter where you live, with a little investigation that will take a year or two to fine tune, you can narrow the frenzy period down and plan to hunt it. Throughout New England, you can bet it will fall between November 10th and November 15th (give or take a few days either way) each year. One of the best ways to determine if the frenzy period has begun is to read the vehicle accident report section of your local newspaper a few days before Halloween. If you live in the city, have someone start mailing you a local paper from the area you hunt about the same time. Each week, you will see a definite increase in the number of car/deer accidents reported. As the number of accidents climbs, you can bet it's because bucks are seeking out does as they are emitting more estrus pheromones. It is no surprise that most buck/car accidents occur during the dates I gave you above.

Remember that there will always be controversy among hunters about the rut and when it occurs throughout North America. Don't let that dissuade you from confidently believing in and applying what you have just read. To sum it up, you can take the above information about the rut to the Deer Hunting Bank.

PRE-RUT

Generally begins about October 13th and has a high activity level for 24 to 48 hours, extending an additional day or two depending on variable factors. Then it abruptly ends.

PRIMARY RUT

Starts with the frenzy period around November 10th to the 15th–give or take a few days either way. It then continues into the period where both bucks and does are matched up for a week and then experiences a slight decline in breeding activity around November 22nd or 23rd.

LATE RUT

Approximately December 13th or so, sexual activity rises again with bucks going into an excited state for two or three days and declines until around the 25th of the month. Generally, if a hunter counts 28 days between peaks of sexual activity, he will discover the heart of the frenzy period during each of the three phases.

6. And You Thought Bucks Were Wily

*M*ost hunters today have taken the fun out of their hunting by worrying constantly that they have to take a mature buck in order to be considered a "trophy hunter." Taking a young buck or a doe is considered by many hunters less of a hunting achievement. That is very regrettable.

Hunting for a buck or doe can be equally challenging and should be enjoyed and viewed as such. Hunting antlerless deer not only aids in good deer management, it also provides valuable experience for beginning hunters and even for long-time hunters. As the old adage goes, "You're never too old to learn, and a mature, matriarchal doe can teach us all a few tricks! No one should be embarrassed about shooting does. It doesn't mean you are any less of a deer hunter, in fact, it may prove the exact opposite!"

The trouble is most hunters are brainwashed into thinking that they have to kill big bucks to be recognized as valid deer hunters. What horse crap that is! Don't let yourself be a victim of media overplay. Many pros who make videos, or who are on television or write magazine articles exalt the taking of a mature whitetail buck as being the most wily and savvy deer in the woods. As I have mentioned, the most mature bucks get that way because they inherit a gene that makes them afraid of their own shadows. This is not so for a mature doe. She is destined to protect her family group and, by doing so, her senses are much more sharply tuned than a buck.

With that said, I want to be clear that big bucks are certainly crafty, but they don't have anything over on a veteran doe who has made it through several hunting seasons. I believe that mature does are the most cautious deer in the woods. A mature buck only has to look out for himself, and even then, he becomes a knot head during the rut. Not so for a mature doe. She's always on high alert, mostly because by instinct she knows she has to protect her offspring and other deer in her family group. Taking a mature doe also requires the hunter to get past more than the senses of a single buck. When you are hunting a mature doe, you have to not only fool her senses, but all the vigilant senses of the other deer she is traveling with. Have you ever considered those odds when your friends criticize you for taking a doe? Don't let anyone tell you that a mature doe isn't an ultra-wary deer.

As part of our QDM program on our farm, we plan to take at least four mature does (between 3½ and 5½ years old) each year unless there is a heavy winter kill. We have learned these does are hard to kill. Since our deer herd is fed a wide variety of crops including alfalfa, soybeans, turnips, chicory, sunflowers, and corn, the deer herd is healthy. Many of our mature does that we have harvested dress out around 155 pounds.

Over the last two years there were two does that we called Chubbsy-Ubbsie and Godzilla. Each of them had fat, low-hanging bellies and stood as tall as many of the 1½- to 3½-year-old bucks. Two years ago my wife set her sights on taking Chubbsie-Ubbsie.

◀ This mature doe has survived long enough to learn the ins and outs of hunting season. She would provide a challenging hunt and make a fine trophy for anyone!
(credit: Ted Rose)

Chubby, as I called her, could be seen contently feeding with her group in our fields all spring and summer. But soon after bow season opened she became a lot more cautious. On several occasions, she gave Kate the slip. On other occasions, her sixth sense told her something was up, even though she couldn't see or wind Kate and she vanished into the thickets. On another hunt, Chubby was within bow range but as Kate slowly raised her bow (after Chubby had passed her stand), the big doe knew something was wrong and blasted out of range doing warp 9.9. She stopped 75 yards away, looked back, made an alarm-distress snort and, with the rest of her group, bolted in to the nearby cover. Chubby was proving to be quite the challenge. She continued to stay out of harm's way all of the bow season and never showed up in areas that Kate was hunting. She instinctively knew that the hunt was on!

During the opening day of firearm season, Kate posted on a ledge in an area of the farm where Chubby was rarely encountered. Sure enough, around 9 am Chubby and her family group picked their way slowly through the heavy brush and cedars below Kate. With one clean shot from her Kimber .308, Chubby was heading to the butcher. It turned out when we got to the butcher, a biologist aged Chubby. She was 5½ years old and dressed out at an impressive 163 pounds! That's as large as most bucks dress on our farm.

Godzilla was taken by Kate the following year during the firearm season. Godzilla was so crafty that she gave most of us the slip from bow season through the general firearm season. Once again, Kate planned a hunt in an area that was not where Godzilla was normally seen.

Around 10:00 am, Godzilla was traveling with five other deer, she emerged from my neighbor John Fritz's property and passed through a patch of pines 50 yards from Kate's stand. With the wind blowing Kate's scent directly away from Godzilla, the doe came to an abrupt halt in the pines. She constantly scanned the woods for danger and she stood statuesquely in place while scent-checking the breeze. We had all seen her exhibit this type of behavior before, especially when she was about to enter the fields during hunting season. Sometimes Godzilla would remain motionless for fifteen minutes without moving a muscle before she felt it was safe to take her group into the pasture to feed.

The morning Kate saw the doe, Godzilla's instincts told her something wasn't right. According to Kate, she remained there frozen in place for nearly 20 minutes before feeling it was safe to move. As she left the pines she whirled, looked directly at Kate, snorted and was about to bolt when one shot from her Kimber .308 dropped Godzilla in her tracks. She turned out to be 4½ years old and dressed out at 157 pounds–clearly a savvy old matriarchal doe who met her match with Kate.

Other equally hard to kill mature does on our farm have been taken by my cousin Leo, my son Cody and Cody's best friend Alex. All were tough hunts and proved as challenging as any buck hunt. Each hunter not only felt they helped with the herd management plan, but they also felt these does taught them more about deer hunting as well.

That's because mature does often display buck-like behaviors once they know they're being hunted. After many hours of observation, I determined that the only way I could kill this type of doe was to limit my hunts to days with a straight west or slight southwest wind. I also had to reposition my tree stand three times before finding a spot that put me in bow range of one of her preferred travel routes.

When it comes to good deer management and QDM practices, what's the answer? Controlling the doe population and taking the right number of mature does from your hunting lands. Taking female deer is necessary in order to keep the herd and the food sources in balance. With whitetail population levels at an all-time high, not taking some does on your land can lead to disease, heavy winter kills, and an unbalanced buck-to-doe ratio. It's easy to see why we've come to understand the importance of taking antlerless deer.

If you take up the challenge of taking a mature deer from the land you hunt, here are a few ideas that may help you in bagging the Chubby or Godzilla that inhabits your land. Plan to scout two or three days around preferred food sources in order to locate the larger-bodied does on your land. Observe and note the big doe's behavior. Try to find some type of body part or coloration of the doe that will help you identify her or any other does you want to harvest. Be sure to cre-

ADVANCED TACTICS

ate shooting lanes before hunting season to help you ambush her. I have learned that while I never cut too much from my shooting lanes before hunting season, it is wiser to make the least amount of cutting you can within a month or so of the hunting season. It is better to try to pick an opening rather than cut so much growth that it looks "different" to mature bucks and does. In fact, a mature doe will react more negatively to an over-cut shooting lane than a buck will. When the hunt starts, don't hunt the same area or stand every day. Let it rest for two days before hunting it again, which will help you keep the hunting pressure low and allow the deer to move more naturally.

When planning to take mature does, it is crucial not to hunt the stand or blind unless wind conditions are favorable–as it is when hunting mature bucks. On the other hand, if you are hunting for any age doe than this suggestion isn't as important. I can tell you that the mature does I have hunted rarely make the same mistake twice. That sounds like the behavior of mature bucks, doesn't it?

Remember that when you decide to take a mature doe, it may be wise not to shoot the first one you see unless it's a big-bodied, mature doe. I have noted when I'm hunting (especially during the beginning of the season) that deer activity is pretty much predictable. Often buck fawns and yearling does are the first deer to emerge from the woods and enter the fields or the food plot. While a mature doe may come out any time, she is usually the last to come into the field. Patience pays off when you're trying to outsmart the oldest doe of a large group of antlerless deer.

▼ This old doe gave Kate the slip on several bow hunts. "Chubby" made her mistake on opening day 2005 when one shot from Kate's nail-driving .308 sent "Chubby" to the butcher. Kate is as proud of her hunt for this mature doe as she is of any buck she has shot.

▲ Leo Somma poses with a 3½-year-old doe taken on our farm in 2006. The doe proved to be "worthy prey" as the Hirogen's would say on Star Trek Voyager. Taking her also helped to keep our doe harvest numbers in place for the year. She dressed out at 143 pounds.

White-tailed does live in maternally related groups. They are often intricate and include deer that are of different social classes. The first three categories include fawns, yearlings, and young or first-time mothers. Then there are the "dispersers," which are second-time mothers. These does usually take up residence as far away as a quarter-mile or more from where they were born. The last group includes three levels of matriarchs and the senior females. Matriarchs are prime-age does ranging from 4 to 10 years old. A doe doesn't classify for senior status until she reaches age 12–which, in most northern areas of the country, is hard to find unless doe hunting is not allowed. Like bucks who reach six or seven years old, these does are almost un-killable. They have seen it all and haven't survived by accident. Their senses are as sharp as any mature buck's senses. A hunter would have a better chance at taking a mature buck that dropped his guard during the rut than he would of killing a senior doe.

Taking matriarchal does is the best management tool to deer management programs. They represent the pinnacle in physical fitness and health. Through many years of close calls and experience, they have become the survivors who allow a population to grow at its best level.

With all this said, hunters shouldn't become fixated on taking only mature does or the fun goes out of the hunt again. Herd management can still be done when a hunter kills any doe from his property. Female deer quickly adapt to hunting pressure and rely on their inherent survival techniques to dodge hunters pursuing them.

To outsmart mature does as the season progresses, you will need to be flexible. Hunt the social areas, overgrown fields, the edges, and the fringes of cover as the season gets older. The most productive stands are in what I term as social areas but are often called staging areas. These are patches of thick cover adjacent to feeding areas. I have said many times that the late afternoon is usually the best time to hunt social areas. Deer congregate in these areas waiting for low light to arrive before moving toward the fields, apple orchards, and other food sources. A social area can be quite small in size. Sometimes it is less than an acre. But I guarantee you that both older does and bucks seek them and use them on a regular basis.

Bowhunters often find that hunting the edge of a crop field can be frustrating because does enter the fields from positions that allow them to scan for danger well in advance. We've all seen them pause at the wood's edge and race out into the middle of the field and then begin eating. I believe this behavior demonstrates that they instinctively (there's that word again), know they're safer from the middle of the field where they can see danger approaching for long distances in any direction.

Mature does are even harder to kill in big woods. To get the most action when hunting mature does in large tracts of woods, locate oak ridges, travel corridors, and clear-cuts–this is where you will find older does most of the time in bigger forest areas.

One last piece of advice when hunting does is to take your time to unquestionably confirm you are not looking at a button buck. Without question, if you hunt does you will inevitably make the mistake of shooting a buck fawn. It happens. The world doesn't come to an end if it does. Realistically, a healthy herd is one that has an even distribution of deer from all age classes. End of story. Don't be embarrassed or ashamed if you shoot a buck fawn.

So take the challenge this year and do you part to help control the overall health and management of your deer herd. Hunt for a mature doe–or any doe for that matter. Remember, keep it fun and enjoy the hunt as if you had just taken a dandy buck. Oh, by the way, female deer (more often than not) make for better eating too!

7. Only the Nose Knows

Anyone who has ever hunted white-tailed deer knows that in order to be consistently successful year-in and year-out, you must try to reduce human and other foreign odors as much as possible. Totally eliminating human odor is almost impossible, no matter what other people tell you, but keeping it to a bare minimum is not. By paying attention to this one element of your deer hunting strategies, you will immediately see and bag more game the next time you go afield.

Many seasoned deer hunters don't doubt the white-tail's sense of smell as its key to survival. I have long said that busting a buck's nose will enable any hunter to bust a buck! Conversely, if a hunter doesn't pay meticulous attention to the whitetail's olfactory ability to scent human odor, predators, food sources, or a hot doe, you are only limiting your ability to bag a buck or doe. I can promise you this, the whitetail depends more on its sense of smell than any of its other senses—and you can take that information to the deer hunting bank!

Understanding wind and air currents is very important to be consistently successful. When hunters lure deer with deer scent, decoys, rattling, or calling, they must keep wind direction uppermost in their mind. That begins by keeping your body as clean and odor-free as possible as well as eliminating foreign odors from your hunting clothes and boots. To help reduce human and foreign odors, you can use a variety of commercially made attracting, masking, and food scents in addition to non-scented soaps.

You will find there are three distinct camps about using scents. Some, mostly the die-hard old-timers, swear that scents are just a lot of sales hype and are very vocal about them not being effective. The second group is much more practical about using commercially made scent. They feel it has its time and place. And then, there are those who are overly passionate about the use of deer scents and won't hunt without using some type of commercially made deer scent.

I have always had a realistic opinion about using deer scents, odor eliminators, non-scented soaps and the like. I base my support mostly on my past success when using deer scents. I also keep in mind that there are a lot of stories spread around by certain scent manufacturers regarding how their scent is collected and what it can do for the hunter–it's called sales hype. Unfortunately, many of us are sold by the pretty bottles and outrageous claims.

Do I believe using commercially made scents to mask human odor or to attract a buck or doe work? You bet I do. But I temper my thoughts about using deer scent with a healthy dose of good old common sense.

That means that I use scents as smartly as I can. My number one rule about using deer scents, whether I'm using them alone or in combination, is to create the most natural olfactory illusion I can. When the scent or scents that I put out reach the nose of any interested deer, I want them to be in an amount that is so natural smelling that a buck or doe will come into my stand with its guard totally down. By paying attention to this one statement about scent you will have leap-frogged from just a hunter who uses scent to a savvy whitetail hunter who understands the nuances about how to use deer scent.

To begin with, I can guarantee you no matter what type of scent you use, you will have greater success using it sparingly rather than putting out several canisters, rags, or other scent-makers filled with heavy doses of scent around your stand. Too much rut-type deer scent (no matter what type you use) will almost always spook, or at least make wary, any buck approaching your stand, almost as quickly as human odor will. I have found, however, that using commercially made scent wisely has always helped my deer hunting and not hindered it at all.

The old adage I coined years ago, "Bust a buck's nose and you've busted the buck," still applies today. By simply blocking or impeding a buck's ability to pick up human or foreign odors, you are halfway to scoring on your next buck.

I divide deer lures in the following categories: rut-type lures, food scents, cover scents and natural animal lures. Each has its best time to be used alone or in combination during the hunting season depending on where you live and when your deer season actually is.

For instance, in my home state of New York, we begin our bowhunting season around October 15th each year. The bow season runs into our firearm season, which generally starts around the middle of November and runs until the middle of December.

▲ Cody is washing up with a non-scented soap before leaving for a hunt. By doing this, he will help reduce his human odor. Remember, "Bust a buck's nose and you have busted the buck!"

branches. Do not use any other scent on them at this point.

The next morning, I start the day off with a shower and scrub myself using a non-scented soap. I shampoo my hair with the non-scented soap as well. If I shave, I lather the soap up and use it rather than a scented shaving cream.

Next, I eat breakfast in my PJs so I don't get food odors on my hunting clothes. Most mornings, if not all, we all eat a cold breakfast to prevent the odors of bacon, eggs, toast, butter, etc., from clinging onto our skin and hair.

After breakfast I remove the clothes from the container (or that I hung outside) and I spray them with the Scent Destroyer Spray–lightly. Every other day, or sometimes every three days, I wash the bottoms of my boot soles with a small finger nail brush (that you can buy in any CVS type store) filled with In-Scent's Scent Destroyer Soap. This helps to remove any foreign odors

During this time, different types of scents work when you match them up to what is naturally happening in the woods during the times you are hunting.

In October, I tend to use a combination of scents to help me attract deer, hold down my human scent, and eliminate foreign odors from my clothes and boots. I also use a food scent not only to attract deer but also to cover my presence as well. This is kind of a double whammy approach that has proven successful for me for over 40 years!

During October, bucks are making a lot of rubs and scrapes and other bucks and does are checking them regularly. I take full advantage of these olfactory visual and scent posts–by creating mock scrapes and mock rubs.

I begin the evening before my hunt by making sure my clothing is washed or at least sprayed with a scent eliminator like In-Scent's Scent Destroyer Spray. I hang my clothes outside if the weather allows. If you can't hang them outside, place them in a plastic container filled with freshly fallen leaves and freshly cut pine

I keep the wick hanging on this tree in a zip-lock type plastic bag. That way it retains most of its odor so when I hang it before hunting, I only have to refresh it with a few sprays of In-Scents Love Potion No. 9™. ▶

This is one heck of a buck working on depositing his vomeronasal scent from the organ on the roof of his mouth onto the overhanging branch above his scrape. This scent (along with the other scents he deposits here) will tell other bucks and does visiting the scrape exactly who he is and what state of the rut he is in. (credit: Ted Rose) ▶

on my boots from when I wore them in the barn, on the porch, while driving my vehicle, or in my home.

This winning tactic has helped me control the scent left on the ground, whether I'm wearing rubber or leather boots. However, I use common sense here. After washing the soles, I spray earth scent on the bottom of the soles as well. In my mind, it helps to reduce any residual odors of soap no matter how slight the odors may be. I know, this may be a little over-the-top here, but it gives me confidence that I took every available measure to do what was necessary to prepare correctly.

Once I'm in the field, I apply scent/s that I feel are natural this time of year. If I hunt from my stand and try to rattle in a deer, I might use a combination of attracting rut scents like buck urine and tarsal. I'll also add a food lure like acorn or apple–even when apples don't grow in the area. Any buck hearing the antlers and coming in downwind of me will smell what he instinctively expects to smell: the urine from competing bucks along with a light dose of tarsal scent. Does generally don't hang out with bucks as they spar or fight. They move a good distance away from them, especially when they are accompanied with fawns and yearlings, so I don't use doe urine or estrus scent now. Now, I have created a most natural illusion for any responding buck. (By the way, I have found that using a heavy dose of food scent does not alarm deer like over-using other scents will.)

If I make a mock rub in late October, I use a combination of scents including buck urine, tarsal gland scent, straight doe urine, and an excellent scent made by In-Scents called All-Season Lure. This is a mixture of glandular deer scents and smells like general deer odor to other deer. If one of my hunting buddies has already killed a buck, I use the buck's forehead gland scents on the rub too.

During the peak chase period of the rut (see Getting Into the Rut, chapter 5), things change a bit regarding the way I use scent. I use more food lures to cover my odor than I did earlier. Why? Common sense tactics is why. As available food sources declines, like wild apples, acorns, and domestic corn, deer are more likely to check out a food-scent odor. It also helps keep my scent down as well. I spray the inside of my hat with a food scent as it helps to drastically reduce odors emitting from my head. Body odors from your head account for about 75 percent of all human odor coming off your body.

Then I also use slightly more–and I mean slightly, not much more–doe estrus scent mixed with young buck urine. Love Potion No. 9^{TM} is a combination of a mature doe estrus and the urine of a competitive young buck. I developed this scent in the late 1980's and I have used it successfully over the years. It is designed to instinctively attract mature bucks. They pick up the scent of the hot doe through their vomeronasal organ. By doing so, they can detect the rut status and age of the buck following the hot doe and, by doing so, they know it is an immature buck. These mature bucks are instinctively (there's that word again) motivated to follow the scent knowing they can easily intimidate the younger buck off the trail of the doe, getting the opportunity to have the doe all to themselves.

You can find Love Potion No. 9^{TM} on our website at www.deerdoctor.com or at most sporting goods stores including Wal-Mart. In 2007, I licensed the product to

My son, Cody, makes a false rub—a powerful visual decoy to bucks. By adding a small amount of buck urine near the rub and a few drops of tarsal scent at the base of the tree, you will also create an olfactory illusion. This is one of my most effective buck-hunting tactics. ▶

a new deer scent company (In-Scents) that makes quality deer scent products. Love Potion No. 9™ is also available through their website at www.in-scents.com. But no matter what deer scents you like or buy—use this combination during the rut and it will work for you.

By now you get my meaning. When I use scent, I do so sparingly and with a heavy dose of common sense.

I always try to match the odors a deer instinctively expects to encounter in the woods and in the amounts that will not seem unnatural to deer, especially a nervous buck. But keep in mind here, spooking a matriarchal doe can be just as devastating to a morning or evening's hunt.

If you would like to have better action this season, here is some more information that will help you the next time you're afield.

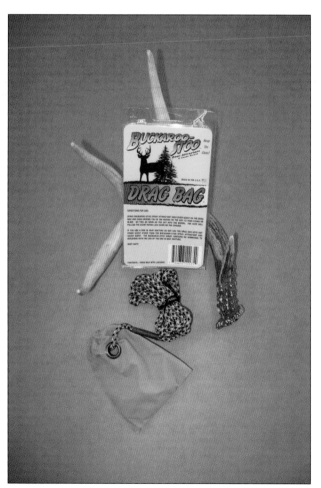

Deer Gland and Organ Scents

White-tailed deer have several external glands and organs that play a significant part in their communication and behavior. These include the more commonly known tarsal, interdigital, and metatarsal glands, and the less commonly known orbital (forehead), nasal, and pre-orbital glands. Three of the least known are the vomeronasal organ, salivary and the preputial glands.

Pheromones created by these glands and organs are received and interpreted by deer to help them decipher everything that is happening in their world. The messages received via the deer's olfactory senses are many. They may alert, calm, attract, or frighten a deer. They can also give the direction of travel of other deer, help establish the exact identity of other deer in their herd, or identify a deer's pecking order, age, estrus, or rut status within the herd.

◀ The most effective way to use commercially made sexual scents (doe estrus urine, buck tarsal or urine, etc.) is to dip them on a rag and drag it behind you. It creates an olfactory illusion that a buck will eagerly follow.

Nasal Glands

New facts are now available about this gland. When I first wrote about the nasal gland, biologists weren't totally sure of its purpose. Over the last 15 years, however, they now believe that the nasal gland serves several functions. They help to lubricate the lining on the inside of the deer's nose and they are also used to leave scent on overhanging branches. Some believe that they are used to leave a buck's specific scent when they make new rubs or refresh old ones. By depositing nasal scent on the overhanging branches above the scrape, a buck can leave his scent to let other bucks know he was the creator of the scrape. The nasal glands, which are located in the nostrils of a deer, consist of two almond shaped glands.

Preputial Gland

Additional information about the preputial gland has emerged as well. The preputial gland, which is located on the inside of the buck's penal sheath, also has researchers believing it serves different purposes. Researchers once felt that this gland didn't play a significant role regarding the rut. That has changed. Now they feel it not only serves to lubricate the penis, but the yellow/gray substance also deposits a scent when the buck urinates. The scent of this substance tells other bucks who the buck is and helps in defining his rutting status, too.

Forehead Gland

The forehead gland is comprised of sebaceous and aprocine hairs. During the rut, these hairs swell up and produce a scent that the buck deposits on trees as he is rubbing. Both bucks and does use this gland as a scent marker. In the 10 years I have videotaped deer, I have seen dozens of bucks rubbing their antlers on trees. To the buck, they all exhibited the same behavior while rubbing. First, they approach the tree or sapling, smell it and then begin to vigorously rub their antlers against the trunk. After rubbing their antlers up and down several times, they pause, step back, smell the trunk and then lick it. Then, if the mood strikes them, they repeat the process over again. Obviously, this behavior is not a random act, but rather a specific behavioral routine bucks seem to stick to when making a rub. The rubbed area often carries an odor for days.

Tarsal Glands

While there is nothing relatively new about these pungent odor glands, the tarsal glands, which are true external glands, are located on the inside of the hind legs of all deer. This tan gland turns almost black as bucks continually urinate on it throughout the rut. I think the combination of the urine mixed with the preputial substance helps in turning the tarsal jet black in color.

Deer use tarsal glands and their pheromones (which are mostly made up of lactones) in several ways: as a

◄ This dandy buck is getting a nose full of something he likes–most likely estrus scent. To fool a buck this big you must control your human scent to the best of your ability. (credit: Ted Rose)

▲ This buck is making a scrape. Hunters can create false scrapes to attract bucks. Sprinkle a mix of tarsal gland and buck urine in a false scrape. The odor convinces any buck visiting it into thinking it was made by a competitive buck.

visual and olfactory signal of a mature buck, as a warning, and as a means of identification of individual deer. In mature deer, the tarsal glands become involved with breeding behavior during the rut. When a buck or doe is excited, the hairs on the tarsal gland stand erect and can be seen for quite a distance by other deer. All deer urinate on their tarsal glands and this contributes to the glands' pungent odor.

To obtain optimum response from tarsal scent during the rut, put several drops of commercially made scent like Tarsal Gland and Buck Urine in a drip boot dispenser, rag, or pad and hang it from a branch close by. Its scent will permeate the area and act as an attracting or agitating smell. Don't place it on your clothing. You don't want the deer's attention to be zoning in on you. Instead, focus his attention or aggressions ten to twenty

yards from you. More information about why I recommend this is at the end of the chapter.

Although the scent from tarsal glands of harvested does attracts bucks, many hunters have had equal success attracting bucks with commercially made tarsal scent. Sometimes (not always), the odor of tarsal agitates bucks so much they respond within a short period of time after putting out the scent.

When creating a mock scrape or hunting over a natural scrape, I use tarsal scent. I also use it when I am hunting with deer decoys, on mock scrapes, and on mock rubs. By placing a few drops on the inside of a buck decoy's legs, it adds to the flavor of realism. I also put some on the ground when I'm using my natural deer tail. Remember the key phrase in all my books and seminars, "Always try to create the *entire* illusion."

I also use tarsal with estrus scents when I am hunting during the rut. Tarsal gland scent has a pungent odor. Use it only during the peak rut and then only sparingly. Using tarsal the wrong time of year and too much of it will be ineffective. The key to all these glandular scents is to try to use them in conjunction with the times of year that deer are accustomed to naturally finding these smells in the woods.

Interdigital Glands

Interdigital is a potent scent that attracts all deer when used sparingly. The interdigital gland is located between the deer's hooves. The gland emits a yellow waxy substance with an offensive potent odor. Interdigital scent is like a human fingerprint: individual to each deer. Although I don't know of documented evidence suggesting the interdigital odor from bucks and does are different, I would speculate the interdigital scent from mature bucks and does is more potent than the scent from immature deer.

Hunters can use interdigital scent two ways. Used sparingly, you can use it as an attracting scent. All deer leave minute amounts of interdigital scent as they walk. Other deer follow trails marked with a normal amount of interdigital scent. Use only one or two drops of a commercially made interdigital scent on a boot pad. When you are within 15 yards of your stand, remove the pad, hang it on a bush, and wait for deer to come and investigate the odor.

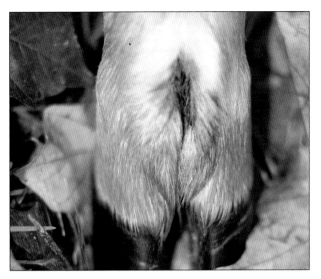

◀ This image clearly shows the location of the interdigital gland in the tuft of black and white hair on this hoof. (credit: Ted Rose)

Deer also use interdigital scent as a warning to other deer. When a deer stomps its hooves, it's warning other deer of danger through sight, sound, and scent. Deer that smell excess interdigital scent often refuse to continue further down the trail. They will mill about nervously for several moments, walk around the scent, or retreat the way they came, while instinctively heeding the pheromone warning left earlier by another deer. Hunters who use interdigital scent incorrectly (in excess of a few drops) will definitely spook, rather than attract, deer.

Here's my favorite way to make deer move out of heavy cover. When I was a guide, I placed clients on known buck escape routes. I moved about 100 yards away, spread excess interdigital scent (about 10 drops), stomped my feet and blew an alarm-distress snort. This imitation of a deer sending out an alarm–through both audible and olfactory scent messages–sent bucks and does sneaking down the posted escape routes while trying to flee the danger signals their ears and noses were receiving. Of course, you would not use this ploy too often or in more than one or two locations in the woods you are hunting. It could have the tendency to genuinely motivate deer to become reluctant to use the area.

To convince you of the potency of this scent, simply spread the toes of the next deer you kill, and with the tip of a knife, dig between the toes. Caution: Don't be brave enough to place the knife tip directly under your nose. You'll regret it–as it may induce the dry heave response or gag reflex. The odor is so foul it can make you nauseous. I use commercially made interdigital scent rather than collecting it from dead deer–it's much safer, easier, and much more practical!

Preorbital Glands

The preorbital gland is located in the front of the deer's eyes. They control the gland via muscles in this area. Its main function is to serve as a tear duct. However, deer continually rub this gland (together with the gland on their forehead) on bushes, branches, and tree limbs, especially during the rut. Biologists now speculate that bucks use it to signal aggressive behavior. They also say that does open the glands "wide" when feeding fawns but do not know why they do it. Deer also use these glands to deposit a specific

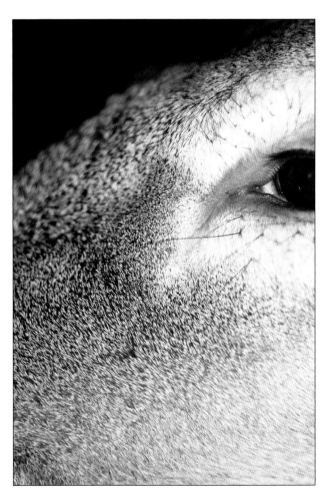

The preorbital gland (in the lower corner of this buck's eye) is what monitors the decrease in daylight helping to trigger chemicals to his brain to begin rutting behavior. (credit: Ted Rose) ▶

ADVANCED TACTICS

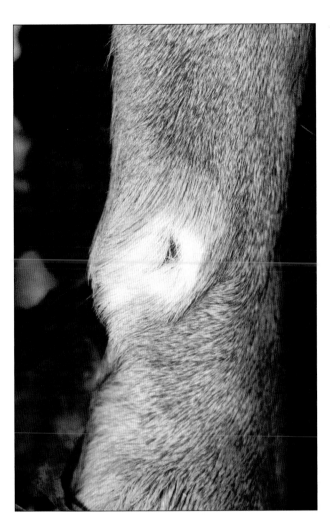

pheromone to mark certain areas and to help identify individual deer to each other.

Metatarsal Glands

The metatarsal glands are no longer as controversial as they were when I first wrote about them. In fact, I have some new thoughts about them. Each gland is within a white tuft of hair located on the outside hind legs just above the dew claws. Now, most all naturalists and biologists I have talked with believe they are atrophying (getting smaller through evolution because deer no longer need them), and therefore, they serve no real purpose.

There is a small camp, however, that still believe the glands omit a pheromone, and it's used by deer for identification. I have smelled these glands on countless deer before and can say that, while they do not smell anywhere as potent as the tarsal glands do, they do emit an odor. In my opinion, any scent a deer omits serves some type of purpose to other deer. In any

event, this gland's function is still not well understood by many hunters.

My suggestion coincides with my philosophy about deer hunting: don't be afraid of being innovative. If you're not sure how this gland will help you during the hunting season, give metatarsal a try and experiment with it this fall.

Over the last dozen years, I have used metatarsal the same way I use tarsal. I have seen both bucks and does walk down a trail where the scent was deposited. For the most part, they have ignored the scent. I may, however, be interpreting their reactions incorrectly. Instead of ignoring it, they may be more docile or relaxed by smelling it. I'm really not sure. So if you use the scent, do so as an experiment and you'll be using it at your own risk.

When using deer scents, especially gland scents, be careful not to mix conflicting pheromones. For example, don't use excess interdigital with attracting scents. Excess interdigital scent is meant to warn deer of danger, not attract them. When a deer stomps its hoof repeatedly, it is sending both a visual and audible message. Biologists say the vibration from the deer's stomping hoof can be heard and felt for a few hundreds yards by other deer feeding or bedding in the area. I use excess interdigital to help me create the entire illusion of real danger when I'm trying to intentionally spook deer from heavy cover while I'm using an alarm-distress snort vocalization. You can, however, use one or two drops of interdigital with an estrus scent, as both are attracting scents.

Sexual Lures

The most overused deer scent is doe-in-estrus. Although estrus scent works, do not use this scent throughout the entire deer season. Estrus works best for a few days prior to each peak period of the three phases of the rut and is effective when it is used sparingly.

I use doe estrus every year. However, I use it sparingly and with an open mind and a lot of common sense. There isn't a buck in the woods that will confuse the estrus scent from a natural hot doe with a commercially-made estrus deer scent. But that doesn't mean you should not use a commercially made doe estrus scent. To the contrary, when they are used correctly, they can be as effective on a buck as natural doe estrus.

◀ I created Love Potion No. 9 fifteen years ago. It is an agitating scent mixed with subordinate young buck urine and doe-in-estrus scent. When a mature buck smells the aroma he instinctively follows it thinking he can run off the younger buck and have the doe to himself.

When used right, big bucks have no hesitation in investigating a scent rag or wick with doe estrus hung near a stand. I think estrus scent works best before the actual peak periods of each phase of the rut–especially during the peak chase periods that happen prior to the actual breeding.

Pheromones from these glands and organs are natural everyday olfactory odors in the woods. Used properly, they will add to your total deer hunting experience. They will create deer hunting opportunities that you may never have had otherwise. In addition, you will have opportunities to witness the amusing and interesting reactions of raccoons, coyotes, foxes, bears, and elk when they stop, smell, and react to scents laid out for deer. By using all the other suggestions within this chapter, you will not only gain an edge, but you will also have an interesting and exciting season watching and learning how does and bucks respond positively to scents when used correctly.

Food Scents

One of my favorite types of lures is food scents. Use food scents with an open mind. I have heard some so-called experts recommend not using food scents that are not native in the area you are hunting. If there is one point of deer hunting hype that annoys me–this is it. It is my pet peeve when it comes to deer hunting. There are those who say you can't use apple scent in a hardwood forest because deer will "know" that apples are not growing there. They are wrong at the least and

I use plastic apples sprayed with apple scent to attract deer. You can hang them anywhere–even where apples don't grow naturally. I put several on a tree and more on the ground. The first deer to see and smell the apples come in quickly to check them out. This is one of my favorite unorthodox decoy tactics. ▶

are bull-crap artists at the worst. Trust me. When used correctly, food type lures are highly effective whether they are native to the area you are hunting or not! And you can take that fact to the deer hunting bank!

If you don't believe apple scent (or any other type of food lure for that matter) attracts deer where wild apples don't grow, you're missing out on a productive hunting strategy. Try this. Before hunting season, take either a couple of real apples or a scent pad soaked in commercially made apple scent (food scents are the only scent you don't have to worry about using too much). Place the lure or fruit in an area you are absolutely sure has no wild apples. I promise you that as deer move through the area they will smell the food source and investigate it whether the scent is natural to the area or not.

Common sense tells you deer instinctively check out odors from potential food sources. If they didn't, they

would have a lot less food available to them. Deer have no way of figuring out if a scent pad laden with apple scent is a lure left by a hunter and not an actual food item. There isn't a buck alive that would make his way through a hardwood forest free of natural wild apples and pick up the odor of the apple lure and say, "A-ha! Apples don't grow here! That must be a fake lure. Yikes! I've been had. I'm outta here," and then run off without looking back. The fact is, they will check out anything, and I mean anything, that smells like it would be good to eat.

Apple scent is my favorite covering and attracting scent–I use it throughout the season, especially in areas where there are no apples. Apple scent not only acts as a food attracting scent, but is also excellent as a cover scent to help mask your human odor. I often place several drops on my cap to help keep my human odor down. You can also use acorn scent in the same way and use it in areas where there are no natural acorns. I use it when I'm hunting in evergreen forests. Guess what? Many deer have walked through the pines, winded the acorn scent pad and walked over to check it out. This is proof that you don't have to use food scents indigenous to the area you're hunting.

It's a simple matter of common sense. If you use apple scent in an apple orchard or acorn scent in a hardwood forest filled with acorns or corn scent in the middle of a cornfield, the only thing you would accomplish is to help mask your human odor. The natural food will attract the deer long before the imitation food scent. My advice is to use natural food scents in areas where they are not naturally present.

I treat food scents (like acorn, apple, corn, wild grape, and vanilla) exactly the way I treat attracting lures. I hang them 10 to 20 yards from my stand. All except apple scent. While I hang apple scent away from me, I also use it on my cap to reduce human odor, as mentioned above.

Woodland Scents

Natural woodland fragrances like hemlock, pine, spruce, cedar, earth, and the like can be worn on clothing without risk of attracting a deer's attention to the hunter. I use them regularly to help mask my odor. I especially like earth scent.

Reducing Your Scent

While I want to remind you there is no way to totally eliminate your human odor, you can reduce it significantly, however, by following some important guidelines. Keep yourself as clean as possible before each hunt. Use a Scent Destroyer Soap on your body and a Scent Destroyer Spray on your clothes and boots. If you can shower between hunts, do so. Use unscented deodorants. During deer season, always use nonscented hair soaps or shampoos. Scrub the soles of your boots every couple of days with a nail brush and unscented sportsmen's soap. In addition, wash your hunting clothes at least every other day. If you can, dry them outdoors. If not, hang them outdoors for a few minutes to remove the odor from the dryer before putting them on to go hunting.

Stay away from foreign odors like gasoline and diesel fuel. Don't let your dog rub up against your hunting clothing. Avoid camp odors like cigarette smoke and cooking odors, as if they were the plague. Also, never get dressed and then take your morning constitutional

ADVANCED TACTICS

▲ Many hunters are fanatics about using only rubber boots. If you wear rubber or leather you can eliminate almost all the odor by washing the soles every few days with an unscented soap. I have done this for 30 years with excellent success and yes, I wear leather boots.

▲ Here are my leather hunting boots packed in my box with fresh conifer branches. The pungent evergreen odor permeates the leather, giving them a natural smell. I wash the soles off every few days, too.

(ugh–how much common sense does that one take?). Instead, wait until afterwards to put on your hunting clothes. Once again, I apologize for this tacky suggestion, but it's better to say it than to not mention it to you. Finally, a savvy hunter always washes himself (not only your hands fellows) thoroughly after the morning constitutional. Get what I mean here?

Deer pick up scents mostly from the foreign odors collected on the soles of your boots. Avoid wearing your hunting boots anywhere else other than the woods. Sometimes I'm even guilty of wearing my hunting boots where I shouldn't. When I do, however, I make sure I wash the soles free of odor. If you are driving to a hunting area, leave your boots in a small cardboard box filled with pine branches, fresh leaves and fresh earth, and change the leaves and earth every two days. When you arrive at your hunting location, remove your sneakers or shoes, put on your boots, and head into the woods. When you return, immediately remove your boots and put them back in the box. By following these suggestions, you will keep your boots totally free of foreign odors. I still wash the soles of my boots every few days to remove any human odor that may have permeated into the soles. By taking these scent suggestions seriously, you will eliminate as much human odor as possible.

Section II

TRACKING

TRACKING

8. Defining Tracking

As with most of the other tactics in this book, the art, or more precisely, the ability, to follow the tracks left by a deer until you actually catch sight of the animal is a crucial tool in becoming a more skillful hunter.

There are two types of tracking to define, however. The first is an absolute necessity for any dedicated, ethical, deer hunter. This is the ability to track a wounded animal by either the blood trail left by the inflicted wound, or by the "sign" left on the forest ground, grass, branches, vegetation, and even rocks along its escape route. This type of tracking ends when the hunter either finds the dead deer or is able to spot it and finish it off.

This is a tracking skill that every hunter must learn in order to lessen the odds of losing a deer that he has wounded. The odds are (whether you are a seasoned veteran or a novice) sometime during your hunting life, you will indeed wound a deer and have to follow its blood trail in order to recover it. That is a fact no long-time hunter escapes. Despite what your friends or anyone else says, the wounding of one, and sometimes even a few, deer over a lifetime of hunting is inevitable. Wounded game has been part of the "hunt" since our cave man ancestors hurled spears and released arrows. As hunters, each and every one of us is morally responsible to know how to make every effort to recover a wounded deer. The recovery begins by understanding how to effectively follow the tracks, blood, and other signs from a wounded deer.

To become proficient at this type of tracking takes a lot of practice, persistence, and patience. With this type of tracking, the more trails of wounded deer you follow, the better you become at finding wounded game. Each and every blood trail is totally unique. But, in the end, the same general information will be garnered each and every time you're afield so that you can log (in your memory or on paper) and refer to it time and again. It will teach those who pay attention something new and different every single time. For this reason, long before you ever have the "call" of having to find a deer you have wounded, learn through first-hand experience when you can.

Anytime you are hunting with a friend who wounds a deer, volunteer to help him trail it. Keep a low profile, especially if the hunter you are assisting is

▲ We all dream about following the tracks of a buck like this until we catch up with him in his bed or he stops to check his back trail to find out what is "dogging" him.

experienced in trailing wounded deer, but stay alert to what is happening. It is important not to feel embarrassed about asking an experienced tracker questions regarding the sign left behind. Take the time to join in on tracking, even when it means giving up some of your valuable hunting time. The experience you gain will make you a more proficient hunter: a hunter other deerstalkers and non-hunters alike will respect and admire. I cover this type of tracking further along in the book in much more detail. It is important information for all hunters, both skilled and beginner, to read carefully.

The second type of tracking is more romantic. It conjures up a spark of adventure lying deep in every hunter. To find a track of a deer and follow it until you are able to get a clean shot at the deer, especially

▶ Following the tracks of a wounded deer even in the snow takes patience and skill only learned after you have tracked several bucks.

a mature buck, is to most hunters, the ultimate deer hunting experience. It is one of the most exhilarating and captivating aspects of deer hunting. To be skilled enough to trail a buck by following his tracks and finally tagging him on his turf, while playing by his rules, is the underlying desire for almost all deer hunters. For most of us, it generates a feeling of satisfaction like no other deer-hunting tactic can.

Through most of my deer-hunting life, when I daydream about taking a wise, old buck with a heavy, wide set of antlers, a long drop tine and a few gnarly kickers, I imagine that I cross his track while I'm slowly still-hunting through the woods after a fresh snow fall. The track is, of course, wide, long, and set deep in the snow. The distance between each hoof print is unusually long. And, there is always some defect in the hoof to set the track apart from other bucks—least I confuse it as I set out to walk him down. My daydream takes me over mountains, through swamps, into thickets, cedar forests, and eventually, back the other way as the buck inevitably tries to circle behind me. Just before legal shooting light comes to an end, I spot him as he stops to check his back trail. Without the buck ever seeing

me, I send a brush-cutting bullet whistling over the blow-downs–and before the big buck can react to the report of the rifle, the bullet finds its mark and the buck crumbles instantly and quietly into the fresh snow. I have had this daydream many times during my hunting life, and I'll bet most of you have had some version of the same fantasy, too.

While most of us romanticize about duplicating the efforts of well-known trackers of Maine and Vermont, like Hal Blood, the Benoits, and Berniers (I often quip that perhaps to be a famous tracker from New England, your last name must begin with the letter "B"), the reality about tracking, however, is that it is a tactic that requires a heavy dose of reality and common sense.

The most overlooked truth about tracking for most buck hunters across the nation, especially those in heavily hunted areas, is to acknowledge that in order to become the next Blood, Benoit, or Bernier, a hunter must have un-pressured hunting space and plenty of it. This is the key element for tracking down bucks as consistently as the trackers mentioned above. A successful tracker must also know how to quickly interpret track signs left by deer. It also requires one to hone his skill of orienteering. And, when tracking bucks in big woods, it demands that the tracker be in above-average physical condition. I often compare it to bighorn sheep hunting, because following a buck up and down ridges, over blow-downs, through thickets, swamps, and bogs can quickly sap the strength of even the most athletic hunter, especially in the legs. Most of all, successful tracking of a buck in the wild backcountry of Maine, or in the remote regions of Vermont, New Hampshire, or the Adirondacks of New York State, requires a lot of patience, more patience than most hunters have. But in the end, it demands diligent persistence. Without this skill, you are better off never taking after the track of a buck in big woods country–period. Therein may be the most overlooked element of a successful big woods tracker.

But those elements are not only what it takes to be a skilled tracker. Equally as important, a hunter must know when to give up on the track. I know you have all read that some trackers follow the prints overnight and into the next morning. While that makes good reading, and is very romantic, it is impractical and never really a tactic used by anyone. The fact is, in

TRACKING

▲ Hal Blood, Master Maine Guide, is recognized as one of the leading trackers in North America. He has the endurance and strength necessary to track a buck for long hours in deep snow over mountains, swamps, and lowlands. This buck scored 1661 8 B&C points. (credit Debbie Blood)

most states, such activity is illegal. Even without a firearm and gun, following a buck during the night can be considered "harassment of wildlife" by most state game departments. Chasing after a buck at night, by the mere definition of pursuit, is hunting. As far as I know, hunting at night is prohibited in every state. An ethical sportsman should understand that he has lost the battle of the chase for the day if by legal sun set the hunter has not caught up with the buck and killed it. It doesn't mean that by legal sunset you hand someone else your firearm and continue to harass the buck, with flashlight in hand, through the night—as far-fetched as that might be.

Anything less presses against the ethical edges of hunting and fair chase. Again, a hunter would be wise to remember that in many states, dogging a buck overnight carrying a firearm and packing a flashlight (even one that is stowed away in your backpack) will test the patience of almost any game warden. The nonsense of some hunters tracking a buck overnight and staying

with the track until shooting light the next morning is, in my mind's eye, a vast exaggeration of the truth and of the ethics of hunting as well. It is also not sporting to the deer, despite the glamour it evokes. It also taxes my patience. Staying with the deer through the dead of night over hill and dale and running him ragged until you spot him the next morning, then shooting him, and then still being in good enough shape to drag out this 300-pound buck—is just down right hooey! It is meant to sell magazines and to make other trackers feel less of themselves. That crawls under my skin. Anyone can track a deer at night. There's no magic involved, as the deer is less spooky of what's on his back trail.

To prove this point, I know we have all walked out of the woods after leaving our stand once legal shooting hours are over. During the egress, many of us have bumped into a buck or doe. Inevitably, instead of snorting and immediately running away, many times, these deer will remain frozen in their tracks, trying to "make you out." I have even had mature bucks walk within feet of me trying to identify what I was. Even though this may be hard to believe, I am sure there are many hunters who can collaborate. I have even had deer stand there with the wind blowing my scent directly to them. Darkness just seems to make deer less afraid of human scent and/or human outlines than during daylight. So, dogging a buck at night isn't "the ultimate challenge" it has been hyped-up to be.

The fact is, the longer you track a buck, the greater the chances become that another hunter will shoot him. I can't tell you how many times I have taken up the trail of a buck in the snow, in country that is under-hunted, only to hear the inevitable report of a firearm coming from the direction the track was heading. In most cases, I have followed the track until it leads me to the dead buck and the hunter who shot him. In my

▼ Posted signs are a reality check that means the chase has come to an end in places other than big woods.

conversation with the successful hunter, he usually winds up telling me he shot the buck as it was "check-ing its back-trail." Sad as it is, undressing the mystique of tracking leaves the bare facts–tracking isn't always what it's cracked up to be!

I share these negatives not to discourage you from becoming a tracker, but rather to give you confidence and to share some common sense about the tactic.

Know Your Terrain

If you have ever hunted deer in Maine, you have learned a few things about just how wild that state can be. For the most part, western Maine is a maze of thick wilderness. Even its system of logging roads can be confusing to the first-time hunter. Let me share a story with you of just how confusing the logging roads can be. This is a story that is embarrassing for me to tell, but it is the truth, and as such has its value in sharing with you, no matter how foolish it makes me feel.

Several years ago while bear hunting in Maine, I drove my truck into the hunting area by following my outfitter who was driving ahead of me. Once we reached the area, he directed me to my stand and told me "just reverse the directions to find your way out without any trouble." Having a great sense of direc-tion, I didn't think twice about it and headed to my stand. I made sure I noted each turn on the many log-ging roads we took on a tape recorder as we traveled. Just before the outfitter left, he asked, "Do you think you'll be able to find your way back?" I smiled with confidence and said, "Of course."

By now you surmise that when I tried to drive out in the pitch dark, all the logging roads looked the same. It was hard to differentiate the landmarks I logged during daylight on my way in. Each turn left me feeling like I made a mistake. I couldn't recognize anything–nothing looked familiar in the dark. You guessed it. I became hopelessly lost. So lost that after four hours of trying in vein to find my way back to the main road, I had to radio for help. Not that I wasn't calling in earlier–I was. But I couldn't raise the base camp. Finally, I got to a high point on a small knoll where the radio worked and I reached the lodge. When I told them what had happened, I heard the howls of laughter of the other hunters in camp, including my guest–former baseball great, Wade Boggs. Over the radio, the outfitter told me, "Stop where you are and don't move again. When you see my lights, beep your horn and call me on the radio." It took him (and several other hunters who came along for the ride to see the hunter who was lost in his truck) over an hour to locate me! When they did, I wasn't embarrassed or ashamed of getting lost.

The fact is, this is big–very big–country that all looks exactly the same. And unless a person is very familiar with traveling the systems of logging roads in the back-country, getting lost even in daylight, never mind the dead of night, is a reality. The same holds true when hunting through the big woods of Maine or any other state or area that is new to you. The fact is, before you set out on a track of a deer in strange country, you'd better think twice–no, make that three times. You must have years of experience with the land you hunt before attempting to track a buck (or in my case drive a truck), for miles and miles. Actually, that's good advice anytime you're thinking of picking up a buck track in wilderness country.

If you are tracking a buck in the snow and you think you can re-trace your footsteps to get out, this still can be problematic. Moreover, an unsuspecting snow storm or heavy rain can eliminate all your foot prints. There goes your back trail, making it impossible to fol-low your steps back out of the woods.

I learned that lesson early in my deer-hunting career. When I was 17 (back in the '60s), I was on my first hunt in the Adirondack Mountains in New York. This is a vast wilderness that, in places, compares to anything Maine offers. I was hunting in the town of Childwold on a 50,000-acre tree farm owned by International Paper. It was the fourth day of the hunt. That afternoon, on the way to my stand, which was about 500 yards from a logging road and about 1,000 yards from where I parked my truck, I cut a big track in the fresh snow (in those days, there was usually snow on the ground by mid-October).

Thinking I could follow my back trail out, because I thought I had learned enough about the area to do so, I took off after the deer. It was 2:30 pm when I began tracking. That was my first mistake. I slowly walked off to the side of the deer track–cutting back to it every so often to check that it was the same print. After an hour or so, I spotted the buck. I remember his rack even

to this day. I probably recall it bigger than it actually was, but he was the first buck I had ever tracked in the "big" woods.

As I slowly raised my rifle, he casually disappeared into a stand of heavy pine trees. I followed him in. The stand of evergreens was immense and the buck lead me on a wild goose chase as he constantly circled around me. I spotted him two more times–each time only for a moment. The last time I saw him, I realized how dark it was getting. I could hardly see him in the scope. I glanced at my watch and it was only 4 pm Fear instantly over took me. That was my next mistake.

I instinctively knew I had to immediately abandon the track and try to get back to my truck. I never found my way out that day. Even following my back trail became hard as the light faded. I spent the most har-rowing night of my young life hopelessly lost in the big woods of the Adirondacks. I walked and walked (I didn't know better back then that I should have remained where I was), and called and called for help. No one answered. I shot most of my shells, keeping only a few in case I met up with a bear who was in a foul mood.

At dawn I was tired, scared, hungry, wet, disoriented and about to freak out when I heard voices. I ran toward them and to my joy and shock, I emerged on a trail that boy scouts–little boy scouts–were happily walking along. The scoutmaster quickly scolded me for carrying a firearm on the Boy Scout's property. It didn't take him long, after sizing me up, to realize my story was true. In the end, I had walked miles from my truck overnight–many miles. The scout leader took me to camp, warmed me up, fed me, calmed me down, and drove me back to my truck. I won't tell you how far. My lesson and the lesson any one who wants to track deer should take from this is to know your hunt-ing area.

With all that said, tracking down a buck and bagging him can be the most challenging and satisfying of all deer hunting tactics. It takes a conditioned hunter, with experience in several areas of survival and hunting skills to become a seasoned, consistently successful deerstalker. Once accomplished, however, the art of stalking a buck can help you bag your deer when other hunters can't seem to tag out.

▲ When a wounded deer finds its way into standing corn like this, keep a keen eye out, not only for the blood on the stalks and ground, but also for him possibly being bedded ahead of you.

9. Tracking on Farmlands and Small Woods

The best strategy for successful tracking in heavily pressured areas (or for that matter in wilderness areas) is to know the travel routes of the deer. Know what to expect from a wise old buck that has you dogging his trail. Know what he'll do under that type of pressure. What are his favorite escape trails? Where will he head when he's nervous about being followed? How will he react to your pressure? If you know these things in advance, you can plan a tracking tactic that will work.

Even the best tracker will cut a trail and then stop to lay out a plan. In some cases, he calls for reinforcements. Once a track is found, a call over the radio brings a few other ardent trackers together. The stalker with the most stamina is elected to take up the track. Before he does, where legal, the other two or three hunters plan to take up stands–sometimes a long distance away from the track, far enough away as to require the stalker to wait an hour or so before starting after the buck. Once in place, they signal each other and the tracking begins. As the primary stalker gets on the track, he stays with it until he either jumps the buck and shoots it himself or until he pressures the buck enough that it becomes so worried about its back trail

that it begins to forget to pay as much attention to what is ahead of him. Often, the buck winds up walking into one of the hunters who has taken a stand on a known escape route or on a logging road that crosses from one section of property to another.

This is, in fact, how most trackers get their bucks. It is a rewarding hunt, filled with skill and challenges. This strategy is not for the unskilled or those who lack the ability to be patient and persistent. It is especially not for those who cannot keep the ethics of hunting upper-most in their minds and know enough to call off the stalk in fairness to both the sport and the game–if and when that time does arrive.

During my several decades of hunting, I have tracked elk, moose, mule deer, white-tailed deer and even a few bear. Aside from whitetails, I have only successfully tracked and shot two bull elk. But when it comes to tracking whitetails, I have had much better success. I have tried to get the drop on 75 whitetails by following their tracks. Now that may not seem like a lot of deer tracking, but I suggest, for my type of hunting, and for the areas I hunt, it is. Remember, some hunt bucks, like the famous trackers of New England, almost exclusively by tracking

▼ I shot this mule deer after tracking him in soft sand and dirt. His tracks were easy to follow not only because they were left in soft earth, but also because one hoof was chipped.

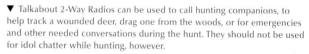
▼ Talkabout 2-Way Radios can be used to call hunting companions, to help track a wounded deer, drag one from the woods, or for emergencies and other needed conversations during the hunt. They should not be used for idol chatter while hunting, however.

TRACKING

them. In real-world deer hunting, a majority of deer hunters track deer only incidentally to a more usual type of hunt. They pick up what appears to be a big, fresh, buck track in the snow while on their way to their stand, or on a deer drive, or as they slowly still-hunt through the woods, hoping to spot or jump a deer from cover. That is the hard-core truth. It is how I generally decide to follow a deer track anyway. It is rare that I leave the camp with the absolute intention of riding along a logging road or walking down a trail looking for a buck track. It is very rare for me to pass up what looks like a good track to continue to search for an ever larger track, like so many of the more famous trackers say they do. So, I guess when compared to some, I'm a casual tracker or perhaps an incidental one. I track, but only when the spirit or sign moves me. For my type of hunting, it works perfectly for me.

Even though I have taken up the track of 75 deer, I can count the number of successful hunts (where following the trail ended up with me actually killing a buck) on one hand.

One was shot as I caught him feeding off-guard on the branch of a cedar tree. Another buck met his fate when I noticed his prints were getting closer together in the snow, suggesting he was slowing down. I shot him as he tried to sneak away as he slowly walked up a small creek. I shot another tracked buck as I spotted him trying to circle downwind to see what was dogging him. I quickly, but quietly, got to a spot where I thought I could cut him off—which I did. An interesting note here is that all bucks were tracked in snow that was at least three inches and not more than eight inches deep.

Each and every tracking experience taught me something and helped me become a better tracker in the heavily-hunted areas and type of terrain that I track deer in. I learned more from the numerous deer I tracked that eventually gave me the slip, than I did from the bucks I outsmarted.

Lesson Passed On

A couple of years ago, I was hunting on my farm in the southern tier of New York. I was hunting with my long-time hunting companions, my wife Kate and twin cousins Leo and Ralph Somma. Opening day dawned

▲ I took this 12-point buck after tracking him on a mountain in Warwick, New York. I wait until the pressure drives bucks to this hard-to-get-to area on the backside of a steep mountain where the chance of seeing another is slim.

▼ Ralph Somma shot this buck the first season on our farm. We had to track the buck for over a mile before Ralph made the finishing shot. It was bedded down with a doe!

with about 18 inches of fallen snow and more was still falling. It was not too much later, when my cousin Ralph called on the radio and asked me to meet him by his stand. When I got there, he told me he shot a nice eight-point buck and wanted some help tracking it. So, I brought along his brother Leo and my son Cody (who was 14 at the time). After discussing our strategy, Ralph suggested that since we did not know the land well enough yet (it was our first season hunting the land), he would take a stand where we suspected the buck might circle back to. I was going to slowly pick up the buck's track and blood trail and follow after the deer.

I brought my son along with me to give him a first-hand experience of tracking a wounded deer. We weren't on the track more than 100 yards when I turned and said to Cody, "Judging by the tracks and the blood in the snow, this buck is slowing down. He should be close by." Those words barely left my mouth when the buck jumped up from behind a deadfall not ten yards to my left. In the surprise and excitement of the moment, I fired and missed. The buck ran off in a different direction.

Again, we picked up the track. This time, there was much less blood to help us. I could see from the hoof prints that the buck was about to bed down ahead of us. I told Cody to keep a sharp eye out. Fifty yards later, Cody spotted the buck sneaking off to our left through some heavy pines. The buck didn't offer a shot, but he was, in fact, heading in a direction that would soon put him in Ralph's path. Each time we jumped the buck, the possibility of him being shot by another hunter on adjoining property became more and more realistic, especially since it was opening day. With this in mind, we slowed our pace and hoped that the buck would slow his pace, too. Just then, a single, muffled report from Ralph's 12-gauge Browning Deer Stalker rang out not 100 yards from us. I took a moment to share with Cody that with a little patience, knowledge to not pressure the buck, and good planning skills, we put together a good tracking effort to get this buck.

Remember what I said earlier about "real-world" tracking. Well, that's what I do. I don't get the chance to track deer in remote, wilderness areas like Maine or the Adirondacks on a regular basis. In fact, when I'm hunting with an outfitter while taping a television segment for our TV show, *Woods N' Water*, no matter how remote the area, we don't track a mature buck with me, the guide, and a cameraman. It cuts the odds of bagging a buck down to a percentage neither the guide nor I can accept. I have a limited amount of time to produce the show and we stand a better chance of scoring if I take a stand, rattle, or call.

All the bucks that I have tracked and shot were in areas where other hunters were. In my view, that is just as much of an achievement as picking up a track of a wilderness buck and taking it to the final confrontation. In my mind, it requires more hunting and tracking skills than wilderness tracking. But in the end, both are challenging and require specialized hunting skills, equipment, and tactics to be successful.

Play the Odds

In the numerous times that I have cut a track and followed it, I managed to see the buck I was following about 70 percent of the time. This is a testament to how successful tracking can be under the right circumstances. About 30 percent of the bucks were never spotted, nor was I able to tell if anyone else shot at or killed them. I simply never caught up with the elusive phantoms. Each beguiled all my attempts at running them down and won the match by giving me–and everyone else around them–the slip.

Even though a majority of the bucks I have tracked and killed lived on lands that could be hunted by others, the one element that remained constant is that they were taken in hard-to-reach places. Most bucks were taken in mountainous areas that I consider to be under-hunted ground–lands that I like to call "tough terrain" where most hunters don't like to go. They are lands that are high and steep and once a hunter gets that high and that far back in, there is usually very little other hunting pressure to contend with. Only one of the bucks was taken in "big woods wilderness country." In fact, several other bucks were shot within 50 miles of Manhattan, New York in southern Orange County! I attribute my success in catching up with all of these bucks, however, almost solely to the element of low hunting pressure. Don't let anyone ever tell you anything different about tracking. Consistent successful tracking goes hand-and-hand with unpressured big woods hunting grounds. You can take that statement

◀ Kate is examining tracks left by a big deer on our farm. She followed the track but never caught up to the deer. The snow was perfect: soft, fresh, and not too deep.

mud, snow, or sand. A mature buck puts most of his weight on his front quarters when walking. It's obvious then that his front feet will sink deeper into the ground than his rear feet. If the track you're following has prints that indicate the front feet are deeper than the rear feet, you're most likely on a mature buck track. Mature bucks swagger as they walk, too. This means there will be a stagger effect between their front right and front left legs–another indication you're following an older buck. Smaller does and bucks leave tracks that are much closer together. Learn the importance of determining if the buck is walking, trotting, or running by knowing how far apart the tracks will be when a deer is in a walking stride or in a trotting or running gait.

Learn to detect what other factors indicate whether the track you are looking at actually belongs to a buck and not a mature, heavy doe. Remember a mature buck is a totally different animal than even a mature doe. He acts differently, instinctively thinks differently, eats differently, and walks differently. Bucks walk in a random way often stopping to make or freshen a rub or scrape. In snow cover, you will see where he has urinated between his tracks. You'll also discover that

to the deer hunting bank–period. These types of areas can be found anywhere you hunt, no matter how populated the area is. There is always some type of terrain that other hunters just won't hunt in (swamps, steep mountains and the like). Find such areas and the chances of catching up to a buck whose tracks you are following increases ten-fold.

Hoof Tracks

There are, of course, other elements that help make a tracker more successful. First and foremost, understand an overwhelming majority of successful tracking is done in fresh, soft, snow that isn't too deep. Next, make it your business to learn all you can about a deer's hoof prints. For instance, is the length of a track of significant importance? It isn't to me. Is the width of a track what really determines a big track? From my experience it is. If it is 3 to 3½ inches wide, I have learned that I am following a mature deer. Learn what the significance is of how deep a track is that is left in

▼ The splayed hoof, deep dewclaws and over length of this print suggest its maker was most likely a buck. The savvy tracker checks other available sign to confirm this.

TRACKING

does, even mature does, usually leave almost perfect heart-shaped tracks. They also walk in a straight line.

A crucial element to tracking is to learn to identify the track as soon as you have picked it up. Know what makes the track you're following unique from other deer tracks around it. Burn its image in your mind quickly. If the deer joins up with other deer, identifying and singling out its track from the other tracks will keep you on the correct trail.

Is It a Fresh Track?

Keep in mind that if you are on a track during a snow-fall and then the snow suddenly stops, and you find tracks that the snow hasn't filled yet, your buck probably isn't very far ahead of you. In fact, depending on what the buck is doing, he may only be 15 to 30 minutes in front of you! A fresh track is always more defined, too, especially around the edges. Older tracks begin to crumble and are less definable. One very important element in this learning process is to understand what tracks are fresh enough to set out after, and what aren't. Only experience will help you here. It took me a long time to learn this part of tracking. I eventually learned to place my boot print next to the buck track and compare the two. If the deer track looked a lot less definable than my track, I guessed it was too old to follow. If it is somewhat less sharp than the boot print, but reasonably close, it usually is worth stalking. Of course, if it is as sharp as your boot print, then get on it quickly.

Know the Escape Routes

It bears repeating that you have to know your hunting area. Even more important, know where deer escape routes are. This is especially true for the real-world type of tracking most of us will do. Knowing an escape route of a wilderness buck is somewhat less important, simply because the buck has so many choices available to it when covering a lot of ground in big woods. This is not true, however, when it comes to hunting bucks with a lot less territory available to them. They are more inclined to quickly head toward an escape route than their big woods cousins. This simply means that a hunter who knows where these escape routes are, increases his chances tremendously when tracking bucks in heavily hunted areas.

Learn where deer head when they are being pressured by something on their back trail. Know as many escape routes as possible. Learn to anticipate what a buck being followed by a predator will do and what he might not do, or where he will head in good weather or in bad weather, on wet ground or in snow. Bucks have a sixth sense about snow. They instinctively know they are easier to follow in snow and will react differently when pursued in it.

Perseverance

Next come the elements that separate the really good trackers from the casual ones. These are the elements of the mind and body. A truly good tracker has character. He or she is able to muster the spirit to go on when the body and mind wants nothing more than to quit. This person has the ability to stay totally focused on the job at hand and is able to dig deep when everything else tells him to turn back. A good tracker has the competitive spirit. He or she wants to succeed—he has to have a will to win. The buck has almost the same determination to put as much distance between it and whatever is on its back trail. It has an intense will to survive.

▼ Master tracker Hal Blood with a buck he tracked and killed. Once Hal is on a buck's track, the buck might as well make out his will. (credit: Hal Blood)

One of the most impressive trackers in big-woods country I know has all of the above qualifications: Hal Blood. In his book, "*Hunting Big Woods Bucks,*" Blood emphasizes his dogged approach to following a track. In several of his stories about taking up the chase in big, wild country, Blood makes it clear that his tenacity for outlasting bitter cold temperatures, deep snow, mountainous terrain, wind, and even rain, overcomes any desire his body sends to his mind to quit the trail. For anyone who intends to track mature bucks in big woods, he must first commit to being a determined tracker like Hal Blood.

Another example of a single-minded tracker who hunts in heavily pressured areas, is my long-time hunting companion, Ralph Somma. His ability to focus on nothing else other than staying on the track and sign is second-to-none. In the many years I have hunted with him, I have seen other hunters quit a trail, only to have Ralph pick it up, follow the track, and find the animal. This type of concentration is absolutely important when you're trailing a buck in heavily hunted areas. It is absolutely crucial when trailing the tracks and blood trail in areas where there are numerous other hunters.

Keep Your Pace

One of the most critical points to becoming a consistently good tracker is knowing how to effectively follow a track. There are times when you want to pick up the pace and move fast. Other times it is much better to slow down and move at a snail's pace, almost like you're in slow motion. By watching a buck's tracks closely, you will know what he is doing and how you should proceed.

If you make the wrong decision, one of two conditions will develop. You will either see a flash of brown or glimpse at the glare of an antler as it drifts into a patch of cover as the buck escapes. Don't expect a mature buck to flag as it sneaks away. A wise old buck has learned to tuck his tail between his legs, especially when he has a predator on his back trail. That's what a tracker is to a buck—nothing more than a predator. I mention this because it is a little-known fact that mature male game animals—like whitetail, mule bucks, bull elk, and moose—that are predated upon learn to live secretive lives. They instinctively avoid being caught with a group or herd of their kin. They are lon-

ers and live within the boundaries of being stalked by predators. They have evolved with an intense instinct to out-maneuver their pursuer rather than blindly run from danger in their attempt to get away. The older the animal, the more ingrained this behavior is in his psyche.

Therefore, the wise or seasoned tracker rarely expects to see a flagging, running buck as he tracks his prey. He knows that he is more inclined to see a buck sneaking off ahead of him. On the other hand, if you track too slowly, you will never see the deer at all.

But, if tracking is done correctly, the reward will be getting a shot at your trophy. For instance, if the buck's tracks have a longer stride than what you have been following, he has picked up speed. Once you determine this has happened, you have to increase your speed, too. If his tracks begin to wander, or pace around nervously in a very small area, or begin to circle, he's on to you and is preparing to give you the slip. Now is the time to slow down to fine tune your pursuit by keeping all your senses at full alert and moving with one cautious step at a time. Keep your eyes scanning the surrounding terrain. Proceed with extreme caution—he most likely is not far away. Learning when to do what, will help make you a better tracker. Again, experience will help you.

Also remember to concentrate at looking at what is in front of you—but not directly in front of you. Most bucks that are being tracked have a habit—a natural instinct—to move off their track and watch for their pursuer's approach from one side or the other. Another problem is that too many first-time trackers, and even some who have been at it awhile, often become over-involved with studying the tracks. This is one of the most common and costly mistakes a tracker can make. Surprisingly, bucks who are being trailed for a long time will often slow up and hide to check out what is after them. This is why hunters who track sometimes see the deer several times during a stalk. This is what makes tracking a fascinating hunting strategy.

Looking Down On You

Bucks prefer to get higher than the pursuers on their back trail—even if it is only slightly higher. While I was hunting whitetails in Montana, we were following a track through a clear-cut. The terrain was flat, but there were several piles of blowdowns made up of tree tops

▲ Bedded bucks will use the slightest rise on the ground to get a better view. When tracking, keep a keen eye out for small rises in the terrain. (credit: Ted Rose)

as well as piles of brush. The clear-cut twisted and turned for over a mile in front of us. Each time we rounded a bend into a new clearing, I expected to see a buck sneaking off from behind a blowdown or pile of brush. Halfway through the clear-cut, I noticed the buck's tracks were getting much closer together and were milling about before moving off again. I realized he couldn't be too far off and I slowed my pace. As I scanned the blowdowns, a movement caught my attention. As I looked over, I saw the buck staring at me as he stood on the only bare ground rise in the entire clear cut. It was not more than two feet high and five feet wide. It offered him, however, what the blow downs could not–a clear unobstructed view of the predator on his back trail. Before I could react, he was gone. I logged the incident in my mind and have never forgotten it. Many times since, I have seen mature bucks use this tactic to help escape their pursuer.

If you are tracking a buck even in the flattest of terrain and you come to a knoll or even the slightest increase in elevation in the topography, pay particular attention to it. If you do, you'll never get caught with your pants down. It is crucial to keep a keen eye on the

natural cover off to the side and ahead of you. Glance from side to side, look for an antler, an eye, a nose, or even the entire deer. I know you have read that it is better to look for parts of deer when still-hunting. But, when you're tracking a deer, be ready for anything. Many times I have been surprised and even shocked to come around a bend or enter a stand of pines to see the buck standing there looking back over his shoulder at me. Sometimes, I have come up on them while they were facing their back trail. This usually happens after they have been dogged for a longer period than they want to tolerate. Seasoned trackers always know to be alert to what's ahead of them when they're following a set of tracks.

One-of-a-Kind Track

Several years ago, just after a snow had stopped late in the day, around 3:00 pm, I immediately went hunting on a ridge behind my old house. I found an unusual track with a very defined chip in the left hoof. It led me to a ravine that I knew well. Most times, only young bucks occupied it. (I firmly believe that certain grounds attract young bucks and other parts of the terrain attract mature bucks.) Even though the track was indicative of an older deer, I wasn't convinced since I rarely saw big bucks in this area. As I approached the ledge, a huge-racked buck sprung up from beneath me. Before I could get my Knight blackpowder rifle up, he was gone. By that time, it was already late and I decided not to give chase in hopes he would return to this spot over the next few days.

The following day it snowed again. When the snow finally stopped, at about 10:00 in the morning, I left to go hunting. Once again, I picked up the chipped hoof tracks heading in the same direction. I approached with extreme caution. As I got to the deep ravine, I glanced at the tracks and saw that they meandered down between the rocks on the ledge toward the spot he had jumped up from the day before. I was looking for the buck when out of the corner of my eye, I saw him just slightly above me and to my right! He went down the ledge, then doubled back up and bedded at the highest spot just off to the right. In this spot he could watch anything that came up from the valley below. Pretty cagey, huh? Again, he was gone before I had a chance to react. This time, I had plenty of time to follow his

▲ I followed this buck's fresh tracks in snow and was able to get a shot at him two hours later. I had its tooth aged and the results said he was 10.5 years old, which may be why his antlers dropped earlier than usual. To age your deer accurately visit www.deerage.com.

TRACKING

tracks. Over the next several hours, I saw him twice. I was tired, however, and my reaction time was much slower than his. Again, the buck had won the match. I figured he had out-played me and that the chances of him returning to this location would be slim to none. I did plan on getting some rest and hoped I could cut his very unusual track again in the same area.

The following day, I left at the break of daylight. I took a new route to where I had stopped the hunt the day before. But as I began to climb the mountain, I again cut the fresh tracks of the buck I was hunting. The tracks were coming from the cornfields across the road. He, too, was heading up the mountain. Taking a good guess as to where he was heading, I quickly walked and trotted to the spot where I had jumped him twice before. I'd hoped the buck was taking his time, meandering, and stopping to browse on his way up the mountain. As I reached the area, I set up my deer-tail decoy for insurance. If I was successful in cutting the buck off, I intended to distract him by twitching the deer tail as I made my shot. I no sooner hung the tail from a branch and settled into my ground blind when I saw the buck walking parallel to my back trail!

For some reason, he decided to take his usual route to the ravine and ledge where he bedded down at the top of the mountain. Before reaching the area where he started to travel down the ledge, he made a sharp turn and started down the ravine. I moved up to the edge and peaked down. The buck moved off so suddenly because a hot doe was 50 yards below. He chased after her and they went up the other side. I watched as another buck with a slightly smaller rack chased my buck down the other side of the ridge and ran off with the doe.

The chase was on again. I followed his track for exactly three hours back and forth over several ridges. Luckily, I leased the 500 acres I was hunting and it bordered 1,000 acres of land no one had permission to hunt on. His tracks eventually lead me back to the spot where I had previously jumped him twice. Just as I crested the top of the ridge, I noticed his tracks stopped on the side of the ridge. The tracks appeared to indicate that he had paced around and then headed toward the flat on top of the ridge. I circled off to the side and approached the knoll slowly, carefully scanning back and forth for him. Then, I saw him looking over the ridge away from my direction and down into the ravine—almost like he expected me to be coming up any minute. The .50 caliber echoed through the valley as the 200 grain Sabot hit its mark. The big buck never lifted his head. He died in his bed looking over the ledge for his pursuer. If I hadn't noticed how his tracks paused and then headed away, I would have never known to slow up and cut off to the side.

One point to note. I also knew when to quit the track as darkness settled in the first day. I knew I didn't have the strength nor the focus to stay on the track the second day and I knew I had him when I was able to read what his tracks meant the third day of this amazing hunt.

The buck had 12 points. His antlers were heavy and palmated. His body was bone-thin though and when I went to drag him out, one of his antlers pulled off. I guessed he was an old buck that had seen better days. I confirmed this when I sent a tooth to a lab and they aged it at an incredible ten years and four months old! No wonder he was hanging out in an area where younger bucks frequented. He was probably run out of his old haunts by other mature bucks that were just too strong for him any more. In any case, being able to read sign from his track enabled me to take this handsome and savvy buck.

10. Recovering Wounded Deer

One of the most important elements to becoming a good tracker of wounded deer is to become intimately familiar with a deer's anatomy. This includes knowing everything you can about its internal organs and its skeletal, muscular, arterial, and cardiovascular systems. It is also crucial to learn all you can about the deer's hide. Understanding where certain hair has come from on the animal will help you identify or ID the part of the body you hit. Knowing deer hair ID will help you make an educated guess at the hit sight and as to what the deer will do, where it might go and how long it might take for the deer to bed down or expire.

Understanding the skeletal structure of a whitetail is probably one of the most crucial elements to eliminating the possibility of wounding a deer to begin with. This is especially true for the bow hunter, who might put a broadhead through bone. There are

▼ Understanding how to track a blood trail effectively will end in a recovered animal. Also learning to interpret all the other clues left by a wounded buck is equally as important to a successful recovery.

times when a broadhead or a projectile does not penetrate the body cavity and the wound ends up being superficial. A good wounded-deer tracker has a chance of recovering the deer with a skeletal or muscular wound if the proper tracking techniques are employed from the onset. For instance, if you identify that the buck you shot has a superficial wound, your first obligation is to follow the deer to the best of your ability in order to recover it. Stay on the blood trail until it absolutely evaporates and all other sign is hopeless to find.

Remember that recovering a deer that has been hit in a non-vital area requires persistence and patience. Equally important, it requires an in-depth understanding of the wound itself. Wounds from different parts of a deer's body often leave different types of blood sign. The color of the blood can range from very dark–almost black–to light pink. Each of the different colors provides a clue as to where the deer was hit. Understanding the colors will help you quickly determine how to track the buck you are after.

▲ This buck's tracks indicated he was walking slowly without concern for his back trail. I was able to keep a slow pace and concentrate on scanning the woods ahead of me carefully.

For instance, bright, red, crimson-colored blood calls for immediate tracking. While pinkish-colored blood, especially with tiny bubbles in it, indicates that the deer was hit in the lungs and should be allowed to rest before pursuit.

Know Your Deer Hair

The same holds true when identifying deer hair and determining from which part of the body it came. Once a deer is hit, a good tracker marks the exact spot (or as close to the exact spot as possible) the deer was hit and immediately seeks to locate the hair that has fallen from the impact of the broadhead or bullet. Here is where a lot of novice blood-trail trackers make their first mistake. They often look for blood before looking for hair. A good tracker always looks for hair first.

I can recall wounding a deer high in its back. I knew this was where I had hit the deer because of two clues I picked up when I approached the location where I shot the deer. First, there was an absence of blood and there was a lot of hair on the ground. Looking closely at the hair, I noticed it was very coarse, hollow, long and was dark-gray with black tips. I suspected it was hair from the top of the deer's back. To make sure, I checked my pocket-sized deer hair ID chart. This is a wallet-sized portfolio with deer hair laminated on white, business-size cards with descriptions of each type of hair and from which part of the body it came. I confirmed that this was hair from the top of the deer's back. This also explained why there was no blood at the site of impact.

Often, deer that are hit high in the back won't begin to bleed until they run 25 to 50 yards. Knowing this, I began to slowly and carefully search for more sign as I picked up the track of the running deer on hard ground. It was easy to see the direction the deer took from the scattered leaves and kicked-up dirt left behind. Within 100 yards, I found blood and was able to follow it until I found the wounded buck in a bed. I shot him as he stood up.

Upon closer examination, I found I hit him above the spine and while the wound was enough to slow him down, it wasn't a killing shot. The buck would have eventually recovered. By being able to identify the hair and knowing that the blood trail was not far

ahead of me, I was able to get a second chance at this buck.

Go Slow–Be Vigilant

When following a wounded deer, I can absolutely guarantee that all good things come to those trackers who are extremely patient and even more diligent. Following the trail of a wounded deer requires a hunter to move slowly and observe all sign when moving forward. This includes not allowing too many of your hunting buddies to join in tracking the animal before you have established some crucial evidence: where the buck was hit (by locating the hair), the color of the blood and the direction in which the deer moved off (whether in snow or on bare ground). By letting others help you, no matter how good their intentions, crucial sign will be unintentionally disturbed or eliminated when too many hunters join the search too early.

Some of the best advice I can give is to simply focus on the job at hand. Stop. Take a deep breath. Begin at the precise location where the deer was shot–this bears repeating. Once you've located hair and blood, it's important to remember to keep looking for blood in places other than on the ground. Look for sign on branches, brush, and hanging vegetation. Your next task will be to determine whether the track you're following is from a walking or a running deer. Never assume anything about the wounded animal you are following.

Lots of Blood Doesn't Mean Dead

One of the biggest misnomers and errors when following a blood trail, is thinking the heavier the blood trail, the greater the possibility the deer was fatally hit. Through experience, many of us learn this is not always the case. Many times a deer leaves a lot of blood sign, especially when the wound is superficial, but isn't fatal.

Years ago, I shot a buck from a difficult angle from a tree stand. My bullet hit the buck and I saw the buck go down. I watched it for several minutes as it laid motionless and thought it was mortally wounded. As soon as I lowered my rifle, the buck jumped to its feet and ran off. Upon approaching the site of the hit, I took my time to look for hair and blood. I find plenty of hair and an immediate blood trail. The deer hair was stiff, very

▲ This hair indicated that the buck was shot high in the back. Being able to identify what part of the body the hair you find at a hit site is from, will help you know where the buck was hit, which will help you decide on how to track it.

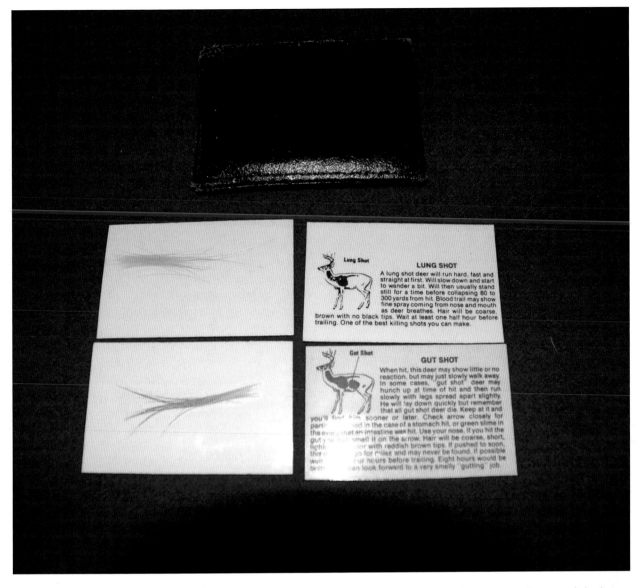

▲ This deer hair chart has over a dozen hair samples identifying where on the deer's body they come from and suggestions on how to track the deer according to where on the body the deer was hit.

coarse, dark-gray with dark tips, and was about 2½ inches long. It indicated the buck had been shot in the brisket. I knew then and there that I would have a long tracking job and would have to pay strict attention to the trail ahead if I was to get a second shot at this buck.

My cousin, Ralph, joined me on the trail and we tracked the buck for several hundred yards. After we had been on the trail for a long time, the buck's wound appeared to have stopped bleeding. This left us with following only his tracks on the bare ground and through a few patches of snow that were left here and there. Occasionally, we found a droplet or two of blood in areas where he stood still to watch his back trail. The buck actually passed within 20 yards of 14 of our tree stands along his escape route! Take a moment

to think about that. I am not exaggerating when I tell you that this buck passed 14 of our tree stands. This is a classic example of Murphy's Law when it comes to following a wounded buck. Somehow, they instinctively know where to go and where not to go in their attempt to escape.

The only stand he did not go by, of course, was the stand my wife Kate was sitting in. Eventually, the buck's trail took him on to private land. Unfortunately, we did not have permission to hunt this property. As we stood there discussing who would go back to ask for permission from the landowner, we heard a single shot ring out from the woods less than 100 yards ahead of us. As it turned out, the owner of the neighboring property shot the buck.

▲ Get to know the neighbors surrounding your hunting land. Offer to help post their property. If they won't let you hunt, at least they may let you track a wounded deer on it.

Understanding the blood, hair, and track sign that we were looking at enabled us to pursue the buck for a few hours. If he didn't go on to private property, we would have eventually gotten a second opportunity to finish him off.

Some of the most frequently asked questions about trailing deer are about when and where a deer will bed down, do they circle, do they travel up hill or down hill and do they go to water? It is important to note that there are no absolutes when it comes to the behavior of a wounded deer, especially a mature buck. As any seasoned hunter knows, big bucks have a tenacity for life and because of this, they tend to "die hard." I have found that the body weight of the animal often determines how far it will move after being wounded before it has to bed down or succumbs to its wound.

I remember shooting a buck in my hometown in a spot I named The Bowl. It is a unique area that often attracts mature bucks because of its extreme cover. One time, a buck about 50 yards from me was walking slowly across The Bowl. I stopped the buck with a blat call and I took my shot. I could clearly see that I hit the buck in the boiler room and was absolutely sure I would recover him within a short distance from where I hit him. When I checked the location of impact, I found blood and hair that supported the fact that I had made an excellent shot. Again, I was confident I would find the buck only a short distance away. But I did not.

I followed a heavy blood trail until the end of the day when it got too dark to trail him any further. I did everything right. I gave the buck enough time to bed down. I stayed on the track and moved slowly and methodically, keeping my eyes out in front of me. But each time I got close to the buck, I either saw or heard him slip away. I decided to let the buck bed down overnight. I was quite sure I would find him the next morning.

I picked up his blood trail at first light the next morning. To my utter amazement, I found the buck bedded, but still alive. He strained to get up. But he was, for all intents and purposes, dead on his feet. One final shot put the buck down in his tracks.

After I field dressed the buck, I was amazed to see that I hit the buck squarely in the boiler room. The bullet entered through the rib cage, took out a lung and ricocheted into the liver. How the buck survived for the length of time it did, still amazes me today.

I have experienced similar situations like this with mature bucks over the years. The old adage, "Big bucks die hard," should be remembered by anyone trailing a mature wounded whitetail buck. Whether it is hit with a broadhead or a bullet, a big deer's tenacity for life enables it to perform feats that younger deer simply can not. The point to remember here is that you should never become disillusioned when you hit a big buck well, only to find a long and arduous tracking job ahead. The fact is big deer have more stamina than their smaller brethren and use the energy in amazing ways.

Bedding Down

Deer that are severely hit try to bed down in thick cover as soon as they can. Even when shot in open hardwoods, a deer often moves to the security of a dense area before it beds down. This behavior some-

▲ Despite being double lung shot this buck managed to travel several hundred yards to where I found him dead. Knowing to track him slowly from the sign he left paid off in big dividends.

times changes if a deer detects that a tracker is following it. Through my years of tracking wounded bucks, I have found they even seek out certain types of dense cover. My long-time hunting companions, Ralph and Leo Somma, have substantiated this. Both of these hunters have tracked their fair share of wounded deer. Ralph lives and hunts in an area in New Jersey loaded with horse and agricultural farms surrounded by dense cover. Leo, on the other hand, lives and hunts on the eastern part of Long Island. The area he hunts is also filled with dense cover. We also have a wide variety of terrain on our farms in upstate New York. Leo's farm has a lot of dense cover on it. They both told me that bucks they tracked, whether they were in New Jersey, Long Island, southern New York state or even central New York state, headed to thick cover soon after being hit. Believe it or not, dense cover includes standing fields of corn. We have all found that a wounded deer will head to standing corn. Standing corn, to a wary old buck, represents security. He instinctively knows that he can hide there safely. Be cautious when tracking a wounded deer into standing corn. It's hard to locate blood in a cornfield when the ground is bare. Be observant as you enter the corn and look for blood smeared on the stalks and leaves of the plant.

Other times, wounded deer will head to the thickest cover around. The pursuers will either pass him up or find it hard to penetrate the cover to disturb him. I have often seen bucks use this type of cover to bed in when they know they are being pursued after being hit. As soon as they enter cover like this, they will bed down. Whenever you find a bed with blood in it, be vigilant. I always recommend standing in the spot and slowly eyeballing the area carefully before picking up the trail again. Oftentimes, bucks will rise from a bed, go 30 yards, and because of the wound, bed down again. Paying attention to this detail can often put a wounded buck in your sights.

Up- and Downhill

There seems to be a never-ending controversy about whether or not deer travel up- or downhill after being wounded. It is similar to the argument about whether or not all wounded deer immediately head for water. I can only relate what I have witnessed with the deer I have tracked.

I have trailed many wounded bucks up the side of a mountain, despite the fact that most experts will tell you that a wounded deer rarely, if ever, heads uphill. I discovered that deer that head uphill after being wounded leave a blood trail as they climb that is less than the blood trail found on level or declining ground. Why? I don't know. But it is a fact.

My wife, Kate, shot a buck at the base of a mountain behind our old house on opening morning. She called on the radio to let me know that the buck ran off into the pines. She was going to wait 15 minutes and then pick up the blood trail. About a half hour later, she called me back to let me know she was about 200 yards into the blood trail and it was heading half way up the side of the ridge. Kate mentioned that she was worried that the buck was not mortally hit because the blood sign was dwindling. Knowing that even a heavy blood trail lessens as a buck goes uphill, I asked her to stop and wait.

We picked up the blood trail and we followed it another 200 yards up the ridge to the first plateau. I asked Kate to stay behind while I slowly and methodically poked my head over the top to look around the plateau for more blood sign. Following the trail, I picked up a lot of blood within 75 yards. Kate re-joined me and again we took up the trail. The blood remained significant for another 100 or so yards until the buck once again started up again towards the next plateau.

As we reached the second table, the buck must have been running out of gas, as he was only bedded 30 yards from where he walked onto the plateau and was laying with his head flat on the ground.

Kate never even had to take a finishing shot. The buck expired in his bed, within minutes thereafter. Upon field dressing him, we found that Kate's shot was indeed a fatal wound and should have left a significant amount of blood throughout the entire trail. The fact is that it left an easy-to-follow blood trail only on flat ground.

Another interesting fact about blood trails of wounded deer going up- or downhill is that for some oddball reason, deer do not seem to bleed any less when going downhill. The blood trail always seems to be as significant as it is on flat terrain. I have never been able to put my finger on exactly why this is, or why a deer bleeds less going uphill.

▲ Although it is crucial to have snow to track a buck effectively in many parts of the country, in places where soft, dry soil exists like in Texas, deserts and beaches, and in the red clay of the south, a deer print is also easy to follow. I tracked this Wyoming buck for two hours over dry loose soil before I found him bedded down in a patch of scrub oak.

You would think the mere fact that the deer is exerting itself walking uphill would make its heart race more and thereby pump out more blood. But that's just not the case.

A different case was documented on a TV show I produced in Canada in 1988. Viewers saw a large-bodied, 140–155 class buck break the rules about traveling uphill after being shot. I shot the buck in the chest and he immediately took off in high gear through the woodlot. The camera followed the action as the buck ran through the woods for about 100 yards, down an embankment, through a small stream, and then up a very steep embankment on the other side, heading toward an open field.

As the buck started up the steep hill, it was noticeable that his back legs were giving way. Yet, he continued his ascent with a mindset that seemed irreversible. Just shy of the top of the hill, about 50 yards above the stream, the buck's life force began to ebb. He collapsed. To our surprise, he then staggered to his feet and turned to look down toward the stream. At that point, I thought he was going to head downhill to the water. Instead, he tried to climb the last several yards uphill. Within a dozen yards, the buck's back legs slowly gave out and he slid all the way back down the hill and into the stream.

I believe he died on his feet as he tried to climb the last few yards to the steep embankment. Why the buck chose to run up this steep hill rather than stay on level ground or run along the stream is beyond me. But, what it did prove is that, once again, every deer's reaction to being wounded is unique. Hunters must keep this in mind when trailing a wounded animal. Nothing about wounded game is written in stone.

Seeking Water

What I found out about wounded deer heading for water is like the rest of the adages about wounded deer: nothing is ever written in stone. Most fatally hit deer do not immediately head toward water. They are simply not thinking about liquid at this point. Instead, they are preoccupied with escape and survival. It isn't until a deer begins to become feverish that it will actually seek water. Most of the time, this occurs when a deer has either a fatal wounded that may not result in death right away or has just a minor wound. In either case, the wound is severe enough to raise the temperature of the deer. This is the only lesson I have learned about wounded deer and water.

11. Tracking Strategies

*N*ow that I have covered the fundamentals of tracking, I would like to get to the "real meat" of stalking after a buck's prints–the tips and strategies that will put a buck you are trailing in your crosshairs. I'm sure many of you have heard and read that some hunters can absolutely tell the difference between a buck and a doe track. Some, especially biologists, steadfastly agree that it is impossible to absolutely tell the difference between a buck and a doe track. I agree with this but only in a general sense.

Doe Versus Buck

There are indicators to help you separate a buck's track from a doe's track. These indicators all have to do with the size, width, splay, and depth of the print.

▲ These splayed tracks were accompanied by drag marks and deer hair. A savvy tracker keeps one eye out for any changes in the tracks or drag marks while using his other eye to spot a buck before *it* sees him!

▲ Dewclaw marks left deep in soil or snow suggest the deer that left it may be a heavy mature buck or it could be from an old matriarchal doe. (credit: Ted Rose)

Hunters often overlook other indicators that will help differentiate between a buck and doe track and can tip the odds in your favor. If you elevate your detective work to visualize not only the track itself more but also the sign that surrounds it, you will, more often than not, be able to tell a buck track from a doe track.

What Size is the Track?

The first thing a tracker should look at is the size of the hoof print. No matter how big a doe may get, it is a rare thing that she will achieve the body weight of a big buck. Therefore, her track will rarely be as large as a big buck's track–but it can be confused with a medium-sized buck's track. Occasionally, an old doe that has made it through eight or more seasons may actually be big enough to have a track that is comparable to that of a mature whitetail buck.

Dewclaws

Another factor to consider when identifying a buck or doe track is the depth of the snow. If there is less than two or three inches of snow, a doe walking at a normal pace usually doesn't leave tracks with the dewclaw marks. This is not so with a mature buck. He always leaves tracks with his dewclaw imprints, despite the snow's depth. I have noticed that the heavier the buck is, the deeper the dewclaw's imprints will be in the snow. Keep in mind that the dewclaw imprints will always be present if the deer was running in the snow no matter if they are left by a buck or doe. Again, a good tracking detective will soon discover that a buck's dewclaws–even when running–are larger in size than a doe's dewclaws. They also leave marks in the snow that exceed the width of the buck print it.

Distance Between Prints

Another good indicator of whether or not you are following a mature buck or just an average one is the distance between the left print and the right print. If it's eight inches, it's a good-sized buck. Ten inches and you know you are following a really good-sized animal. Twelve inches or more and you're on the trail of a trophy-class whitetail.

You can know this because as a buck matures, several physical characteristics stand out and help determine or estimate his age. At 3½ years old, a buck's chest appears deeper than the hindquarters, giving the appearance of a well-conditioned racehorse. At 4½ years old, his fully muscled neck blends into the shoulders and his waistline is as deep as his chest. At 5½ and 6½ years old, a buck's neck blends completely into its shoulders and the front of its body appears to be one large mass. A buck older than this is a conundrum and can be misleading. Once a buck is older than 6½ years, its tracks are often mistaken for a younger buck's tracks due to the lack of muscularity in the older buck's shoulders.

The difference in distance between tracks, therefore, develops as the buck matures. His chest gets deeper which puts more weight on his fore legs and often causes him to have a flat-footed, long stride.

Another indication of an older buck is drag marks. If a buck is dragging his hoofs when he is walking, even in a very light snowfall, it's a good bet that he is an older buck. Older deer, 4½ years and older, will have a tendency to drag their feet more than younger bucks.

When the snow is more than a few inches deep, all deer appear to drag their feet. Bucks will still drag their feet more than does. But it is hard to identify buck from doe tracks in several inches of snow.

I also see this sign when hunting in Texas on dry, dusty sundaroes. There is always a top layer of loose soil where a buck's prints are sharp and identifiable.

▼ The deep chest, thick neck, girth, big belly and the body weight of this buck show that he is a mature buck that is at least 4½ years old and maybe older. (credit: Ted Rose)

▲ Whenever a buck urinates, he drips urine on the soil or snow. When tracking a buck, look for drops of urine for several feet after a spot of urine is found. It will be a very good indication that you're trailing a buck. (credit: Ted Rose)

Older bucks, even on this type of terrain, still tend to drag their hooves.

A buck tends to swagger when he walks. The greater the swag, the bigger the buck. Unlike a doe that will travel through and under brush, a big buck is more likely to go around such vegetation to avoid tangling his antlers, rather than go through or under it. This is especially true for wide-racked bucks. Some bucks are too lazy, however, to go around an obstacle and will push their way through it. In this instance, it is important to see how a buck moves through the brush. Usually, one hoof will be off to one side as he steps to work his rack through the tangles. A good tracking detective deciphers small clues like this to help interpret the track he is following.

Urine

An additional way to help identify whether or not a track belongs to a buck is to look for urine. A buck urinates as he walks. There will be dribble marks in the snow. I often laugh to myself when I see this, because it reminds me of any guy who is over 50 and has any kind of prostate problem. Dribbling becomes part of everyday life for older males–bucks and men alike.

The reason a buck urinates like this is because he is marking his scent as he travels through areas. We have all seen how a dog marks each and every tree or hydrant on his morning walk. A buck is doing the same thing. These dribbled urine marks can sometimes go as far as three to five feet. A doe, on the other hand, will almost always squat and urinate in one place. Even when a buck is urinating to relieve himself, the urine leaves a different pattern than that of a doe. A doe's urine will be concentrated in a small area and in a relatively small spot. The urine mark will show up behind or centered on her tracks. A buck's urine appears in front of his tracks. As any male knows, the penis is not as stationary as we would sometimes like it to be. Therefore, the hanging appendage will wobble around much like a fire hose that the fireman does not have control of, causing urine to be scattered over a large area in the snow. While what I have said may seem like the urine is spread over quite a distance, it's only a matter of several inches.

Use your nose when following a large track–especially during the rut. A big, mature whitetail's urine exudes a strong, musky odor. It is unmistakable once you have learned to identify it. Over the years, while hunting with friends, I have stopped in my tracks and taken a long deep sniff of the air. When I do this, in almost every case, I have been able to find either a marking of urine in the snow or in a scrape. At the time, the odor is so powerful and potent it can be tasted in the molecules of the air. This may seem hard to believe, but I promise you that once you have learned to identify this scent, you, too, will have the same reaction.

The ability to pick up this scent is a learned skill, which will pay off big dividends to those who pay attention to it. It can direct you to a hot primary scrape, a trail of a buck following a doe, into a buck's core area, and many times, to his mid-day bed. The tactic works on bare ground and in snow.

Other Sign

Many times a buck will leave sign that is not as obvious as his tracks or scat. This type of sign is harder to see especially for the novice tracker and, therefore, often goes unnoticed. This is unfortunate because this sign provides as much information about the direction the buck is heading, what size his antlers might be, if he's after a doe and much more. To discover this type of information, a tracker needs to be more of a detective than he or she is when simply following a buck's hoof prints.

Antler Tip Marks in Snow

For instance, I once tracked a set of hoof prints that were wide, set deep in the snow, and had splayed toes. This indicated to me that the track probably belonged to a mature buck. At that time, as long as a buck had points on his rack, he was fair game as far as I was concerned. So, I set out after the prints in earnest. After a few hours walking all over the mountain, I was about to give up. The weather was getting colder and I only had a couple hours of light left. Just then, I looked more closely at the track which was at the base of a log where the buck had been nibbling some fungus.

I clearly saw his nose print in the snow. As I examined it more closely, I noticed that the tips of his

▲ As a buck lowers his head to sniff or feed, especially in snow, the tips of his antlers will often make an imprint in the snow or soft earth. (credit: Ted Rose)

antlers were imprinted in the snow on either side of his nose print. This really caught my attention because most often, the tips from the main beams don't leave imprints in the snow. It's usually the second, third, and fourth tines that leave their mark.

I had to look twice at the width between the points. I pulled out my tiny tape measure (which is always in my pack) and discovered that the points were 22 inches from tip to tip. I also saw several other marks in the snow that were obviously from other tines on his rack. To quit following his trail now was absolutely out of the question.

As it turned out, I jumped the buck on his trail just an hour later. Unfortunately, this was one of those occasions where the thrill of the chase ended with the buck escaping. My mind was briefly diverted by studying his track too hard and I never saw the buck jump from behind a blow down and run off before I could get a clean shot.

The point is, there are a lot of other clues that a buck leaves behind for a tracker to decipher other than his hoof prints. I mention this because many of us become so mesmerized by the hoof prints when we are on the track of a buck, that we often overlook other equally important messages that we should pick up.

For instance, I have learned that antler imprints in the snow can suggest how many points are on the buck's rack. As mentioned above, the imprints in snow are usually left by the second, third, and fourth tines and not the brow tines nor tips of the main beams. Therefore, if you see three points on each side, the buck you are trailing is most likely a ten-pointer.

Buck Antlers in Bed

Bucks that lie in their beds will most often leave an imprint of one side of their antler in the snow. Seasoned hunters and some biologists say that this will usually be from the left side of the buck's head, as most bucks will lay out and put the left side of their head down to sleep. Not that this makes any difference here–I just thought I'd mention this particular behavior.

Back Print in the Front

New trackers are often confused as to exactly what they are looking at. They are often confused as to whether they are looking at the front hoof or the back hoof. You are always looking at the back hoof. The reason is simple; a deer (buck or doe) will always put its back foot in the same spot its front hoof just made. Therefore, the front track is always covered by the back hoof track. Remember that the back hoof of a deer is always smaller than the front.

This is a good point to know for two reasons. One–you will learn to look for unique markings of a hoof such as chips, splits, shape, size, etc., to help you identify one buck's tracks from others as you continue on the trail. Two–if you are not sure about the track you are following, stay with it long enough until you come to a spot where the buck stops or mills about. As soon as this happens, the buck will leave a front hoof print that you can size up to help determine how big of an animal he might be. Once you have determined that

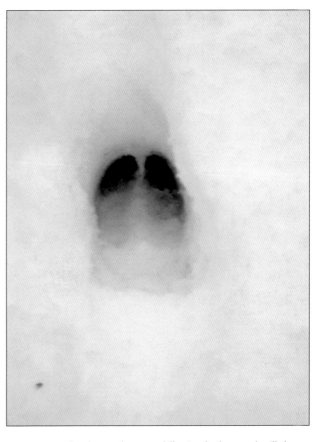

▲ No matter what deer track you are following the front track will always be covered by the deer's back hooves. A deer's back hoof is always smaller than the front hoof, too.

the track you are on is a buck track and it is the size that you want to follow, you can once again take up your search on its trail.

Is That Track Fresh?

Once of the most-often asked questions from hunters who are interested in tracking deer is, "How can you determine whether a track is fresh or not?" The only way to determine if a track has been made "only moments ago"–is if you see the buck standing in the tracks!

Basically, there are many variables when it comes to aging a track in the snow or on bare ground. A wet snow will help keep the track sharp for a longer period than a dry snow. Sometimes this can be problematic when the tracker believes the track is fresher than it actually is. In a dry snow, a track will often have crystals of ice forming in it. So, if you know how long the snow has been on the ground, it will help you gauge the age of the track more reliably.

Tracks that are constantly blown over with new snow are most difficult to age. Under these conditions, any tracker will have a hard time locating a good set of tracks and aging them correctly.

Finally, trying to identify tracks in snow that has been affected by a warmer temperature–or even rain–can be alluding. Under these conditions, the tracks will look older and in some instances, appear larger than they really are because of melting conditions.

Tracks and Droppings

This is where you separate the men trackers from the boy trackers. This tactic requires one to feel and smell deer droppings. Sometimes I squeeze the droppings between my fingers and break them apart to look for the type of forage the deer has been eating. By doing

▲ Foul weather (ice, snow, and rain) distort deer tracks making it difficult to tell how long ago they were made.

this, you can get a good idea of how close the buck is in front of you. On a cold day, droppings freeze quicker than normal. The easier the scat squashes and the wetter it is, the fresher the scat. When it has a mucous texture on the outside and has a fresh odor, drop the crap, and scan for the buck with your eyes. He may be really close!

I know many trackers who swear they can tell the difference between a buck dropping and a doe dropping. Other seasoned trackers are absolutely adamant that there is no difference between dung that is stuck together in clumps as opposed to individual pellets.

I fall squarely in the middle of these two camps. As with anything else with tracking, clumpy scat and single pellet droppings are once again only indicators. Nothing about tracking sign is absolutely written in stone. Droppings change from season to season and from what the animals are currently feeding on.

For instance, in the summer when foliage is greener, the dropping will more likely be clumped together. But herein lies the quandary. Some say that because of that, you can't tell the difference between buck and doe scat. But I have noticed that a buck's scat is like everything else about a buck, whether it is his track, his chest, his stride, his neck, whatever–it is usually larger than a doe's. In the case of his poop, may I delicately suggest–here, too, he has a heavier load.

But this doesn't necessarily mean that he will leave a large, elongated clump of dung. I learned this when I started keeping stats on my Deer Diary Stat cards in 1975. Each time I field dressed a decent-sized buck, I noticed the scat in his colon was usually comprised of individual pellets. I got so curious about this that I decided to do some research on my own. Over the remaining part of the year, I field dressed several fresh road-killed bucks to see if this phenomenon was different than during the hunting season. It wasn't. Each buck had single pellets in its colon. As the years passed, the stat cards clearly indicated a pattern that demonstrated that most of the time, most of the bucks had single pellets in their colons. However, there were times when this did not hold true, but not enough times to change the overall findings.

I noticed that buck scat was larger than the pellets from does (in areas I hunt). That may be different in

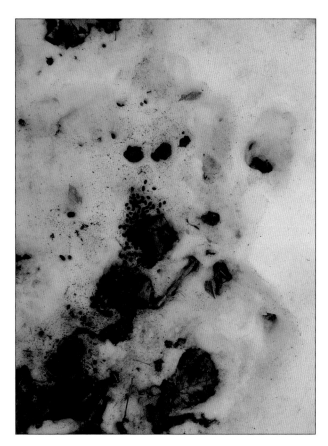

▲ Although there isn't a steadfast way to identify the sex of a deer by its scat, there are indicators that suggest if it was left by a buck or doe.

wilderness areas, but I would not know since I do most of my tracking in farmlands or in the suburbs.

It bears repeating here that unlike my tracker colleagues who trail bucks in wilderness areas, I'm following bucks that more than likely will run into other hunters or enter private land. And so will you, if you find yourself tracking in the real-world conditions in which most of us hunt.

I mention this because when I find a track I want to follow, I have other elements to consider than the trackers who live in Maine and Vermont. Time is against me and with them. The longer I'm on a trail, the less likely the tracking will end in the taking of the buck. That may be depressing to hear, but if you're tracking on a limited number of acres, it is reality. And if you want to be a tracker, you have to own up to that fact early on. Once you do, you will become a better tracker in pressured hunting country and a very good tracker in wilderness areas.

Let me give you a comparison. For the sake of this example, I will refer to big woods or wilderness trackers as BWTs (big woods trackers) and other trackers as PWTs (pressured woods trackers), as that is mostly how

this type of tactic divides itself. When a BWT takes up after a buck, he has time to follow the quarry without a lot of pressure. PWTs don't have that benefit. The BWT can dog his prey for many hours without much care that he will run it into another hunter. Not so in the areas where a PWT hunts. Big Woods Trackers can even react to sign differently than their PWT comrades.

Let's say either a BWT or PWT picks up a buck track early in the morning. They both can assume the buck is most likely bedded down. The BWT can now make a plan and head off on the trail. The PWT has to first take into account whether or not the buck is bedded down on land he can track on, or if the buck is bedded on his neighbor's posted property. If the BWT gets close to his buck and he notices that the buck is picking up his tempo, the BWT can, without much thought, pick up his pace as well. A PWT can't do that. He has to stop and think about where the buck is heading. If it is circling, he has a chance to continue to follow it even at a quick pace. If, on the other hand, the PWT determines that the buck is headed in a beeline toward another property, he has to slow the chase and give the buck time to settle down and hope that the buck circles back or remains within his hunting area—or the hunt has ended. In fact, so I don't boggle your mind with this comparison, there are a lot of tactical tracking differences between the big woods tracker and the tracker who follows hoof prints within smaller plots of land.

I mention this because I don't want you to become depressed when you lose a buck that moves out of your area when you are tracking him. I also don't want you to feel like you are not a good tracker if you don't score on the first several trails you follow. Wilderness trackers have a way of making a lot of other would-be, real-world trackers feel incompetent. I'm sure they don't mean to, but they do. Don't expect to shoot even a majority of bucks that you track in heavily lived in or hunted places.

In big woods country, you should be able to increase your success to one in ten tracks you take up. The fact is, no matter what the success ratio is in big woods or heavily pressured areas, killing a buck you have tracked is the ultimate deer hunting experience—one that invokes all our primordial feelings.

As trackers, we become one with our surroundings and with our quarry. We are the hunter and they are

▲ I followed this buck's tracks along a sandy embankment on a 5,300-acre ranch in Wyoming. I didn't have to worry that I would push him onto other private land.

the prey. We have stalked them fair and square on their home turf and under their rules and we have come away better for it. Tracking teaches us to be much more patient, observant, diligent, and unrelenting hunters. Like our cavemen ancestors, we become the efficient predators all hunters strive to be.

▲ Most of us do not hunt huge tracts of big woods. Therefore hunters tracking deer in suburbia, farmlands or small tracts of property have to be concerned about forcing the deer to move off their property and onto posted land.
(credit: Ted Rose)

Section III

WIND AND THE MOON

WIND AND THE MOON

12. Catch Wind of This!

*I*first learned how unpredictable wind currents could be many years ago. I was posted in a tree stand that was productive only when the wind was out of the west. Around 4:15 pm, a buck came from the swamp and made his way toward my position. A steady breeze blew from the buck to me. Suddenly, 40 yards out, the buck stopped abruptly, lifted his nose and without hesitation–disappeared.

I was confused. The piece of sewing thread that hung from my bow indicated the wind was blowing in my favor. I hadn't crossed his trail, so he couldn't have picked up my odor, and I took a shower and put on clean clothes before the hunt, so I was reasonably sure I had kept my body and clothing odor to an absolute minimum.

Then I remembered the bottle of powder in my backpack. When I sprayed the powder in the air, what I saw would change what I thought about wind currents for-

ever. At first, I watched as the white powder confirmed that my scent was drifting away from the buck. Then about 15 yards behind my stand, the powder dropped suddenly and quickly blew back past me toward the buck. I was astonished that a low wind current could move in the opposite direction of the prevailing winds and was strong enough to even spook a buck.

What I learned from reading and talking about wind and air currents with certified biologists like Jay McAninch, the President and CEO of the Archery Trade Association (ATA), was as profound as it was enlightening and helpful. The information below will help you not only understand wind currents better, it will help you see and bag more deer this season.

Prevailing Winds

In every area you hunt, there will be a prevailing wind direction during the hunting season. It is the predictable breeze that we are all told to keep in our

▼ This big boy likes what he is smelling. If he was getting a nose full of human odor, however, he would have bolted instantly. (credit: Ted Rose)

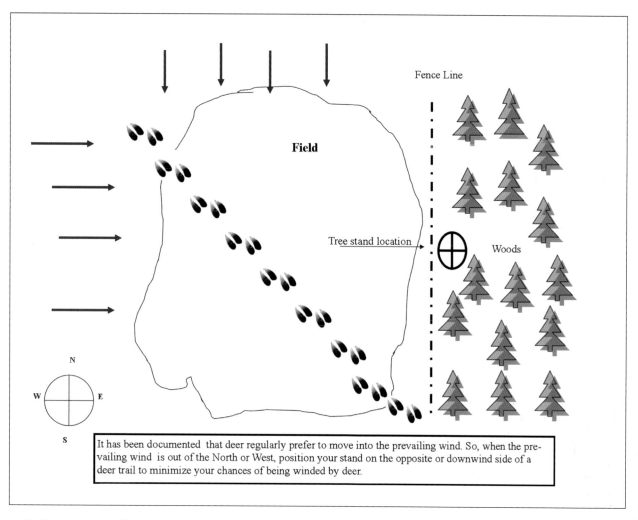

It has been documented that deer regularly prefer to move into the prevailing wind. So, when the prevailing wind is out of the North or West, position your stand on the opposite or downwind side of a deer trail to minimize your chances of being winded by deer.

▲ It has been documented that deer regularly prefer to move into the prevailing wind. So, when the prevailing wind is out of the north or west, position your stand on the opposite or downwind side of a deer trail to minimize your chances of being winded by deer.

faces in order to prevent deer from scenting hunters who are on stand, still-hunting or making a drive. Over most of North America, the prevailing wind is from the north, west, or northwest. This wind can often be the strongest of all the winds that blow during deer season. Other times, it is nothing more than a continuous light breeze. It has been documented that even though deer will move in all directions in relation to the wind, they prefer to move into the wind whenever they can. Seasoned hunters know that deer trails match the prevailing wind direction and customary wind changes.

Knowing the prevailing winds is especially important in more open habitats. Choosing which side of a bottle neck or funnel will be determined by the prevailing winds. When posting along the edges of agricultural fields, pay attention to the prevailing wind because most of the time the does and fawns enter first. If they don't pick up your scent, a buck may soon come into the field as well.

Deflective/Convection Currents

Deflective wind currents are the product of the prevailing wind flowing over an obstruction or flowing into an obstacle that changes the direction of the airflow. For instance, if your stand is in front of a thick group of tall pines or a steep rise or depression, these obstructions can disrupt the flow of a prevailing breeze. For hunters, wind current that is deflected downward is trouble because, if the velocity is strong enough, that current can create a back draft much like

▲ The rock behind this hunter will definitely cause a deflective current to take place. When posting in places with obstructions, remember your scent may blow against the prevailing wind!

the undertow on ocean beaches. If you are in a tree stand, you might never know that the wind current deflected after it passed you and actually flowed back "under" the prevailing stream.

Deflective currents result in many "micro" wind currents that become isolated and localized over relatively small areas. Imagine how water directly hitting a surface splashes in all directions until its initial velocity is lost–and that is what happens when wind hits an obstacle. These small pockets of air are called convection cells and are capable of going in any direction–which spells trouble for the unaware hunter.

Deflective currents are prevalent under low pressure centers, which are common as the days cool and cold

fronts start pushing south from Canada. Beginning in October, deflective wind currents are the predominant air movements and that means deer hunters should not only know these flows exist but also how they work.

When hunting from the ground or from a tree stand, you should take into account the terrain or structure that lies behind the stand. Consider how the prevailing wind will be deflected in the vicinity of your stand. Be sure to test the currents using a fine spray powder from each stand and record your findings in a daily log book. After noting the wind flows, position each stand to maximize your ability to predict what the air currents will be doing.

If the airflow in an area seems unpredictable, then you must move completely from the area. Remember, deflective currents don't occur all the time and they vary in speed. After sitting in a stand several times, you will begin to learn how to use a convection cell or deflective wind flow to your advantage.

"The hunters I've known who consistently take mature bucks are guys whose stand placement strategy is dictated first by the direction of the prevailing winds and, second, by the air flows in and around each stand. Knowing how deer will be receiving wind- borne scents is the key to successful hunting," said Jay McAninch, CEO/President of the Archery Trade Association.

Thermal Currents

Thermal winds are airflows that occur as the air temperature increases in the morning (hot air rises–cool air falls). All hunters are affected by thermal winds, which result from temperature differentials between the ground or water bodies and the air close to the earth. Thermal activity is usually highest during the first and last hours of daylight and it lasts until the circulating air and the ground and water are similar in tempera-

ture. This means thermals are most active during the prime times that deer hunters are on stand.

At sunrise, the ground and water are still cool from the nighttime temperatures. So, as the sun warms the air, there will be a rising wind current. You will have an advantage if you sit on the high side of a stand on a slope and if you approach your stand from a ridge top; your scent will drift up. Used to your advantage, early morning thermals can contribute to a couple of hours of action-packed hunting.

In the evening, the opposite effect takes place. The air cools quickly as the sun sets, while the ground and water bodies remain warm for several hours. In this situation, a down draft will occur as the cool air sinks (we've all felt that sudden quick chill as we pass by an area that is lower than the higher ground we came from). During this time you should enter your stand from the valley bottoms and not the ridge tops and it pays to take a stand below a hillside trail. Within a short time you will see that deer will pass your stand undisturbed because your scent is not carried to them.

According to McAninch, "Hunting from stands in forest areas where there is water and hilly terrain is ideal for taking advantage of morning and evening thermals. Once deer travel patterns are known, the experienced hunter can move in and out of the area and can hunt in positions where deer are at a serious disadvantage. In addition, using thermals can mean the movements of other hunters can be used to your advantage."

The Bottom Line

Hunters who ignore wind directions and currents often see fewer deer. And, the deer they do see are nervous and quick to spook. The seasoned hunter always keeps wind uppermost in his mind. To consistently see more deer, consider the prevailing winds, deflective winds, and thermals and how they will affect your hunt each time you go afield. If you become wind savvy, you will immediately improve your deer hunting success ten-fold. You will see far more whitetails standing calmly within range, which will be the key to bagging your next trophy buck!

◀ I always check how the wind is blowing before heading to my stand. Once in the stand I check the wind every 30 minutes with a powder to be sure it has not changed direction or that a convection current doesn't have it blowing against the prevailing wind.

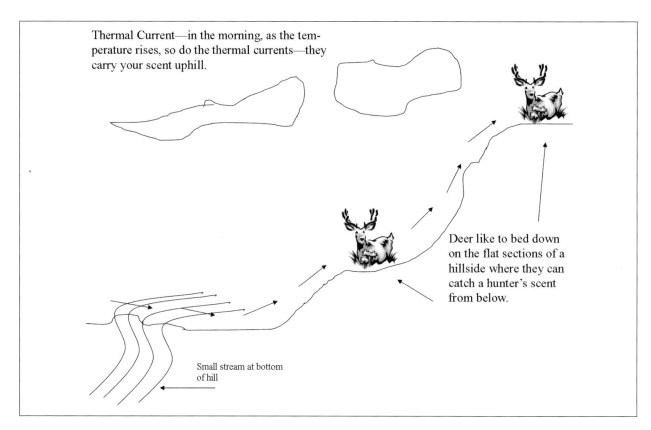

Thermal Current—in the morning, as the temperature rises, so do the thermal currents—they carry your scent uphill.

Deer like to bed down on the flat sections of a hillside where they can catch a hunter's scent from below.

Small stream at bottom of hill

▲ In the morning, as the temperature rises, so do the thermal currents . . . they carry your scent uphill.

▼ Note how the hunter walks to his stand, against the prevailing wind.

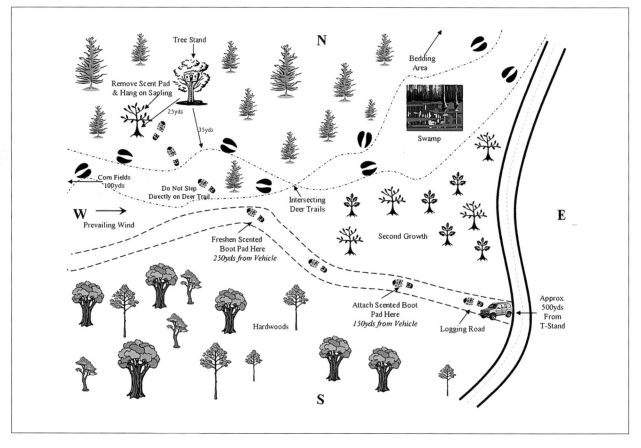

Tree Stand

N

Bedding Area

Remove Scent Pad & Hang on Sapling

25yds

35yds

Swamp

Corn Fields 100yds

Do Not Step Directly on Deer Trail

Intersecting Deer Trails

Second Growth

E

W → Prevailing Wind

Freshen Scented Boot Pad Here *250yds from Vehicle*

Attach Scented Boot Pad Here *150yds from Vehicle*

Hardwoods

Logging Road

Approx. 500yds From T-Stand

S

BEAUFORT SCALE OF WIND SPEEDS

WIND SPEEDS	DESIGNATION	DESCRIPTION
0 to 1 mph	Dead Calm	Wind detector powder rises almost vertically.
2 to 12 mph	Light Breeze	Powder moves slowly in one direction or another Deer movement natural.
13 to 18 mph	Moderate Breeze	Small branches move freely. Deer movement continues to be normal.
19 to 24 mph	Fresh Breeze	Small trees begin to sway. Deer move but begin to use their ears and eyes more to detect danger.
25 to 31 mph	Strong Breeze	Large branches and treetops begin to sway, small trees begin to bend, wind whistles in wires. Deer move more cautiously, stopping often to detect danger.
32 to 38 mph	Moderate Gale	Whole trees move and creak. Deer move, but not as freely. Noises make them more nervous.
39 to 46 mph	Fresh Gale	Twigs and small branches begin to break off trees. Deer movement begins to slow, flee response heightens.
47 to 54 mph	Strong Gale	Larger branches break, small trees bend severely, larger trees are in constant motion. Deer seek cover. Any movement is limited to short distances.
55 to 63 mph	Whole Gale	Trees uprooted, ground debris becomes airborne. Deer remain bedded down.

WIND DETECTING/CHECKING PRODUCTS

- H. S. Archery Accessories–Windicator–www.huntersspecialties.com
- Primos–Wind Checker–www.primos.com
- Buck-Studs–Wind Marker–www.buckstuds.com
- Turkey Creek Trails–Wind Scout–www.eders.com
- Wind Chaser–www.eders.com
- King-Wind Walker Wind-Detector Orange–www.eders.com
- Contractor's Powdered Chalk–Local hardware store, Home Depot, Lowes
- Common Black Sewing Thread

13. By the Light of the Moon

*L*et me start by saying that I'm a firm believer that different phases or cycles of the moon do influence deer activity throughout the year. To some degree, I think that the moon also plays a role in feeding behavior as well. I don't place a lot of confidence in the belief that the moon dictates precise dates of activity levels of the whitetail rut. A moon cycle might coincide with an active rut one year more than another. But I can't base my hunting strategies and hunting time to align with the different cycles of the moon.

With that said, I must admit that I have been a long time enthusiast and student of the planets and other aspects of the solar system. In fact, it is because of my penchant for studying the planets that I accidentally came upon the terms "perihelion" and "aphelion." These two terms describe the continual cycle of the

▼ What effect does the moon really have on the activities of deer?

▲ This is a buck I followed and shot on our farm the morning after a night with a full moon.

earth slowly moving closer to the sun year by year and then retreating back from it again over an eleven-year period. It is this cycle, I believe, that actually influences whether the whitetail rut will be active or lethargic. But I will cover more about this later.

Here are some moon facts-The moon appears to travel from east to west when we observe it in the night sky. However, it travels from west to east in its orbit around Earth.

Understanding many different moon phases can mix-up even the most savvy hunters. A new moon isn't visible and a first or quarter moon is actually a half full moon.

The moon makes one full rotation on its axis in the same time it takes to orbit Earth (which is referred to as a synchronous rotation). This accounts for why we see the same "face" of the moon from Earth at all times.

The moon completes one revolution (around Earth) in only 29 days, 12 hours, 44 minutes and 2.8 seconds, but actually returns to its original position opposite Earth in 27.3 days.

The moon holds an elliptical orbit that varies in distance to Earth from 225,742 miles to 251,968 miles with the average distance being 238,856 miles.

The moon is responsible for creating tidal friction on Earth that slows our planet's axial rotation by .002 seconds, thereby lengthening a day by that much every century. It also keeps Earth from wobbling out of control.

Additionally, it has a day that differs from a 24-hour Earth day, instead averaging a slightly longer day of 24 hours and 50 minutes.

The moon rises and sets at different times every 24 hours.

While Earth turns on its axis the moon moves about 12 degrees eastward in its orbit, causing it to rise an average of 51 minutes later each day.

As if that isn't enough, the moon's height above the horizon varies through the seasons. In early spring, the first quarter moon is highest, the last quarter is the lowest and the new and full moons are about equal. However, in the fall, it changes significantly. Around September, the last quarter is highest, first quarter is lowest, and a new and full moon coincide with the sun's midday high-point. In December, the full moon is highest, the new moon is lowest and the two quarters are in-between. The terms "directly overhead or underfoot," really mean how high or low the moon gets above and below Earth.

So you can see that despite over 20 years of countless articles written about the moon, it remains confusing to most—especially when it includes its influence over white-tailed deer and their movement and breeding. There are volumes of articles, books, calendars, graphs, DVDs and even reference charts to carry afield that are all dedicated to how the moon influences whitetails—especially during their breeding season. By getting to the bottom of this issue, it can help you make better hunting decisions.

For many hunters, the question about planning their hunting time and strategies around the status or influence of the moon's cycle or phase has become of paramount importance to them. Unbelievably, some will not even go deer hunting if they feel the moon's cycle isn't at the right stage to encourage movement or

rut activity. How wrong is that? Very wrong! One never knows what can happen once you are afield. I have either seen or killed plenty of bucks that came past my stand by some other hunter moving in the woods, after a deer drive on neighboring properties, and even some that were chased by coyotes. My point is, if the moon's cycle predicts that activity levels will be slow and rutting behavior will be at its lowest level–it doesn't pay to not go hunting.

In fact, on one occasion when the "charts" told me that the moon's cycle predicted a slow rut and mostly nonexistent activity–I went hunting anyway. On the way to my stand, I accidentally drove a deer to myself as I walked in. The buck was crossing a logging road and when he saw me, he ran back in the direction

▼ Ralph Somma with a buck shot during a moon cycle when buck activity was supposedly going to be slow. That's why I hunt, rather than worry about what phase the moon is in.

from which he came. I hid behind a large boulder and waited. Forty minutes later, the eight-point buck reappeared and started to cross the logging road. He never made it to the other side! So there you have it, a day afield hunting beats the hell out of a day at the office or reading about hunting in camp because the moon's cycle is "wrong."

The gravitational pull of the moon is strong. Its pull affects many life forms and natural wonders in our world–there is no doubt in my mind about that. There is also no denying that the moon's pull affects the tides in the oceans. But does the moon's lunar cycle play an important enough role to have hunters plan their entire deer season around the stages of its cycle? This is the question that needs to be answered once and for all.

Many deer stalkers are convinced that significant whitetail activity is greatest during specific moon phases. Many hunters tell me they are certain they see more deer moving during midday after especially dark nights, solely due to the cycle of a new moon.

The assumption is that dark nights make it difficult for deer to move easily within their range, forcing them to move more during daylight hours. Still others are certain the primary rut takes place during the rutting moon (which is close to the second full moon after the autumn equinox).

Many devoted hunters have been convinced by so-called authorities that lunar phases are critical for timing deer movement during specific moon phases, but believe me, there are many facts that suggest that is simply not the case.

Researchers from the University of Georgia's School of Forest Resources examined how the moon's lunar phases affect the timing of the white-tailed deer's breeding behavior. They wanted to find out if deer hunters who strive to bag a buck should concentrate their hunting tactics during a full, new, or partial moon.

David Osborn, Dr. Karl Miller, and Robert Warren, UGA wildlife research biologists, used breeding-date data from a variety of state wildlife agencies to determine if moon phases had any effect on whitetail doe estrous cycles and, therefore, the rutting activities and behavior of bucks. Breeding dates were gathered from captive deer in four states and more than 2,000 free-ranging does in seven others. Believe it or not, this information took between three to nineteen years

to compile. It was then compared to lunar cycles throughout the birth date ranges.

"We would expect annual breeding dates for a population to be similar if the calendar date and therefore, the same length of daylight, was the driving influence," explained Osborn. "We would expect annual breeding to be less similar if moon phase is the driving influence because a particular moon phase might vary as much as 28 days across years."

The fact is, and many of you have heard me preach this for years, biologists and scientists have long agreed that photoperiod (the length of daylight) is the overriding influence on whitetail breeding activity. There are no bones about it–the evidence is quite clear. Scientists and biologists agree that the phase of the moon has virtually nothing to do with the timing of whitetail breeding activity.

For years, state wildlife biologists all over North America regularly and confidently use calendar dates to help hunters plan their vacations and time afield to match with the peak rut activities. The state of Virginia shows November 15th as the peak of the rut and Minnesota hunters need to be in their deer stands the first week of November. In my first book, I listed the prime rutting dates in most of the northern states and provinces as November 10th through the 15th give or take a few days on either end.

But while any of the dates provided can be used as reliable guidelines, they should not be taken as the last word on rutting activity. As I have often said, there are just too many other outside factors to consider. The rut can be delayed by extremes. Matt Knox, Virginia's deer project leader said, "It's really impossible to choose a specific date because of a variety of outside factors. I'd say that November 15th is a pretty consistent date for the peak, but it's going to vary a few days on either side."

Dr. Warren of the University of Georgia said, "The timing of the rut is influenced by various factors, but moon phase doesn't appear to be one of them." The study found there was no hard evidence to support theories that breeding behavior is controlled by lunar cycles. Dr. Warren says weather, food availability, human activity and a variety of other factors all play a role in the timing of the rut, but breeding activity typically happens within a relatively predictable period, no matter what the moon phase happens to

▲ On full moon nights like this, it seems as though deer wait until much later in the evening to come out into large fields.

be. It is controlled more by the length of daylight than anything else.

New England deer biologist Gary Levigne, who works with Maine's Department of Inland Fish and Game, contributed to the UGA study and he also echoed the theory that the timing of the rut is based almost entirely on photoperiodism.

Again, if you have ever heard my seminars, read my articles, or the chapter in my book about the rut, I strongly emphasize that Mother Nature (perfect in her design) has planned through evolution to perpetuate the species. That means making sure the fawns are born during times of good weather and good sources of food availability for the doe. The bottom line is that evolution has developed a plan where the fawn survival rates are maximized. If fawns are born too early in the year, when it may still be too cold or wet, the does may not be able to gather enough food to provide vital nutrition in their milk. If they are born too late, the

fawns may encounter early snowfalls and won't have enough time to become healthy enough to survive the oncoming winter. So, the 28-day disparity that would coincide with the moon phase theory would mean that fawns could be born 28 days before or after the peak fawn birth date. Most hunters who watch when does drop their fawns, know birthing takes place pretty much the same time every year.

It is important to note that the while the rut may be about the same dates in Montana as they are in Maine, breeding activity in the more northern latitudes like Saskatchewan and Alberta typically takes place over a short period of time, but activity tends to be a lot more intense. On the other side of the coin, deer that live in southern states like southern Texas and Florida have a much longer breeding season, sometimes lasting as long as four or more months. Trying to pin down an actual date of the peak rut may be much more difficult in southern areas because there tends to be less concentrated rut activity around a specific time. But the general conviction among most whitetail experts and almost all of the biologists and scientists I have talked with, is that no matter where deer live, they don't seem to pay attention to the phase of the moon.

The question about whether the breeding activity is influenced by the gravitational pull of the moon has been answered. There are, however, still other questions hunters regularly pose to me, "What about the moon's influence on other deer activities? Do deer feed more during the day during a new moon phase because they can't gather enough forage during extra dark nights? And do the moon's lunar cycles have any affect on deer movement in general?"

Well, not according to my deer observations over the last 40 years, and not according to the many biologists that I have talked with either. No one I know or have interviewed has found any distinct or predictable patterns in wildlife activity during various phases of the moon. Deer movement in general might remain fairly regular if weather, hunting pressure, and food sources remain constant, but the chances of that are slim as deer live in a world of continual change.

Most biologists agree that the most influential factor not only on breeding patterns, but in a deer's life in general, is the availability of high-quality forage. Again, Mother Nature makes sure that the driving force behind the life of every doe is procreation. Therefore, they are designed to respond to changing food sources in order to provide the maximum amount of energy for their fetuses or fawns, depending on the season.

There have been several studies (both private and public) that have demonstrated without question that breeding activity can take place either very early or very late, depending on the quality of the mast crop. When the mast crop is heavy and very early, does come into heat earlier than normal. If there is a total mast crop failure, breeding activity can be delayed, sometimes by a month or more."

So with all that said, what should a hunter do? My advice is (as it has always been), "A good day afield hunting deer beats one at home!" I strongly recommend that hunters stop worrying about how the moon's cycle or phase affects their deer hunting and forget all the hype that goes along with it. You can take this advice to the deer hunting bank because the information I just shared with you is a good as gold–hunt the calendar, not the moon. Remember this–researchers across the country agree–whitetail breeding behavior is controlled by photoperiodism, not the moon phases.

As many of you know, I start hunting as soon as the season opens. Like many of you, I hunt right through to the end of the season as well. As I mentioned in my first book, if you happen to be on the way to work and you see a big buck out and about at 10:00 in the morning, call in sick! The rut is on and you need to spend all day in the woods if you can.

So, there it is, my feelings about placing too much reliability on the moon cycles or phases and deer activity and the rut. In a sentence–it's nothing to really worry about.

Section IV

LAND AND DEER MANAGEMENT

LAND AND DEER MANAGEMENT

14. Creating Sanctuaries on Small Properties

Although most hunters think that a lot of land is needed to create a place for deer to hide and feel secure, that's not the case. The fact is, only very small tracts of good cover are required to create a sanctuary that deer and other wildlife will use to escape from hunting pressure. The key is to plan these areas wisely in order for them to be useful to deer. In order to attract and hold deer on small tracts of land that are 175 acres or less, you must create habitat that deer want to both feed and bed down in and most importantly don't want to leave often.

▼ This is our second sanctuary about 10 acres in size. It includes a large beaver pond and wet area as well as pines and thick cover.

LAND AND DEER MANAGEMENT

Few properties are suited for Quality Deer Management (QDM) programs. I speak from experience, since my farm is only 200 acres. I was worried that 200 acres would not be enough to create and maintain a workable QDM plan. So, I kept looking and found a 500-acre farm in Steuben County, New York that I was considering. Steuben County is one of the best counties in New York for quantity and quality when it comes to deer. The problem for me was the farm was more than six hours away from my home. I knew that the average 3½-year-old buck in the area would score about 135 Boone and Crockett (B&C) points. But, I decided that I wanted a place closer to

home in order to get in as many weekends as I could to plant, hunt, build tree stands and blinds, trails and play in the dirt.

I ended up buying the 200-acre farm that was only a two-and-a-half hour drive. I decided that I would get much more time on the land and would be able to keep better control of the property as well. I knew the average 3½-year-old buck on our farm was only going to be around 115 to 120 B&C points. Through good deer management and land stewardship, I felt we could raise that average to 120 to 125, especially over a few years time. I thought if we could convince the neighbors to follow a good QDM program, I might

▼ After posting your sanctuary, never penetrate it again. If a wounded deer seeks cover there, look for it only at night after other deer have left the area to feed elsewhere.

▲ This photo was taken by a friend on his land in Indiana. The buck is following the does out of my friend's sanctuary and into a hunting zone. He let the buck pass because he knew there were "bigger bucks on the place"! (credit: Ted Rose)

even have the possibility to increase the antler scores to about 130 to 140 points.

After five years of owning our farm, none of the neighbors have conformed to implementing a QDM program. But it hasn't hurt the deer numbers of the quality bucks on our farm that much. By following our goals and guidelines, including creating watering holes, food plots, pasture land, fields planted in vegetables, legumes, grasses, grains, brassicas, clovers and creating secure sanctuaries, we have made our land "deer friendly." We have even increased the size of the land as well. My cousin Leo Somma purchased 110 acres and we lease another 130; so we have 440 contiguous acres on which to practice QDM.

One of our rules is anyone who hunts our land may kill only bucks that are 2½ years old or older and who have at least eight-point racks. We require that at least five older does are taken off the land each year as well.

Although all these elements helped us to bring our deer levels and antler sizes up considerably over the last five years, the one strategy that has helped the most was creating non-hunting zones. Kate, Cody and I walked the farm several times before and right after we purchased it. We marked off two parcels of land in the middle of the east side of the property and in the middle of the west side and created two secure sanctuaries. Each parcel is between five and six acres. One is located in a hard-to-hunt swamp with ankle-deep water. The other is located off a big field and is in an overgrown abandoned apple orchard with thick second growth cover where we found a lot of deer trails and bedding sign. After posting them with signs, "Keep Out–Sanctuary," we never hunted or entered them again over the last five years!

In a further attempt to keep these sanctuaries totally pressure free, we don't allow anyone to follow in a wounded deer during day light hours. If a wounded deer enters either area (this happened only once since we created them), we look for it at night when the other deer have left the area to go feed.

These two spots have developed into high traffic areas. There are countless deer trails leading into and out of both sanctuaries. Deer can often be seen bedding or standing in the areas as we work the fields nearby or walk the trails above them. They have learned that over a five-year period, no matter what is happening outside their protected area–they are safe and sound inside the sanctuary. It only took them two seasons to figure out where to run when the pressure started from neighboring farms. Our deer numbers go up during hunting season instead of down! To our surprise, not only do deer use the areas for safety, so do turkey, and, in the swamp, waterfowl.

Since that time, we have learned a lot about how to attract and hold deer on a smaller property. Our food plots are strategically located near thick bedding areas and the plots are only hunted over during the archery season. While the plot areas required a lot of forethought, it was worth the time and effort. The same goes for all the different plantings we plan each year that go into our pasture fields.

During the spring and summer, we even try to maintain a low profile on the land by not hiking around a lot. With deer, out of sight means out of mind, and it only helps them to want to remain on the property more.

When it comes to creating a sanctuary on your land, make sure you have sections with heavy, impenetrable cover. By creating these areas you will offer doe groups places to find safety year-round. Once you attract the does, bucks will naturally follow. Since creating our first two sanctuaries, we have since cordoned off eight more off-limit areas that are all less than two acres each. By doing so, we offer other doe groups small, but safe, areas for cover. During the rut, the additional does bring in transient bucks. Over the 310 acres we own (we do not create sanctuaries on the leased land), that's less than 10 percent of the land dedicated to refuges. We can realistically bring that percentage to 20 percent of a property without hurting our hunting at all.

The key for our safe haven success program is that we enforce the strictly off-limits policy not only among ourselves, but also with all guests. If any guest is foolish enough to break the rule and get caught–he or she is asked to leave the farm immediately and is never invited back again. This, too, only happened one time over the last five years. Leo and I ultimately want to set a goal to make at least 100 of the 300 acres a refuge. Because of our tread lightly policy which we enforce throughout the entire year, we are close to that now as we mostly hunt the perimeters of our lands, and hardly ever penetrate the interior.

If your land doesn't have an overgrown area to create a sanctuary, you can make one by cutting down less-desirable trees within a two- to five-acre area. Then, plant a lot of thick and fast-growing shrubs like bayberry that grows 6 to 9 feet high; high brush cranberry which grows between 10 and 15 feet tall; a shrub called sandbar willow that can grow to 20 feet tall and is excellent forage for deer; as well as sumac and dogwood. Deer will eat and bed in all these plantings. The trees you cut will also stimulate new ground cover within the first year or two. Your goal is to create abundant cover that is hard to see and walk through. I tell this to clients who bring me in as a consultant to develop QDM programs to enhance their hunting. Here you get it for only the cost of the book! Use it wisely.

Create The Illusion of Safety–Plant Pines

Another way to create a sanctuary or a protected area that can be hunted is to plant evergreen trees. I like to use a variety of pines including the fastest growing conifer white pine. I also plant red pine, scotch pine, norway spruce, white spruce, and douglas fir.

When I plant them, I don't place the trees in straight lines. In order to make it more natural looking and to attract deer to bed there and to seek shelter when the weather turns sour, I plant them haphazardly and a little closer together than recommended. Once the conifers grow, they will quickly attract deer that are seeking shelter, an escape area and a bedding area.

In order to help them grow more quickly, I fertilize them twice a year with an evergreen mix of 10-15-15. You can also use a general fertilizer mix of 16-4-8 which can be used on trees and shrubs as well. Fertilize them in the spring and then again in the fall. In just a few short years your evergreens (especially the white pine) will grow to six feet or more! You can purchase conifer seedlings very inexpensively from many state agencies. I buy them from the New York State Department of Environmental Conservation's Saratoga Tree Nursery. You can get 100 unit bags of 5-inch to 14-inch trees for about $30 per 100 trees or $45.00 for 250 trees!

We have two post-hole drills: one that is 6 inches and one that is 12 inches that we put on the tractor. With the PTO we can drill 100 small 6-inch holes for the seedlings in an hour or so. In each hole, we put some loose potting soil, add a little fertilizer and then plant the seedling. For larger 5–6-foot conifers or trees, we use the larger 12-inch post-hole digger. This is where owning a tractor comes in handy. It makes very short work of planting trees. Otherwise, you can use some brawn-power by using a hand-held post-hole digger. It will take a lot more time and work, but it will be well worth the effort.

Close It Down with Visual Conifer Breaks

The total number of agricultural fields on my farm is exactly 41.0 acres. In the area we call Big View and Finger Field, I have one huge field that is 8.1 acres long. On my south line, it is bordered by the woods of a neighbor (and I use that term lightly) that has two shooting houses within 100 yards and both are 50 feet of my line. The other three sides of this field are bordered by woods with mature timber.

When deer enter this field from my woods they do so cautiously because the 8.1 acres is so large they are uncomfortable with the lack of cover. Even though the field is broken down to eight one-acre food plots (sugar beets, Big N' Beasty, Lab-Lab, carrots, chicory, winter wheat, turnips and clover). While the deer eagerly come into the fields to feed, they are still skittish as they leave the woods. They often stand motionless for several minutes at the woods edge and then trot into the middle of the field. One day it dawned on me—I could create a feeling of security by sizing down each field to look smaller by planting pine trees to act as a visual breakup of the larger field.

I began by planting about two acres with 150 pine tree seedlings and about two dozen 5-foot conifers along my neighbor's south border at the top of Big View field. (This was mostly to block the view along the south line that looks over the entire 8.1 acre field.) The trees also helped to reduce the vast emptiness at the top of the field from the remaining six acres that are below.

To offer a greater feeling of security for the remaining six acres, I decided to border each plot with conifers so that each one was bordered by my woods on three sides and the pines on one side. I planted two rows of staggered pines; mostly white pines so the border will grow quickly.

I cut the most northern end of the Finger Field (which is the narrowest end of the entire 8.1 acres) into a sheltered food plot. On three sides, the woods are no more than 10 feet from the plot. When the conifers grow in a few years, they will block out the view of the remaining six acres and close off the last side as well. The Lower Finger Field, as we call it, will become a concealed food plot! The deer will be fooled into thinking they are entering an obscured area—when, in fact, the other six acres will be divided by the pines.

This year, I also started to plant pines to create other "masked" food plots in that field. I am positive that within a few short years, the evergreen trees I plant now will grow tall and thick enough to give the appearance that each of the food plots is an off-the-beaten trail restaurant that offers security and cover to any deer, even a savvy old buck.

I'm also planning to plant another 250 conifer trees in a lower field that borders the other side of the woods between the 8.1-acre field and another field that is 15.7 acres. This is in an area we call Future Pond. This will help establish a refuge for deer after the pines grow to five feet or so–which won't take more than five years. While it won't be off limits to hunt, it will attract deer in bad weather and as a general bedding area between the fields and woods.

This tactic will work when you want to reduce the size and view of a larger field to help create a more secretive looking spot for your deer. It will fool them every time as long as it is not hunted hard or over-pressured.

I promise you can take everything I mentioned in this chapter to the deer hunting bank for immediate success. Create refuges or visual conifer breaks on your land and you will see the difference in the numbers of deer in just one season. The trick is not to put

▲ Cody plants two rows of Eastern Red Cedar trees on our farm. When the trees mature in five years, they will divide one of our larger fields making it look smaller and more secure for deer leaving the woods and entering the field to feed for the evening.

▲ Kate helps plant over 100 conifers on our farm. Once the trees get above 6 feet, they will split two large fields into smaller ones. The deer, especially wary mature bucks, will feel more comfortable entering the more secretive looking smaller fields than larger fields.

excess pressure on your fields and to stick strictly to the rules of the sanctuary. Don't give in to peer pressure to hunt the area when the deer seek cover in the refuge. When this happens, deer sightings drop in the hunted area of your land and everyone gets "antsy" to hunt the sanctuary. Remind them that when deer sightings drop (as the pressure of hunting season grows) it means your refuge is doing its job! The excitement is that you may be in the right place and the right time one morning or evening when a hot doe forces a buck to leave your safe haven and walk past your stand! Then you will realize the importance and practicality of creating a place of safety for deer to escape to without being hunted on your land.

15. Plant It *Right* and They *Will* Come!

This chapter is a prelude to the information that will appear in my next book, "The Practical Guide to Successful Food Plots." It will be a detailed book on all aspects of planning, planting, andgrowing quality food plots, woodlot management and deer management. With Quality Deer Management (QDM) being such a hot topic today, I felt it was important for me to at least include one chapter in this book that addresses this subject. So, if quality deer management is among your strategies, then you're probably going to enjoy this chapter. It will help you make good decisions when it comes to planting food plots and the overall enhancement of the natural vegetation on your hunting lands.

It doesn't matter if you own, lease, or hunt public land. There are ways to improve the food sources for deer, turkey, bear, waterfowl, and other wildlife that doesn't require a lot of brains or brawn. Trust me, a little knowledge coupled with a lot of time and willingness to work at planting and enhancing natural vegetation can improve your deer hunting ten-fold. The following chapter is just an overview of the many elements that must not only be considered but employed to grow food plots successfully.

Decisions, Decisions, Decisions

Once you make the choice to develop a QDM program on your land, you should understand what a QDM program entails. It is an agenda that takes in four crucial elements: habitat management, hunter control, herd administration, and herd monitoring. All four components help you improve the overall health, nutrition, and quality of your land and deer herd. Once you undertake a QDM program you become a game and land steward.

▼ Planting food plots on large plots like this, or on small half- to one-acre tracts of land, to attract and hold deer is catching on all across the country. (credit: Windigo Images)

▲ Several does in a corn field left standing. I leave several acres of corn standing on our farm to help feed deer and other wildlife through the tough winter months.

Contrary to what most QDM would-be hunters believe, you do not need a huge piece of land to begin practicing QDM. While it helps to have a big piece of property of 500 acres or more to practice QDM, it can be done with 100 acres or less. The only difference between the two is that on the larger piece you can almost assure yourself that a greater portion of the deer on your land will remain there even during the hunting season. On smaller pieces, the deer you have fed and groomed to have better body weights and antlers will also be using the neighbor's property. That is why if you have a piece of land between 50 and 100 acres you should try to enlist the cooperation of your bordering neighbors to undertake a QDM program as well.

Whatever size property you have, all you need to do is set aside one percent on small pieces to five percent on very large tracts of land. On the combined acreage that my cousin Leo and I own (actually our wives own them), we have dedicated about two to ten percent of

the land to plantings and other habitat improvement. For the guy who owns 50 acres or less, planning to set aside two to three acres is certainly practical.

It is important to remember before you make a decision about undertaking a QDM program that not all lands will benefit from such an agenda. QDM is not a magic pill that will fix all ills concerning your deer herd. If your property is located in areas with very high deer densities, growing food plots may only bring on more problems by increasing the overall deer numbers even further! As any qualified biologist or land manager consultant will tell you, the land can only support so many deer and anyone considering a QDM program must keep this in mind before moving forward. If this is the case, then you must undertake a very serious deer reduction plan including taking as many does as is practical to get the numbers down for at least two to three years before planning a QDM program. Most of us, however, don't have that problem. In fact, we have the exact opposite complication.

Your next consideration is to decide on exactly what level of management you should undertake. I recommend to all my clients (those who hire me to consult with them about QDM) to walk before you run. Basically, you must decide if an involved management program is practical for you. If you start small by just planting a few green plots in the woods, along trails, or perhaps in a small open field, you will get your hands in the dirt and soon find out if playing in the dirt is for you.

Once most people get the feel of planting they enjoy it. It doesn't take long before someone who was planting to just attract deer during the hunting season, turns into a full-fledged deer manager. Now, his planting plans are focused on understanding nutrition, population control, water management, ecology, and deer behavior. He has made a complete metamorphosis from hunter to land steward.

Time to Plant

Okay, now you have made the assessment of what you intend to plant. No matter how big or small your land is, or whether you are clearing small patches of property in the woods or planting in fields, the very first step is to remember the adage "tools make the job easier." When it comes to playing in the dirt, nothing could be more profound! Knowing where to plant is a detail that requires a lot of planning. There is not enough space in this book to discuss it thoroughly here. Just remember that knowing where to plant is as important as any thing you have to consider when planting crops.

For now, let's just say that there are a few options. If you already have crop fields–that's a plus. If not, you can turn over old fields that have not been used in a while. You can also brush hog overgrown fields and

▼ Using Arctic Cat ATVs and food plot planting SpeedPoint accessories helps to reduce the workload and ensures that your plots will grow to their maximum potential. (Credit: Arctic Cat.com)

▲ When planting seeds in a small plot of up to one acre using a seeder like this, is much better than a hand seeder as it will broadcast the seed further and more evenly.

turn them under to create plots. It is also possible to create plots in the middle of woodlots but this takes a lot of work, time, and money on your part. I have found it is better to hire out this type of work.

Hire a Dozer to Clear Woodlots

For hunters who have property that is entirely wooded and you want to create food plots, heed this suggestion carefully. If you have to remove trees and brush to plant a plot in the woods, hire a dozer and an operator. In the end, it will cost you a lot less time, money, and aggravation. It is also safer. A dozer can create several half-acre to one-acre stands in a ten-hour day (depending on the size of the trees removed). Even if you need to hire a dozer for a couple of days, it is worth the money.

Plots created and surrounded by the cover of woods are secure and a major attraction to deer and other wildlife. You can also have a dozer create differently shaped plots. You can have a long and narrow strip 20 yards wide by 100 or more yards long, or a square, round, rectangular, or even a zigzag-shaped plot. All of these types of plots in areas of cover make deer feel comfortable when feeding in them because with one jump, they can be back in the safety of the surrounding cover.

Broadcasting by Hand

If you believe you can plant healthy crops that will produce nutrition and tonnage for your deer by simply broadcasting seeds over the solid ground–boy do I have a bridge to sell you! With that said, there are some instances when you can broadcast seed, but only on ground that has been prepared to accept the seedlings (if you want them to grow to the best of their potential).

When you decide to become a food-plot planter and begin the work to reclaim fields or woodlot clearings, the very next step is to recognize that using the right tools for the job at hand is a crucial element of planting success. Using a 35-HP tractor with large attachments to plant a small plot in the middle of a woodlot is overkill and not practical. Neither would it be realistic for you to use a rake and seeder to plant a five-acre field of clover!

▼ This long narrow strip was cleared by hand and planted with clover. It is 50 yards from one of our fields. It is protected by woods on all sides and is regularly used by bucks during the hunting season that wait until low light or dark to enter the fields.

The prudent thing to do before you begin your plantings is to think through exactly what type of equipment will work best on your land, provide you top quality crops, and will offer you the least amount of labor. Also think about what equipment you can afford to purchase without breaking the bank or getting a divorce.

Over and over again, I have witnessed sportsmen get frustrated or even give up on planting food plots because they don't know what equipment to use to plant the crops they want to grow. Many of them take the "broadcast by hand" advice too literally. While broadcasting seed over bare ground works at times, it never works as well as when you prepare the ground before seeding.

If you have small areas to plant by hand, the best advice I can give you is to understand that, in order to grow a crop that will provide nutritional value and maximum tonnage, there will be some labor involved. In some instances, the labor you put into some plots can be downright back-breaking. It should be noted here that the more work you put into planting a plot, the more you will get out of it and that is a hard-core fact.

For instance, if I'm planting a small quarter acre or smaller spot that I want to clear out in the woods, I begin by thinking through everything I will need in the way of equipment to make the plot grow to its maximum potential. I always take a sturdy hand rake with iron claws to spots like this. It will quickly help me determine how much work will be involved in planting a plot in a rocky or root-filled area in the woods.

You can determine what type of plot you will have by "test-raking" the area. Rake two or three places within the given area you want to plant. If a majority of the spots you rake cause the teeth of the rake to constantly get hooked up on a lot of large or strong roots of trees or turn up rock after rock, you can be sure this will be an area that will take a lot of energy and time to prepare in order for it to grow seeds correctly. If you do not find a lot of rocks just an inch or so under ground and the tree roots are not getting caught on your rake teeth, the area may be a prime spot for planting as long as the soil pH is not extremely low. (You can ignore roots of low brush when testing the spot because they are easier to pull up and don't require the hard labor needed to remove tree roots.)

▲ We hand cleared this planting lane of all brush, small trees, large rocks and tree roots with a chain saw, pruning shear and back labor and then raked the soil and planted it with clover.

Good choices of equipment include a soil test kit, a strong leaf rake, a sturdy garden rake with iron teeth, a heavy four-pronged pitch fork, a sharp, pointed spade, a large pair of pruning sheers, a small hand-held pair of pruning sheers, a chain saw, a hand-held or two-wheeled seeder, and a seed compactor (something as simple as a piece of fence with a cinder block and rope to pull over the planted area to smooth it out). You will also need a small hand-held weed killer and fertilizer spreader.

Once the soil is broken up and raked, make sure to rake it over several more times in order to make the soil as loose as possible. The finer the soil is before you plant it, the better it allows the seed to germinate and grow. Of course, it should not be so fine that it will blow off after a strong wind. The next step is to remove all the remaining roots that you find up to a depth of about a half-inch to just below the surface. You can cut them back with the pruning sheers as the rake pulls them free from the ground. Also, remove as many large rocks from the area as possible. Do not get rock crazy here. You're not looking to build a stone wall with the rocks. It is not necessary to remove stones that are smaller than the size of an open hand, unless they are at the surface and easy to rake away.

Once the soil in the plot begins to look like a small garden patch and the soil breaks easily in your hands, it is ready for the next step. Fill your weed-killer with a solution that will eliminate all the unwanted weeds and other growth in the area you have raked. Make sure you spray it thoroughly, not only in the plot but along the borders of the plot as well. Spray broadleaf and grass weeds. This will prevent weeds, roots, and other unwanted plant material from invading your plot and taking it over as the seeds grow. Don't use weed killer if you know it is going to rain within a day or two of spraying because it will lessen the destruction of the weeds and other unwanted plant material.

Check your spot a week or so later. If the unwanted plant material is brown and looks dead you are ready for the next step. If not, you may have to repeat the weed killing process again. Once you are satisfied that the weeds are controlled, it is advisable to take the garden rake and rake the area again as it will probably have hardened at the surface since the last time you raked it.

Now it is time to lime the area heavily in order to get the pH to the desired level (which your soil test kit determined when you started the plot). If the soil sample is less than 6.0, the soil is acidic and may not be beneficial or it can even be toxic to some species of plants that you might use. You should try to get the pH to about 6.0 or ideally 7.0 which is neutral. Once you have accomplished that, only then can you can move to the next step of putting lime in the plot.

No matter what you read or hear, this is a fact: It takes a considerable amount of lime in order to change the soil's pH. It also takes time. If you lime an area in hopes of having the soil's pH benefit from the lime within a few weeks or even months, you're fooling

▲ Using a small lime spreader you'll be able to get to hard-to-reach plots easier. If you have large fields to lime (20 acres or more), hiring a commercial truck to spread your lime is more practical.

▲ We cleared this spot of low lying brush and second growth and fertilized and limed it for a year before planting it.

planting equipment. Most of you will opt for using an ATV and planting attachments. I can tell you–without hesitation–there is nothing wrong with using ATVs and attachments to plant your ground. In fact, I used them exclusively for a few years before I decided to move up to a 35 HP tractor. In fact, I still use my an ATV to get into tight spaces where my tractor won't go.

If your budget or the size of your land and the plots you are planting do not require a tractor, then buy yourself a quality ATV with enough horsepower to pull disk harrows, brush hogs, grass cutters, compactors, and other heavy attachments. Most of you will plant several one-quarter acre to half-acre plots in woodlot clearings, long clover patches in the woods, in small fields, or reclaim overgrown grass fields. If that sounds like your land–then my friend–you will have to invest in several pieces of equipment in order to do the job right and not to lose the investment you make in time, money, seed, and labor.

I use an Arctic Cat 700 cc and a Firmiseeder by Modern Habitat Solutions. It requires and ATV with at least 500 ccs. They are must-have pieces of equipment for me on my place. Whatever brand ATV you purchase, make sure it will pull an attachment that will disk the ground, seed, compact the soil, mow, and much more. With a little research you will find plenty of companies that make (s) all types of farm attachments. Recently, however, I discovered that Modern Habitat Solutions, Inc., developed a planter specifically designed for outdoorsmen who want to plant food plots but don't need a tractor and large attachments to do so.

Don't kid yourself. If you are going to take planting crops seriously and don't have either the budget or the need for a tractor, you will need an ATV and a Firmiseeder (or a similar type of unit) to get the job done right. It pays to spend a little extra money to buy the right tools. Because if you don't, not only will you waste time and effort, your crops will not grow to their potential. ATVs and quality attachments are very effective tools for planting food plots. Just be sure to give them the maintenance they deserve and warrant for performing the hard work of planting crops. A machine and its attachments will only work as well as you take care of them.

yourself. It takes a lot of lime and at least six months for lime to do its job correctly. But, to start a plot, even with slightly acidic soil, it's worth it.

To plant in a clearing you have made in the woods, in an overgrown reclaimed field, or in an old field of grass, you will need to consider abandoning the hand tools for an ATV with small planting attachments.

The bottom line about planting any crop and making it worth the time, money, and hard work you pour into it, is "plant it right and they will come!" Any seed you put in the ground should be put in the ground and not on top of it. You will get a much better crop when you break the soil and plant the seed under the freshly broken earth to the proper depth (as noted on the bag) and then smooth over the rough soil as gently as possible.

Medium Size Machines

There is no doubt in my mind that a vast majority of you do not have unlimited funds for purchasing

▲ The wise food plot manager realizes to save time, money, and a lot of frustration, it pays to invest in buying quality equipment like this implement, called the Firminator (www.firminator.com). (credit: Firminator)

Small Tractors

For a variety of reasons, including buying larger property or having land with a lot of agricultural fields to plant, the time may come when you want to move up to a tractor. When it comes to planting and tilling large acreage, turning old fields into crop-producing pastures, removing large rocks from fields with a bucket loader, or pushing down brush on your property, the practical land manager understands that the wisest move is to invest in a 25 to 50 horsepower tractor when the time and budget allows.

Tractors are reliable pieces of equipment that make the job quicker and easier. But there are many choices. Agricultural tractors are large, heavy-duty machines suited more toward commercial farming than food plot planting. The smaller utility tractors are less powerful but are built to withstand much of the same hard work their larger brothers do only on a smaller scale. Then

there are the really small tractors called "compact" tractors. These units are for guys who own 100 acres of land (with about 20 percent tillable fields). They are less powerful than both the agricultural and utility tractors but they can still get the job done as long as they aren't used on large tracts of land.

The best feature tractors offer is the Power Take Off (PTO). A PTO enables the tractor to drive implements such as brush cutters, post-hole diggers, and wood chippers. Tractors also have several types of tires that help it work better in different types of soil. An important "opt-in" to consider when getting any tractor is to purchase one with four-wheel drive.

The utility and compact tractors (like our New Holland) are small-farm friendly and will enable you to develop and grow the very best possible food plots as well. Small tractors and attachments like a disk harrow (tiller), hay and brush cutter, a one- or two-point plow, brush hog, spraying rig, bucket loader and a primary seeder and compactor are good start-up choices of equipment attachments.

No matter what you decide to plant with, an ATV with attachments, a tractor, or even by hand, I highly recommend getting a utility vehicle (when your budget can afford it). They are the most useful non-planting vehicle you can own when you have a lot of acreage to plant and woods to maintain. Work on the farm you being able to depend on a work horse of a machine. A good utility vehicle should be able to hold plenty of planting equipment (shovels, rakes, bags of seed, fertilizer, lime, etc.)and (later in the year) hunting equipment, hunters and harvested deer, too.

You can check out the utility vehicles mentioned at www.firminator.com. Pay your local dealer a visit. They will give you the best advice available and will help you make the right choice in purchasing the type of equipment that will work best for your land, needs, and budget.

Now that you have chosen the type of equipment you need for planting, there are very specific steps you must use before planting even a single seed. Next, you must decide where to put your food plots. This is an often overlooked element of QDM. Depending on what you are planting, consider the soil content, the amount of runoff the plot has to deal with, how it lies in relationship to prevailing winds and your stand locations, etc. With an aerial photograph of your land (you can start with Google maps), mark out the different plots and what you think you would like to plant.

Next, before planting, start the process for growing crops that will provide maximum nutrition and yield

▼ If you plant 20 acres or more, consider using larger equipment and implements. It will decrease your planting time and workload.

▲ Having a Power Take Off (PTO) feature enables the tractor to drive rotary implements.

(known as tonnage) for the time and work that will be invested. To do this, you must commit to following specific planting guidelines of all plantings.

Test Your Soil First

Exactly what is a soil test? That may seem like a no-brainer of a question to you. But it is surprising how many people actually don't know the complete answer to that question. A soil test is a method a lab uses to chemically remove the elements from your soil (phosphorus, potassium, calcium, magnesium, sodium, sulfur, manganese, copper, and zinc) and then determines how well a plant or plants will grow with the available elements found in your soil. The quantity of available nutrients in the sample determines the amount of fertilizer that should be added to improve the soil. A soil

test also calculates the soil pH levels, which include humic matter and exchangeable acidity. This analysis will determine if lime is needed and, if so, how much to apply to the soil.

So is it really important to get a soil test? You bet it is. It encourages plant growth by telling you exactly how much lime and fertilizer you need. In the end, this will save you time and, more importantly, money! I often wind up seeing growers guess how much lime and fertilizer is needed. This is a real common error made by a lot of food plot planters. If you use too much lime for instance, the pH levels may get too high. When the pH levels are too high, this may cause the nutrients like iron, manganese, boron, copper, and zinc to become less available to plants! Therefore, applying too much lime and fertilizer not only isn't going to grow better crops it is also cost ineffective. By simply using a soil sample report, you will be able to eliminate the guessing-game aspect. In addition, many food plot planters don't realize just how much lime it takes to raise the pH levels. Tons are required per acre. Most times, I see folks apply several bags of lime per acre and that has little affect on soil pH.

Start by taking a small soil sample of each area you intend to plant. You do not need a lot of soil. Most places only test a tablespoon of soil to get the pH level. It is important, however, that you get soil from a few inches below the surface. Then send your soil sample to your local farm supply dealer or to any of the seed

▼ On my farm, I depend on my Arctic Cat Prowler and the TBX 700 LTD (EPS). They are tough and dependable machines. The bed on the TBX has a 300 lb. capacity that makes short work of anything you want to load, haul, or dump!

A kit like this helps you get soil sample and fertilizer results quickly and easily. They are available in Wal-Mart and other sporting goods retailers.

were slightly off. If you do want to use a hand-held pH tester, they are available at Cabela's, Bass Pro Shops, Gander Mountain, and other retailers. It is the simplest and easiest way to test your soil quickly without having to send the soil out to a lab. But for total accuracy, I would recommend using a lab.

The key here is to be sure your pH levels are as close to neutral (7.0) as possible. Remember that lime takes time to absorb into the soil and the best results are only realized after a year or so, although there can be minor positive results sooner than that.. Although there are some minor positive results quicker than that. Once you have limed the soil, you can prepare for the next step to successful planting. To avoid choking, coughing, burning eyes and getting lime everywhere but where you want it (including in all the working parts of your equipment), you may want to use lime pellets instead of powdered lime (although I have always gone the choking, coughing, and burning eyes way).

No matter what method you choose to test your pH levels, remember that it is the first step to growing the very best crops you can grow. It will help you improve your germination, help to quickly establish the food plot stand, improve forage and yields, and help what you plant last longer.

Soil Preparation

It is also important to know what minerals your soil is lacking. Once you know you, can accurately

companies that sell signature seeds. A company like Crop Production Services (CPS) has locations in 16 states nationwide. If you live anywhere east of Iowa, CPS may be a source for you to work with.

Sending your sample to a company called Building Whitetail Paradise™ is another option. They sell soil test kits that are available in most sporting stores, as well as Wal-Mart. You can take a sample of your soil and send it to them and they will analyze it for phosphorus, potassium, calcium, magnesium, and organic matter. They will send your information back to you in short order for very reasonable rates.

A word of caution here, most hand-held pH testers I have purchased for about $20 didn't consistently provide accurate pH levels. When I did a test by comparing their results to the results of a lab, the soil samplers

▼ This is all the soil you will need to send to a lab for them to take an accurate reading of your soil's nutrients.

LAND AND DEER MANAGEMENT

▲ Spreading minerals even on top of your soil is not legal is some states. Before you put minerals in or on the ground, check with the laws in your state.

plan on what minerals to use to enhance your soil. Remember, putting minerals on top of the soil is unlawful in some states like New York. When I add minerals, I have my farm supply company dump tons on my fields and then I immediately turn them under the soil. Enhancing your mineral content will not only help to grow better crops, it will also quickly help you deer herd's overall health. It will help develop better antler growth on the bucks that live on and around your property!

Each crop you grow also requires specific types of fertilizer (nitrogen, phosphorus and potassium–also known as N-P-K) in order for it to grow to its maximum potential. Crops require these elements in the largest amounts and thus they form the basis of most commercial fertilizers. For instance, an average one-acre plot of turnips requires about 200 pounds or more of 19-19-19 (for every 100 pounds of fertilizer there are 19 pounds of nitrogen, phosphorus and potassium) topped off with about 100 pounds of ammonium

sulfate. Nitrogen is the key element for plant protein production. Calcium and phosphorus are essential building block elements for antler growth, bone, milk, and body growth for deer. So, including these elements in your soil is very important not only for the deer, but the plants as well.

If you grow corn you need to feed it nitrogen. This is a necessary element for healthy foliage and stem growth. It is also crucial in helping make the corn stalks and leaves look a healthy green instead of yellow–nitrogen promotes dark green-leaf color. Phosphorus is an important nutrient for promoting better root development and better flower production. Potassium helps in metabolism and helps the plant make food. You can plainly see why these elements are so important to your crops.

Most legumes like clover contain a legume bacterium (rhizoid). If not, they must be inoculated before planting the seed. If they are not inoculated, they cannot form the root nodules necessary to fix nitrogen from the air and the result will be poor growth potential. Inoculates are simply different types of bacteria that certain plants require mixed into their seeds prior to planting them. There are many different types of bacteria including *sinorhizobium, meliloti, rhizobium, I.b.trifollii, bradyrhizaobium spp* and so on. Knowing which bacterium your plant needs is crucial to its growing success. For instance, white clover which is considered the filet mignon of all the clover seeds, requires rhizobium, *I.b.trifollii* bacterium to grow best. You can purchase a lot of seeds that come already inoculated. If the seed isn't inoculated, then you can purchase the correct bacteria to add to your seed before you plant it.

Spray for Weed Control

The next step is the most crucial element to growing hardy crops. Without it, not even lime, fertilizer, or minerals will help your plants grow to their maximum potential. I'm referring to weeds that overtake the crops. By fertilizing and liming, you not only help your crops growth potential, you also help the weeds grow better. So without a sound thought-out plan to control weeds in your food plots, nothing–and I mean absolutely nothing–will hinder the growth, height, tonnage, and nutrition of the crops you plant more than weeds and unwanted native grasses.

▲ To get the best results when weeding, we spray twice, once after tilling and more importantly again after the weeds have had a chance to grow two or three inches high.

Weeds will compete with your crops and win over any planted area that is not sprayed properly prior to planting every time. The best time to spray is after the weeds and native grasses have had a chance to grow a few inches tall. You will get the best results by spraying then. I usually spray the plots I plant twice. Once with a long spray unit with multi spraying heads that attaches to my Arctic Cat ATV and then I spray the growing weeds and grasses as heavily as possible (according to directions). If I see some random weeds and grasses have grown over the next week, then I spot spray any unwanted native grasses and weeds that I may have missed the week earlier with a hand-held backpack unit. Each time I try to plan it when there will not be rain over the next few days and when there is either little or no wind. Keep in mind, that some of the more recent weed killers allow you to spray as long as it doesn't rain for several hours after you spray. But, they are more expensive and weed killer is expensive to begin with! Even with that said, don't be stingy when you apply weed killer by trying not to use what the directions recommend. The more weeds you kill, the better your crop will be.

It is also important to try to spray with the least amount of disturbance to the soil. Any time you turn the soil under, you encourage weeds and unwanted native grasses to grow. Till lightly and no deeper than the seed needs to be planted according to the directions to avoid over stimulating weed growth.

Planting Choices

Before planting your first crop, you have some more decisions to make. Are you planting to enhance the overall healthy body weight of your herd? Do you want to also improve antler growth? Is making sure your does and fawns have an early season, nutritious food

▲ This buck is what we dream about shooting. Providing a complete quality deer management program on your land including food plots, minerals, lime, watering holes, fruit trees, fertilizing oak trees, sanctuaries, wild grapes and more, a buck like this could be in your future! (credit: Ted Rose)

source important? In other words, are you planning to take on a full QDM program by providing food sources year round for your deer or just in the fall?

If you're like a majority of hunters, you want to plant crops that will attract and hold deer in your area during the time of year that is most beneficial to you–October and November. If that is the case, then I recommend planting fall type crops that will do well during cooler weather. You can also plant a couple of small clover patches and some other plantings for spring and summer–but your attention should mostly be on plots that produce or mature in the fall (see our website for the best seed ideas and plantings at www. woodsnwater.tv).

Once you decide what to plant, remember that the best time to plant is when you know there will be some rain in the near future. Make sure you follow the instructions on the bag–most folks don't and the crop suffers because of it. I like to plant annuals rather than a lot of perennials because I like to change up my plots every year to give the deer and other wildlife something new to eat. It keeps them interested in the area. Once the seed is in the ground (remember most seed doesn't like to be planted too deeply), you now have to think about keeping it fertilized for the best results.

Now that you have taken all the above steps, you need to decide what types of seeds, trees, shrubs and other food plots you want to grow. My strongest recommendation here is to think carefully before planting anything. Consider this, if all your neighbors are growing clover, chicory, corn, and turnips–then your best bet to attract and hold deer on your land is to grow different types of crops along with much smaller plots that include the crops your neighbors are growing! To entice deer to your property from surrounding lands, and to keep your resident herd from leaving your property you must grow things they cannot find elsewhere.

On my farm, I grow sugar beets, turnips, forage rape and kale, chufa, sunflowers, birds' foot trefoil, winter wheat, and canola. I also plant a lot of shrubs that deer like to munch on that cannot be found on any of the neighbor's properties or, for that matter, anywhere within a two square mile radius of our land. I make sure to plant plots of what the farmers grow too, including corn, alfalfa and clover.

Here are some crop ideas that you may consider. I like to plant legumes (a seed pod, or other edible part of a leguminous plant used as food). I found the soybean is the best bet as long as you have enough land to plant at least three to five acres. I also like to plant winter peas.

I also like to plant crops, trees and shrubs that leave a vapor trail from their fruits, nuts, berries, leaves, and grasses. Some choices here are all of the fruit and mast trees, many different types of shrubs, grape vines, alfalfa (ever notice how fast deer will hit a freshly mowed alfalfa field?-many times only minutes after it has been cut), chicory, deer greens, rape, turnip, kale, mustard, and carrots. They are all easy to grow and all have a distinct odor that deer cannot resist. There is a chapter following this one that discusses crops that produce attractive food odors that pull deer in like magnets.

Now I know a lot of you have read that corn doesn't provide a lot of nutrition for deer and hence it should not be given a lot of attention. If you have enough fields, trust me, plant corn–despite what other pros have said about corn not being a valuable food crop. Corn is one of the best fall crops to attract deer. It provides nutrients to deer this time of year, too. Whenever the temperature drops below 28 degrees, deer quickly move off to the corn fields to raise body temperatures and to get needed nutrients from the corn. If you plant corn, spend a little extra money to buy Round-Up ready corn. That way, after it starts growing, you can continue to spray it to keep the weeds from competing with it. Other Round-Up ready crops are also beneficial to plant for the same reason (soybean, etc.).

Don't forget that natural vegetation can also help you improve your deer and deer hunting. For instance, I was the first to write about fertilizing white oak trees in an article in 1983. By simply planting spikes around a tree with a trunk about 16 inches wide or larger, you can encourage that tree to produce larger, sweeter, and more abundant acorns when other trees aren't producing acorns at all! Even in good mast-producing years, your fertilized trees will do better than the other trees.

With a pinch bar, poke holes around the tree where the drip line is. The drip line is directly under the end of the longest branches. Put a dozen or more spikes in the ground around the tree. Break the spikes in half, but do not crush them up. Then cover the soil. I suggest doing this twice a year: once in the spring and again in the fall. I usually wait until I know there will be some rain soon after I put the spikes in the soil.

▼ Tall-growing sunflowers are one of the easiest crops to grow. They provide deer and other wildlife plenty of calories and oil for healthy body development. They also attract honey bees that help pollinate other crops on your land including wild fruit trees.

▲ Deer love apples but they go wild over pears. If you plant several trees, be sure to protect the bark from bucks rubbing it, fertilize, spray for harmful insects and prune when necessary and in a few short years they will bear fruit.

This is one of the best ways to produce acorns that are not only bigger, sweeter, and more abundant, but will also remain on the branches longer because they are healthier. That means when most of the acorns have fallen and been consumed by deer, bear, and turkey, your tree will be dropping mast later in the fall during hunting season!

You can also do this with a lot of natural vegetation like wild grape vines, berry bushes, and other types of plants that deer consume throughout the summer and fall. Find out what plants you have, then ask your local farm store what the best mix of fertilizer is and apply it to the plant. It will increase production of your plants right away.

It also pays to fertilize any wild fruit tree you have. By doing so, you will increase the flavor, size, and abundance of the crop the tree makes. Again, use the right N-P-K mix.

Pruning wild fruit trees, vines, and bushes helps. You should only do this when they are asleep (dormant) in the winter from January through March. If you prune any later than March, you could send the tree or plant into shock and not achieve your goal.

Deer & Habitat Management

Planting food plots is only half the equation when it comes to QDM. Just as important is the other half of the blueprint which includes proper management

▲ This is one of my corn fields. Corn is one of the best crops to attract and hold deer in fall during hunting season. They use it for cover and food. We leave it standing after the season is over to provide a winter food source.

of the habitat on your land, deer management and observation, and hunter management. When these other elements are combined with growing quality food plots they help to lower the over-browsing of native forage so that it has a much better chance to regenerate.

This is another subject that requires a lot more space than I can fairly give in this book, but it is necessary to touch base on it here as well. This is only a summary of what is needed to provide a true management program, but it will help you understand that an overall QDM program must include a detailed agenda of deer and habitat management of both natural and planted vegetation. It must also consider the overall buck population, the doe

population, and most importantly (in my mind's eye), hunter satisfaction.

What is the most important step in deer management? Well, that really depends on your goals. You probably want to see and shoot more bucks on the land you lease or own. And that probably means not shooting yearling bucks and, in some cases, even two-year- old bucks. Most hunters want to be able to take bucks that have eight points or better and have racks that have 16 to 18-inch inside spreads. This is a tall order for sure–but a surprisingly easy one if you follow stringent guidelines.

The most critical aspect is simple–let the smaller yearlings and even two-year-olds go and they will grow! Seems like an easy thing to understand and do

▲ Fertilizing your oak trees will provide bigger, sweeter and more plentiful acorns starting with the first year. By the third year, the tree is so healthy the stems of the acorns hang on longer, falling later than the acorns on other oaks–mostly during the hunting season!

▲ By undertaking a long-term QDM program you will see more bucks each time you go afield in just a few short years. By allowing yearlings and 2½ year olds to pass, it won't be long before you set your sights on a buck like this. (credit: Ted Rose)

but it isn't. After a little pressure of not seeing a buck the first few days of the season, most hunters soon cave- in and take the first legal buck that passes them. This is not a crime and no one should frown on what another man's trophy is. With that said, however, if you are undertaking a true QDM program, this is one way to not only kill the buck but also any hopes of improving the age-class and rack-size of the bucks on the land you hunt.

I bet that most of you, like me, daydream about seeing a lot of bucks during the bow and firearm season. Those dreams include taking a mature buck. Remember that a mature 3½ year old buck in New York is not what a mature buck is in Wisconsin. A 3½ year old buck in the east may only have eight points, a 16-inch wide rack and weigh in at 180 pounds field dressed. The same age buck in Wisconsin may have ten points, an 18-inch wide rack and dress out at more than 200 pounds.

In any event, seeing a lot of bucks and taking a racked buck is what gets our adrenaline flowing. If that is your goal–then you must commit to allowing yearling bucks to pass and to create habitat that also protects them. As many of you know, it isn't fun when you go hunting and don't see deer. It becomes down-right disheartening when you go days or even a season without seeing a buck! Every hunter I know wants to see deer almost every time they go afield

The fact is, in order for that to happen yearling bucks must be allowed to live in order to become two-year-olds and older. The more yearling bucks that are given the opportunity to develop a healthy body and, more importantly, the experience to survive future hunting seasons.

With each passing season, bucks become smarter and more physically fit. They quickly become play-ers in the deer world. They can challenge for the right to breed once they are 2½ years old. They leave their sign (rubs and scrapes) all over the deer woods trying to demonstrate to other bucks they are contenders.

Biologists say that if about 30 to 35 percent of a herd is made up of mature bucks, all the aspects of the rut become more visible and intense. That breaks down to hunters seeing more daytime activity of bucks chasing does and responding to antler rattling (as bucks spar

▼ No matter which of these bucks a hunter decides to shoot, both should be thought of as equal trophies.
(credit: Ted Rose)

▲ The ultimate dream for any deer hunter is to be able to see a group of bucks like this on the land he or she hunts.

and fight with each other). There is more vocalization between bucks which helps hunters have more success using grunts and other deer calls. There are more scrapes and rubs throughout the woods—leaving hunters feeling excited with anticipation of a successful season.

When there are many mature bucks in a herd, more bucks end up surviving the rut, especially after a hard winter. If there are fewer mature bucks to breed, the available bucks undergo a severe decline in their body weight (often not eating during the peak of the rut), thereby becoming much more susceptible to predation and starvation. They will lack the proper health to make it through the winter. Having a good mix of mature bucks also takes the pressure off these bucks, allowing them to keep weight on and maintaining good health to make it past a hard winter. In the end, this means a greater winter survival of mature males, which breaks down to a more enjoyable hunting season the following year.

I know a lot of hunters who use the excuse that spikes have to be removed from the herd because they have bad genetics. Don't let anyone convince you that spikes have inferior genetics. It just isn't always true. A small yearling spike, especially a late-born spike, can turn into a terrific buck if given the chance to become a two or three year old. Many researchers and deer breeders have told me they have seen many spikes develop racks that range from 140- to 170-class size antlers! Let your yearling spikes go. If you really

conform to a buck management program, you will also let four, six and eight point yearling bucks pass as well. I know, right about now many of you are saying, "What?! That might be the only buck I'll see all season." If you can develop the willpower to let yearlings go, you will see more bucks the following year. Even if your neighbors are taking a few of them, the ones you save will help.

On our farm, our policy is not to shoot any bucks with fewer than eight points. In addition, we try hard, although we don't always succeed, to also identify age class as well. If we see an eight point with a 14-inch wide rack and he has the body of a young buck, we let him pass. We know we may be taking a yearling that could be a real "taker" the following season. Sometimes we have been fooled by an eight-point that has a 115 to 120 class rack and appears to be 2½ years old. In this case, he turned out to be a yearling, but this has only happened twice over the last five years. Mistakes happen, but if you can limit them and let yearlings get a year or two under their belts, it won't take but a couple of seasons to see more and larger bucks on your property.

It is not only important to let yearlings walk, you must also provide them with the type of protective habitat that will encourage them to remain on your

▲ Any serious QDM program should include a plan to plant evergreens on the property. Eventually they will provide security and cover from the elements for your deer.

▲ Spike bucks can develop into anything from a 16-inch 8-point at 3½ years old to a ten-point or more at that age. That's one good reason to let them pass!
(credit: Ted Rose)

land. Make them stay on your property, rather than having them seek security on the neighbor's property–especially if the neighbor is close-minded and knuckle-headed about allowing yearlings to survive.

If the land you lease or hunt doesn't offer a lot of secure cover–create it for them! It is easy to do. In one season, you can develop cover by stacking a lot of dead blow downs in several areas of the land. You can plant fast-growing shrubs like bayberry, beach plum, elderberry, locust, buttonbush, high bush cranberry, willow, dogwood, serviceberry, nannyberry, and elderberry. There are trees that grow rapidly to provide thick cover in a few short years like poplar, eastern red cedar, white pine, and white cedar. It also pays to put in some food-source trees like wild apple, pear, and

crabapple. All of these plantings will aid to help safely hide yearlings.

On a longer term plan, creating a mixed conifer forest is also a good way to hold deer on your land and provide cover from hunting pressure, weather, and predators. It takes longer to mature, but a mixed conifer forest is a real plus. It provides yearlings a way to get through the season on your land. On our farm, I started to plant conifers three years ago. I dedicated one of my large fields (about five acres) to the development of conifers. I planted a mix of fast-growing white pines and a slower-growing species of conifers including red, scotch, and pitch pine as well as Norway spruce, white spruce, Douglas fir, and Austrian pine. In a short five years, this planting will hide many deer. In ten years, it will help the deer on my farm evade hunting pressure, and it will also attract deer from my neighbor's lands, especially as a winter storm front approaches.

It is impossible for me to give you all the details you need or want in this book to help you grow quality deer plots and create deer and habitat management goals. However, I hope the information I did give you regarding these subjects has at least made you understand that growing food plots and committing to a deer and habitat management plan takes a long-term pledge as well as a lot of time and work.

It will also require an upfront investment and the right planting tools. Moreover, it will require a considerable investment in lime, fertilizer, seed, and additional minerals, equipment repair and maintenance, shrub and tree plantings, and habitat improvement as well. When it comes to undertaking a complete QDM program of deer and habitat management along with food plots and woodlot management, the amount of time, money, labor, and commitment you plant is what you will sow. Letting yearlings and young bucks pass is what will make you a happy hunter and a true deer manager as well.

Here is a sample chart where you can keep accurate records of your food plot plantings. It contains important bits of information that you can refer to year after year. I found this format to be helpful and I know it will help you in your food plot endeavors, too.

FOOD PLOT RECORD

Plot Name: Big View	Plot Size: 2 acres	Year Planted: 2010

Soil Test Date:	April 5, 2010
Results of Test:	6.5 pH
Lime Applied (lbs./acre):	300 lbs. (150 lbs. per acre)–Soil tested slightly acidic (which turnips like). So I only used 300 lbs. to remain at 6.5 pH
Date of Application:	April 15, 2010
Fertilizer Applied (lbs./acre):	600 lbs. of 19-19-19 (300 lbs./acre)–I also plan to use 150 lbs. of ammonium sulfate (34-0-0) in a couple of months to help increase crop production.
Date of Application:	April 30, 2010
Type of Soil Preparation:	Disk Harrowed–Land Pride Model DH10
Type of Seed Planted:	Turnip (Brassica Rapa)
Planting Rate:	4 lbs. per acre
Depth of Seed:	one-quarter inch below surface level
Planting Method:	Gravity-Fed Primary Seeder with Cultipacker Disks–Land Pride Model PS1572
Weed Control:	Roundup® Super Concentrate Plus–Systemic Grass & Broadleaf Killer. Applied according to directions on container.

LAND AND DEER MANAGEMENT

Additional Notes:

Judging by the success I had with my one-acre turnip crop last year, I've decided to double the size of the food plot this year. Deer fed continually on this crop throughout the fall and into December. I noticed that as soon as we had severe frost, deer activity picked up considerably, and they actively removed the turnips from the ground; eating the bulbs and roots after the frost. This is due to a chemical change that occurs within the bulbous head of the turnip. In cold weather, starches change to sugar compounds. I also noticed that the top growth survived until the temperatures dropped below 15 degrees. It has taken the deer two years to figure out what the turnips are, but now that they have, I expect this year to be the best year ever regarding their attraction to the crop. It has proven to be an excellent cool and even cold-season planting, bringing deer into the food plot long after some of our other plants withered due to frost. I plan to keep turnips as a staple crop in our plantings until I see the deer begin to ignore them–which I do not expect.

▲ Turnips are a like candy to deer, especially after a heavy frost when they contain much more sugar.

16. Non-Traditional Aromatic Food Plots

Growing non-traditional food plots that have a high aromatic value to them can help you attract and hold deer on the land you lease, own, or have permission to hunt. Over the last two decades, more and more hunters have learned the value of planting food plots as part of a Quality Deer Management (QDM) tool to enhance the body weight and antler size of deer on their property. This is also a strategy to attract and hold deer on their lands especially during the hunting seasons. Most hunters plant traditional clover crops as advertised by reliable seed companies and these plots have proven to be very effective in attracting and holding deer to specific areas.

While I regularly plant a variety of what I coined as traditional "signature" seeds, I also incorporate some non-traditional food plot plantings into my strategies as well. I have discovered that some plants offer a natural attractant that a lot of the traditional signature plants don't. They have a high aromatic value especially in the fall—a time when most hunters want their crops to attract deer and other wildlife to their deer hunting stands.

I have included my most successful non-traditional crops that have consistently attracted deer during hunting season. Try these crops in either small or large plots and get ready to draw your bow or flip the safety off on your firearm. They have proven to work on our 300-acre farm season after season!

Sunflowers

Sunflowers are a terrific, tall-growing, aromatic crop. I plant between one to three acres of sunflowers on my farm every year. They are easy to grow and provide deer (and other wildlife) with plenty of calories and oil content needed for healthy body development.

▼ Sunflowers are a very aromatic crop that will attract deer, turkey, bear and almost all other wildlife.

Sunflowers are adaptive and can grow in almost any type of soil. They can be planted in rows or broadcasted in a plot where the soil has been properly prepared and then compacted into the soil. They can be used in large 20-plus acre plots or in plots as small as a one-quarter to a half-acre!

Another plus to sunflowers is that they are most often left alone by wildlife until the seeds begin to mature and drop. Sunflowers will provide food for a lot of deer, turkey, and bear early in the fall (mostly during the bow season). I have witnessed deer and turkey actually run to this crop in order to eat the sunflowers' palatable seeds. Sunflowers mature within 100 days or so of planting. As they do, they emit a pungent odor that is quickly picked up by all types of wildlife. If put in the ground in late June, they will mature in late September and the seeds will attract deer and other wildlife through October. The height of this plant also offers deer a place to bed well into September. Many times, I have seen a buck stand up from its bed in the sunflower plot after I have been watching the field without seeing anything else for two hours! Sunflowers should be planted at the rate of about 40 pounds per acre at a depth of about 1½ inches. If you have apple trees on your land, this crop will also attract hordes of honey bees that will help to pollinate your fruit trees, too. I call these types of plantings companion crops.

Carrots

This is the ice cream crop for deer. Both the seeds and the carrots have a powerful aroma and are unmatched for their vitamin content and sweet flavor for wildlife. Carrots are rich in calcium and iron, which help racks develop. They are tolerant of some negligence after planting as well. It has been my experience that deer will be in a carrot field before they will be in just about any other crop field, including alfalfa, chicory, corn, rye, oats or wheat. That should give you an idea of how much deer like carrots, seeking them out as preferred food sources.

As long as carrots are close to maturity and have a developed carrot root, carrots to deer are unequaled. Their highly aromatic odor also makes them found easily by deer. Carrots are also high in energy and are very palatable as well. Many of the leading seed manufacturers know how well deer enjoy

▲ If you want to open a "candy store" for deer, plant a large or small plot of carrots and watch what happens.

eating carrots and include them in several of their seed blends. You can easily smell carrots in the seed mixes. Imagine how well deer will smell them as they grow and mature. The problem with carrots is that they are sometimes consumed very quickly by deer and rabbits.

Soybeans

Soybeans are another highly aromatic crop. A deer's olfactory senses them easily. Soybeans contain 25 to 35 percent protein, which provides top notch nutritional value for deer. They should be planted in soil that has a pH between 5.8 and 7.0. They must be inoculated with the appropriate Rhizobium (which is strain S) in order for them to grow best. They also should be fertilized with 300 pounds of 0-20-20 phosphorous and potassium per acre for maximum tonnage. They will mature in about 140 days from planting.

Deer love them so much, that unless you have a large plot of four to five acres, they will quickly eat them to the ground before they get started. For that reason, I suggest if you plant soy beans you plan on using repellents such as Milorganite, or better yet, repellent fencing like PlotSaver or electric fencing. I also highly recommend planting soybeans with a companion crop like corn or sunflowers. The heavy stems of both plants provide not only a stalk for the soybeans to climb up on but also the stalks provide the plant protection long enough to get them started. You can plant at a rate of 20 to 30 pounds per acre and not deeper than one-half inch to one inch under the soil.

Deer eat soybeans in both the foliage state and after the beans have matured. Soybeans are an aromatic crop and are highly rated as a fall crop, too. As a plus, many times after the beans fall to the ground as they mature, they will naturally regenerate more plants that will last into fall.

Chufas

Chufas are another highly aromatic crop that require a little more work than the other plants because you may have to help the deer locate the plant the first season. Chufas are similar to peanuts, producing underground tubers to which turkey and deer are attracted. However, wildlife in the colder zones may not be familiar with the tubers, as Chufas are mostly grown in the south. By simply scratching a few tubers just below the surface at maturity, their aroma will waft into the surrounding lands, and turkey and deer

▼ Unless you have a large enough field of five acres or more for soybeans, the deer will eat them to the ground before they can grow. If you do have a large enough field–plant it and they will come!

will locate them quickly and soon learn to scratch the tubers up for themselves. They will return to the Chufas again and again until all edible plants have been eaten.

Chufas can be planted at a rate of about 40 to 50 pounds for one to two acres by broadcasting the seed and disking them into the soil. They grow best in sandy soils and in warm climates. In northern regions, they do best as a warm weather crop, lasting into the first frost. Plant them in south-facing fields that get plenty of sunlight and warmth. If you enjoy hunting turkey, you can't go wrong planting Chufa.

Winter Peas

Winter peas are a terrific biennial cool season crop that are high in protein. Ideally, they can be planted with the traditional clovers like Ladinos, and early rye grass. Winter Peas will tolerate heavy browsing more than their cousin Cowpeas will and for that reason, they are a terrific choice in areas where the deer density is heavy.

I cannot detect an elevated aroma from them unless a substantial plot is planted. Deer, however, can detect the odor of winter peas easily, especially after a hard frost. They will grow well on most soils with little preparation. They are one of the easiest crops to plant in rows or by broadcasting in prepared soil. Many seed companies use them in their traditional mixes. In order to attract deer throughout the fall, plant them in early September. Because of their cold tolerance, winter peas cannot be beat as a fall crop. They should be planted deeper than one inch and must be inoculated with a Rhizobium bacteria that is specific to peas (strain C). They like soil that has a pH level between 6.0 and 7.5. To get the most tonnage they should be fertilized with 0-20-20 fertilizer at 300 pounds per acre (see what I mean about how quickly a QDM program can become expensive?) that is integrated well into the soil. Deer will eat them until they are entirely devoured.

Following are other worthwhile crops that may not be as aromatic as the ones mentioned above. But they still provide some odor and some other benefits as well. These are all crops I have used over the time I have owned my farm and they have proven to be productive and highly attractive to deer and other wildlife.

Forage Chicory

This highly nutritious, broad-leaved perennial herb that belongs to the sunflower family is aromatic. Forage chicory can last up to five years because it develops a deep taproot, which also makes it drought tolerant, too. It will withstand heavy grazing, making it a good choice in areas of high deer density. Chicory is one of the finest forages for extracting nutrients from the soil and transferring them to deer providing bigger body and antler growth. Chicory is an excellent fall and winter crop that is easy to grow in a wide variety of soils. It is drought resistant and has a high protein level that ranges from 10 to 30 percent or more! It is also a good winter crop because it can withstand cool temperatures and should be planted no later than early August if you intend for it to attract deer through the hunting season.

Forage chicory will tolerate low pH levels of about 5.0 to 6.0 but really does best when the pH level is from 6.5 to 7.0. The seed can be drilled or broadcast into prepared soil and should not be planted deeper than one-half inch to one inch for best results. Cultipack the soil to help the seeds get the best seed-to-soil contact. It is recommended that you add a companion crop like clover, a legume, grain, or grass plant. You can fertilize with about 200 pounds per acre of 19-19-19. Good management requires that you mow this plant before the flower stems get bigger than six inches. You can

▼ Chicory is only second to alfalfa on the deer's menu. It provides up to 30 percent protein!
(credit Mossy Oak)

plant about five to seven pounds of chicory seed per acre alone. Or, for a different mix, plant two to three pounds per five to six pounds of clover seed.

Brassicas

Brassicas are excellent broadleaf plant choices for fall plantings. All brassicas can include a mix of several types of seeds. Some of my favorite seeds are carrots and canola (often called rapeseed), forage rape, kale, turnips, cabbage, mustard, and radishes. Most blends are packed with high protein levels. Brassicas are cool- weather tolerant and will thrive in colder temperatures when other food plot plants won't. The key to these plants is to get them into the ground about 45 days before the first chance of a heavy frost. By doing so, you will ensure that the plants will mature during the peak of bow season. As the plant develops, deer will eat the tops and the stalks. Once these plants freeze, the starches in them are converted to sugar as the plant actually begins to decay. At this point, they become even more aromatic and quickly attract deer, including those from your neighbor's property! But after a heavy frost, they will paw the bulbs out of the ground and eat them like candy apples. Like corn, soon after a heavy frost, plan to hunt your stand of brassicas–the deer will!

I always plant at least one acre of turnips. They contain about 15 to 25 percent crude protein and their roots have about 10 to 15 percent protein! They are cold hardy and will last well into the winter. They prefer a slightly acidic soil with a pH level of 6.0 to 6.5. They can be broadcast about four or five pounds per acre into a prepared bed of soil at a depth of no more than one-half inch deep. Then make sure to cultipack the soil after planting. Fertilize with about 300 pounds of 19-19-19 per acre. Some folks top this off with an additional fertilizer of ammonium sulfate (34-0-0) which will markedly increase the production of this plant. They will mature about 90 to 115 days after planting.

Turnips are superb as fall/winter forage that grow well in cool weather and have a good aroma. They are especially good for small woodland or field plots. Again, these are most attractive to deer after a heavy frost when the starch turns to sugar. Turnips have good crisp roots and provide deer with delicious greens.

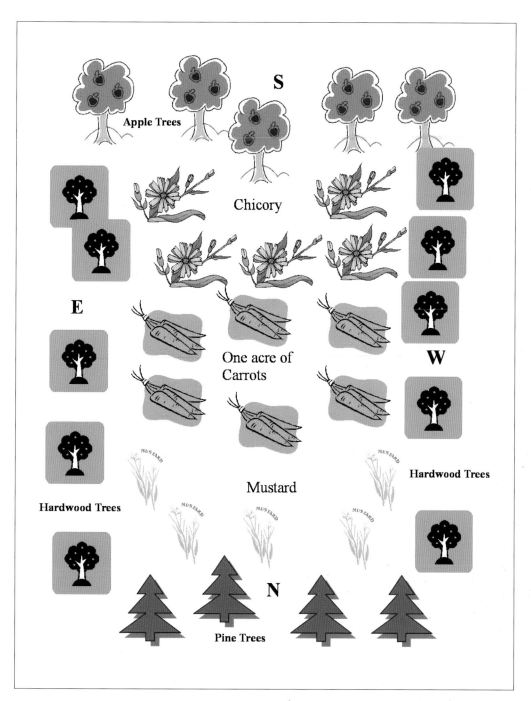

▲ This setup demonstrates how a variety of foods will help attract and hold deer by offering them several items to eat in a given area. The apples, carrots, chicory, mustard, and even the acorns from the hardwoods all emit aromatic aromas when they are ripe or mature and at their peak flavor. Again, a wind break of evergreens at the north protects the crops from harsh winds and weather. All plots are from one-half to one acre in size.

▲ This crop of brassicas is lush and ready for the deer to eat!

Traditional wildlife seed blends use turnips in their brassica blends, but I find it is worthwhile to plant an entire food plot with this crop. Large bags of turnip seeds can be found with other vegetable seeds at most farm seed outlets.

Winter Wheat

Winter wheat is the "mother" of fall crops and is one of the most valuable wildlife plants in America. It is an excellent food plot because of that single reason. It should be planted from September through December at about 100 pounds per acre when planted by itself.

It likes a soil pH of 6.0 and higher and will produce best under these conditions. Fertilize it with about 300 pounds of 19-19-19. Winter wheat sprouts before freezing occurs, then becomes dormant until the soil warms up in the spring. The wheat grows and matures until ready to be harvested by early July. Deer find winter wheat irresistible.

Cabbage

Cabbage is another of the non-traditional crops that deer find attractive throughout the fall. Cabbage is a hardy, easy to grow plant. It is ideal for small and large food plots. Cabbage thrives best in cool weather and should be planted in areas that get some shade during the dog-days of summer. By planting types with different maturity dates, you can ensure this forage will be available during hunting season.

Mustard

I have discovered that deer find this aromatic and leafy vegetable delicious and nutritious. It is easy to grow and an excellent source of vitamins and minerals. Mustard is cold-tolerant and produces green leaves with a pleasing aroma to deer. They can be planted in small or large food plots. Mustard is truly an unorthodox food plot plant. Although some traditional wildlife seed mixes may include some mustard, it is best to plant an entire plot with this crop. Mustard seed can be found with other vegetable seeds at most farm seed outlets.

I also plant a lot of other crops to test how they perform. I recommend that you experiment with a variety of crops to find out what best serves your management needs, too. Each year, I change my planting ideas so that I don't bore the deer with the same-old, same-old, year in and year out. I do, however, sometimes plant a crop a few years in a row if I find the deer really benefit from it and are overly attracted to it, as well. But I never plant the same thing more than two or three years in a row.

Following are some seed companies you can contact to purchase seeds for your land.

SEED COMPANIES

Agassiz Seed Company
(701) 282-8118
lavern@agassizseed.com
www.agassizseed.com

Antler King
(888) 268-5371
antlerking@antlerking.com
www.antlerking.com

Barenburg USA
(Tecomate Seed)
(800) 547-4101
info@barusa.com
www.barusa.com

Frigid Forage
(320) 532-5020
sales@sunrichfarm.com
www.sunrichfarm.com

Hunter's Specialties
(319) 395-0321
website@hunterspec.com
www.hunterspec.com

Mossy Oak BioLogic
(662) 495-9292
todd@plantbiologic.com
www.mossyoakbiologic.com

Preferred Seed Company
(877) 417-7333
info@preferredseed.com
www.preferredseed.com

Purina Mills
(800) 227-8941
customer_service@purinamills.com
www.deerchow.com

Quaker Boy
(800) 544-1600
qbquestions@quakerboy.com
www.quakerboygamecalls.com

Seedland, Inc.
(888) 820-2080
sales@seedland.com
www.seedland.com

The Wildlife Group
(800) 221-9703
wildlifegroup@mindspring.com
www.wildlifegroup.com

Whitetail Institute
(800) 688-3030
info@whitetailinstitute.com
www.whitetailinstitute.com

Section v

TIPS THAT GET TO THE POINT

17. Opening Day

For most of us, thoughts of opening day hold most of our expectations and dreams of bagging a buck. We have all read and heard that up to 80 percent of our chances to kill a buck take place on opening day, with our next best chance on opening weekend.

• With that in mind I thought it would be sensible to include some of my best opening-day hunting tips. These tips are common-sense based and easy to apply. They are meant to give novice hunters some strategies to get the best edge to bag their first buck. They also include some tips that are geared more to the seasoned deer hunting veteran.

▼ An opening-day eight-point buck and a matriarchal doe taken on our farm in 2006.

▲ It pays to remain in your stand on opening day because you never know when a buck like this will show up under your stand.

I hope they make a difference in your success for your next opening day hunt–good hunting!

- During the first few days of deer season (bow or firearm), pack your lunch and stay on your stand all day from sunrise to dark. This is also a good bet for opening weekends as well. Deer will react to the sudden increased hunting pressure and will move continually throughout their habitat, circling hunters and may eventually come into sight of your stand.

- I have always felt that scouting too early can be more harmful than not scouting at all. In places not subjected to intense hunting pressure, scout for sign as close to opening day as is reasonable. By scouting too early, the sign you find may no longer be relevant when the season opens and, more importantly, you can spook, or at least give warning to mature bucks in the area that the hunt is about to start!

- I have longed believed that having several stands in place for opening day and the rest of the deer season is crucial to success. Savvy hunters understand that consistent success depends on how they pay attention to wind direction. With many stands to choose from, you get the edge by being able to select the one that offers the best wind direction before heading out to the woods.

- As I have said for over 40 years, deer, especially mature bucks, move about in strong wind and rain more than most hunters believe. If you get up on opening morning (or any day during the hunting season), to strong wind and hard rain, don't go back to bed. Instead, dress for the weather and go to your stand. Other hunters have waited for opening day too, and even the lousiest weather will not keep them out of the woodlands, so deer will remain on the move. It's later in the season, when hunters are tired, that bad weather keeps them home, but it shouldn't, as deer like to move even in the foulest of weather conditions.

- If you're sitting on stand and another hunter bumbles noisily through your area, don't become discouraged and abandon your stand. He'll undoubtedly keep on moving, and any deer that are in and around the area will circle and give him a wide berth, never realizing that another hunter (you) is there, waiting motionless.

- Whether you're hunting with a bow or firearm, opening day is not the time to take the first legal animal that comes along. There's plenty of time left in the season, so enjoy the hunt, be relatively picky and take the opportunity to look over several animals. It's during the waning days of the season that most hunters begin lowering their standards.

- Deer quickly abandon their normal routines on opening day of the firearms season, especially if there's intense hunting pressure. Because of this, you're likely to have much success grunting in a buck, using rattling antlers or hunting in open feeding areas. So, take a stand on elevated terrain that overlooks a heavily covered funnel or travel corridor. Keep an eye out for bucks using these routes as they elude hunters who have infiltrated their domain.

- When opening day of bowhunting season arrives, bucks are likely to be hanging tight with does that are just about to enter estrus. In this type of situation, your chances of calling a buck to your location are between slim and none. Try using a fawn bleat to call in does instead, any bucks tending them will follow.

18. Little-Known Deer Facts

he old adage that you never stop learning applies to this chapter. While you may already know some of the tips I share here –there may be some that are new to you.

This is a chapter some of you may choose to skip over or browse through. That would be a mistake. I have always felt that consistently successful deer hunters are those who understand their quarry to the ninth degree. Many of the tips in this chapter are geared to providing you that type of information.

You will find some of these tips strategic in orientation, others are biologic in nature, and fact related and others are about the deer's anatomy. All are important for you to have at your finger tips to help you take your deer hunting to the next level.

- According to researchers a mature whitetail buck makes an average of 195 rubs on saplings each fall.

- In the study of whitetail stomach contents, it was determined that the animals regularly feed on more than 600 different varieties of plants.

- The hollow hairs comprising a deer's winter coat are equal in their insulating qualities to the most sophisticated wool or other high-tech fibers developed by man.

- The reason you see fewer bucks during the spring and summer months is because bucks restrict their movements during this time of year in order to

▲ Knowing your quarry inside and out is the key to consistent hunting success.
(credit: Ted Rose)

▲ Research has proven that deer will defecate up to thirteen times every hour. Glad you're not a deer now, aren't you!

avoid injuring their growing antlers. As they grow, antlers remain soft, tender, and pliable and are very easily damaged.

• Scientists tell us that whitetails defecate an average of 13 times every 24 hours. That means even when you locate a lot of scat, it may not indicate that there are a lot of deer leaving the sign. The best way to determine if you have a large herd of deer on your land is to make actual survey counts of deer scat, which is too much trouble for most hunters. I like to see large scat in piles. At the very least, these indicate mature deer–bucks and does.

• There are more than 30 known subspecies of whitetails in North and Central America, all of which are believed to have evolved from the "prototype" Virginia whitetail (*Odocoileus virginianus*) species.

• Many hunters confuse the species and think that *Odocoileus virginianus'* range is widespread especially through the Northeast and New England. This is not so. *Odocoileus virginianus virginianus'* range includes Virginia, West Virginia, Kentucky, Tennessee, North Carolina, South Carolina, Georgia, Alabama, and Mississippi. This is a moderately big deer with fairly heavy antlers.

• The northern whitetail known as *O.v. borealis*, is the largest subspecies of deer and has the darkest coat. It also has the widest range throughout Maryland, Delaware, New Jersey, New York, Pennsylvania, Ohio, Indiana, Illinois, Minnesota,

▲ This buck's rack probably made short work of a lot of the soft bark on the conifer trees he rubbed. (credit: Ted Rose)

Wisconsin, Michigan, Connecticut, Rhode Island, Massachusetts, New Hampshire, Vermont, Maine, and in the Canadian provinces of Quebec, Ontario, Nova Scotia, New Brunswick, and a part of Manitoba.

- The Dakota whitetail, *O.v. dacotensis*, is another very large deer almost as big in body weight as borealis. Interestingly, this deer has more high-ranking trophy heads in the book than the borealis species. The Dakota whitetail's range encompasses North Dakota, South Dakota, Kansas, Wyoming, Montana, parts of Nebraska and the Canadian provinces of Manitoba, Saskatchewan, and Alberta. Unlike borealis, which is known as a woodland deer, dacotensis calls the timbered coulees, gullies, draws, fields, breaks, and river and stream bottoms of the prairies home.

- The Northwest whitetail, *O.v. ochrourus*, is also a large deer. It's range covers parts of Idaho, Montana, Washington, Oregon, California, Nevada, Utah, and the Canadian provinces of British Columbia and Alberta.

- The Columbia whitetail, *O.v. leucurus,* has been declining in numbers for years. They are only found along the Columbia River near Cathlamet, Washington.

- The Coues (pronounced "cows") is also know as the Arizona whitetail (*O.v. couesi*) and is a small deer. This deer is found in the arid areas of southeastern California, southern Arizona, southwestern New Mexico, and in Mexico.

- Other whitetail sub-species include the Texas whitetail, *O.v. texanus*; the Carmen Mountains whitetail *O.v. carminis*; the Avery Island whitetail, *O.v. mcilhennyi*; the Kansas whitetail, *O.v. macrourus*; the Bull's Island whitetail, *O.v. taurinsulae*; the Hunting Island whitetail, *O.v. venatorius*; the Hilton Head Island whitetail, *O.v. hiltonensis*; and the Blackbeard Island whitetail, *O.v. nigribarbis.* All of the last four subspecies have small

antlers. The Florida whitetail, *O.v. seminolus*, is a good size deer that has a fair antler size as well. However, the Florida coastal whitetail *O.v. osceola* is not as large bodied and has slightly smaller antlers. The smallest of all the deer found in North America is the diminutive Florida Key whitetail, *O.v. clavium.*

- I can't give you a reason why, but most researchers say that studies have shown deer respond most frequently to the sounds of grunt calls and/or antler rattling when they must travel uphill or at least remain on level ground. They seldom respond if it'll require downhill travel. I tend to agree to a degree. I have had bucks come down hill to my calling and rattling but not as much as going uphill or on level ground.

- Ninety percent of all antler rubs are made on aromatic or resinous tree species, such as cedar, pine, spruce, shining sumac, cherry, and dogwood. It is believed this happens because the oily cambiums of these trees will hold the buck's forehead gland scent for longer periods of time, even during rain or snow.

- Research by Georgia deer biologist Larry Marchington has documented that during a given year, a buck will make from 69 to 538 antler rubs on trees, with a mature buck averaging 300! (That's a pretty amazing statistic, I know I have never seen that many rubs on my farm!)

- Deer possess a supranuclei ganglion, or an internal clock, in their brains. This allows them to fall into restful sleep just as humans can. But unlike us, deer can spring into total alertness in only a third of a second (Sounds like me when I'm napping and I hear the music of one of the old *Star Trek* shows on television).

- The size of a scrape is a pretty reliable marker of the size and age of the buck that created it. Mature bucks paw scrapes that are minimally 18 inches in diameter, and some up to six feet.

- One of the most argued facts about deer is that deer are not limited to seeing only black and white vision. Recent research has confirmed that deer can see a wide range of colors, including ultraviolet light, which is invisible to humans!

- Chasing does is a lot of fun, but by the end of the rut, an average mature buck will have lost as much as 25 percent of his body weight (Hmm, honey–where are you?)!

- Radio-tracking studies have documented that the largest bucks generally make the largest antler rubs on trees, and they begin engaging in their rubbing behavior a full month before younger bucks. So if you locate a big rub early, the chance is you have probably located a big buck too. To be sure, look at the rub carefully. If it has indents or tiny holes in the tree, they were probably made by the tips of the tines on a buck's antlers. If you look very carefully, you can almost count the number of tines on the buck's rack.

- Many hunters are skeptical about how well deer calls work. Remember, biologists using sophisticated audio recording equipment have identified at least 13 distinct vocalizations that whitetails make to communicate with each other.

- For generations, our fathers, grandfathers, and other old-timers told us that cold air temperatures triggered the rut. Now we know that shorter day lengths trigger the rut because reduced amounts of sunlight entering the pre-orbital glands in the corner of the deer's eyes. These cause changes in a deer's endocrine system, spurring the onset of breeding.

- I'm often asked (mostly by guys who hunt in Maine), "What was the heaviest buck ever killed?" It was a 511 pound buck, taken by a Minnesota deer hunter in 1976. This was followed up by two deer that weighed 491 pounds and 481 pounds from Wisconsin in 1980.

- Laboratory studies of deer suggest their sense of smell is at least ten times more acute than that of a human. Deer are able to separate and analyze seven different odors simultaneously through an organ in the roof of their mouth called the vomeronasal organ.

- Can you look at a pile of deer pellets and learn anything from it? You bet you can! The largest individual pellets are most likely from a buck, because mature bucks are larger in anatomical body size that mature does. Research by a biologist in New Jersey documented that a mature buck will leave a pile of 75 pellets or more.

- As most seasoned veteran deer hunters know, when running, a doe is far more likely than a buck to "flag" with her tail. It helps the fawns, yearlings, and other deer in her group to follow her in dim light or when she is fleeing through thick cover.

- When making rubs, mature bucks a) deposit priming pheromones from their forehead glands, b) drip urine over their tarsal glands and c) deposit more scent from their vomeronasal organ when they lick the rub. These pheromones attract hot does, tell other bucks the particular buck's rutting status and even help to induce late-estrus does into coming into heat. The scents also chemically intimidate younger bucks into submission so they are less inclined to attempt to refresh the rub or try to breed does that are near the rub.

- When the weather turns bitterly cold, seek out places where staghorn sumac grows, if possible. When it gets this cold, deer feed heavily upon staghorn sumac. They instinctively know that this plant is higher in fat than any other native food and thus helps generate body heat.

- Deer have a so-called odor comfort zone of about 250 yards. Beyond this distance, foreign odors, some noises, and even predators are not likely to alert or alarm them.

▲ Use a snort or grunt call when passing heavy cover (standing corn, a patch of laurel, blow-downs, etc.) to coax a buck out of the cover and into the open.

▲ This is the bed of a doe, as it is small and had several smaller beds around it.

- A whitetail's tarsal and interdigital glands carry its unique "signature," just as fingerprints do among humans.

- As most seasoned trackers know, the width of a deer track–not its length–is the most reliable indicator of the animal's age. As a deer's body weight steadily increases with age, a progressively wider based platform to support its weight is also needed.

- Many hunters are unaware that a doe makes good use of a buck rub and scrape. She is able to sniff and chemically analyze all the scents left by the buck that made it, and then evaluate the health, virility, and the exact status of the buck to determine if he would be a worthy sire.

- A lone bed measuring 40 to 60 inches in length is most likely that of a big buck. If the bed you find is barely 40 inches and is accompanied by one or two smaller ones, it's undoubtedly that of a doe with offspring.

- Studies of deer that are penned have shown that they have an attention span of about three minutes, after which they forget whatever it was that frightened them. This is good to know. If you step on a

▲ I was still-hunting through blowdowns when I stopped to rattle. The rattling sounds, along with some grunt calls, got this buck to stand up from behind a downed tree.

branch while still-hunting or walking to your stand, stop and remain motionless for at least three minutes before you take another step. That way, you may keep the deer from running out of the county.

- Immature bucks commonly check their scrapes by walking right up to them. Don't count on that when it comes to a mature buck. They normally scent-check their scrapes from 50 to 75 yards or more downwind while remaining in thick cover.

- Although a whitetail's home range may span several square miles, radio-tracking studies indicate that mature bucks have a core area of approximately 40 acres where they spend up to 90 percent of their time. Hence the term, core area, which refers to where the buck spends most of his life.

- A scrape is always found near a low, overhanging tree branch that has been chewed and broken by the buck that made the scrape. Sometimes, within five feet of the scrape, you will also find a licking stick, which is a very thin sapling about two to three feet high. The tip of the sapling will be chewed and frayed. The buck deposits saliva on both the overhanging branch and the licking stick from his vomeronasal organ and his forehead-gland, as well as scent from his preputial and tarsal glands in order to pass along olfactory information telling other deer that this is his breeding area.

- Whitetails have a vomeronasal organ in the roof of the mouth, which allows them to "taste" odors detected by the nose. After this chemical analysis is performed, the information is then transmitted to the brain for deciphering. The vomeronasal organ is very important and is used throughout the rut to scent hot does, and to deposit saliva scent on rubs and scrapes.

19. Still-Hunting

There are four distinct ways to bag a deer and each way has a specific term.

When a hunter waits for a deer at a specific location on the ground or from above in a tree stand, the term used to describe this hunting method is called *posting*. This hunter depends on knowing the travel routes to and from feeding and bedding areas, as well as the prevailing wind directions and a host of other elements. He often includes calling, rattling, decoying, and patiently sitting and waiting for a deer to walk past his hunting location or tree stand among his list of necessary hunting skills.

Another good tactic involves a hunter picking up a deer's track and following it until he either finds the buck in his bed or jumps him. This is known as *tracking* (discussed thoroughly in chapters 8, 9, 10, and 11). This hunter depends on woodsmanship and hunting skills to bag his buck. He must be able to locate and decipher the smallest amount of fresh sign left by his quarry in order to follow the track to success.

Another strategy entails hunters grouping together to move deer out of the cover of safety and into or past the men who have taken up locations at known escape routes. Of course, the term for this type of hunting is called a *deer drive*.

Finally, there is the hunter who slowly and methodically picks his way through the woods and fields, not so much to find fresh sign or to follow a track, but in hopes of getting into cover where he expects deer to be bedded down. This technique is known as *still-hunting*. This hunter has unlimited patience. He may cover only 100 yards in an hour's time—sometimes longer than that depending on the terrain. His success is solely dependent on his ability to move not only carefully, and slowly, but also his ability to pick out his next step prior to putting his foot down so that he will not spook a deer by accidentally snapping a twig.

The still-hunter watches his back trail constantly and carefully scans for deer that might be lying down, waiting for him to pass by. All his hunting instincts and senses are on full alert from the moment he begins to stalk through the woods until he decides the hunt is over. This hunter is referred to as a still-hunter or stalker.

The image of still-hunting a buck puts goose bumps on most hunter's backs. It conjures up rustic feelings of the skilled

◄ Cody with a deer he hung on our game pole for me. I was still-hunting through a thick patch of pines when I bumped the buck from cover.

hunters from yesteryear. Many of these men entered the woods not for sport, but to put food on the table for their families. Today, some hunters want to relive that vision because it is not only an exciting way to hunt, but it is also demanding and challenging.

For the hunter who still-hunts or for those who want to try the tactic, here are some tips I have garnered over the years through a lot of trial and error. The many flagging tails I have seen while still-hunting dramatically outweighs the number of bucks I have killed using this method. But in the end, the few bucks I have taken like this have etched the deepest memories in my mind over the last 45 years.

- The old Native American adage about still-hunting still applies today "walk little, watch a lot." Keep this one piece of advice in mind when you still-hunt and you will find hunting success.

- Contrary to what most hunters have heard, you don't always have to still-hunt with the wind constantly in your face. With this tactic the wind can also be quartering toward you from the left or right. The key is not to allow your odor to be carried directly ahead of your intended route of movement.

- Some feel that midday is not the best time to still-hunt; I don't. Although it is true that most deer are bedded down then, they are not unapproachable. If you still-hunt during the midday hours, you are also inclined to bump into a buck that has risen out of its bed and is feeding, rubbing a tree, making a scrape, or simply looking for a hot doe. Any time you still-hunt you will have a chance to jump a deer.

◄ Filson wool is our favorite wool to wear. Here Kate is dressed to keep warm in a Filson wool camo hunting jacket.

▲ This deer didn't make an alarm-snort, instead it made an alarm-distress snort and is heading to the next county. (credit: Ted Rose)

- As I have said over and over again, bad weather makes for good hunting. A rainy day, or a steady drizzle or a gentle snowfall seems to relax deer and make them feel safer than they actually are. This is a terrific time to still-hunt as you are more inclined to catch a deer feeding in an open area than on a blue bird type day. The ground is also much quieter during this type of weather, giving you a greater opportunity to surprise a bedded or feeding deer.

- When still-hunting use all available cover. Avoid open, bright places with little cover.

- Always carefully plan your next several steps in advance before moving. Look at the available type of terrain and cover that is ahead of you. Select routes that will muffle your steps such as fallen pine needles, moist leaves, moss, or non-moving rocks.

- Never place your heel down first. The toe end of your boot is more sensitive and it will enable you to feel what is underfoot better.

- For me, there is no other choice than wearing Filson wool when I'm still-hunting. Wool is the quietest fabric you can wear. All other clothes are far too noisy to wear when still-hunting. A good backup for wool clothing is fleece.

- When you're still-hunting and cross fresh tracks, don't hunt directly over them. Immediately adjust your direction and take a route that parallels the tracks to one side. Watch your back trail, as the buck you're following is watching his and may decide to circle around you.

- The savvy still-hunter doesn't spend too much time investigating tracks; he knows they only tell you that the deer passed here earlier. Spend your time looking carefully ahead of you in the distance, in the direction of the tracks. This way, you may just get a good look at the buck that made them.

- Let's say you spot a buck too far ahead of you for a clean shot. If you have enough cover, try to make a wide semicircle to get ahead of him. Then, pick a spot with good cover. Stop and wait without making any movement. There is a good chance the buck may end up walking right past you.

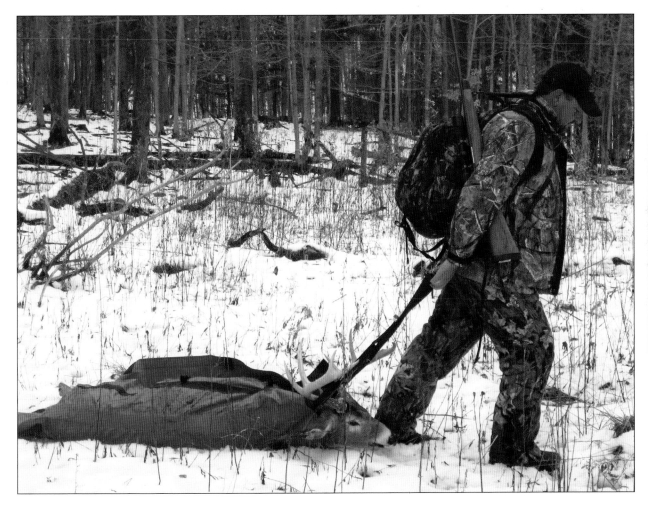

▲ For still-hunters, the Game Sled helps makes dragging deer quick and easy--even over long distances. CEO of Coventry Log Homes, Jeff Elliott, drags out a hefty 9-point with the Game Sled.

- If a deer sees, hears, or smells you and snorts and runs off, snort back at it. This is a good way to not only stop the deer but also attract it. If it doesn't see or wind you it probably won't travel far or it might even start walking your way! If it does walk off–wait about 15 minutes and then begin to slowly make a wide arc to the left or right. You may get an opportunity to intercept the deer within a few hundred yards.

- The worst and the noisiest choice of footwear to wear when still-hunting is a heavy pair of leather boots. They will give your presence away to deer every time. I often wear sneakers in the early fall and light leather or rubber boots later in the season, especially when snow and rain make for slippery terrain.

- If you happen to jump a buck and he isn't aware of you, don't rush to change your position or to take a shot. Rushing usually ends up with the hunter making a careless mistake, which inevitably alerts the buck to your presence. I know what I'm talking about here; I made this mistake countless times as a young, inexperienced still-hunter.

- A seasoned still-hunter isn't always on the move. If you come upon a good spot to watch for deer like a natural bottleneck, deer ravine, or a primary scrape, take a rest. Sit down and quietly watch the area for just about an hour or so before moving on again.

- Deer are most active when the barometric pressure is between 29.80 and 30.29, when the wind is from the south or southwest, and there's a relative humidity of less than 70 percent. This is a good time to still-hunt.

- Researchers say that deer go to water at three specific times each day: around 7:00 am, 11:00 am, and 6:00 pm Why? Because of the deer's body metabolism and cud-chewing periods. If there are water sources in the area you're still-hunting, it pays to check any known water sources during these times, especially during a period where there has been less rain or during a drought.

20. Trophy Hunting

As deer stalkers, we all want to take the biggest bucks we can. To some of us, that simply means bagging a buck that would measure 120 inches. For others, that same quest is for a buck in the 160 and higher trophy-class range. No matter which category you fall in–these tips will help you shoot the buck of your dreams.

This chapter contains more advanced information than the other tip chapters. As such, the information here is tried and true. I have used every tip in this chapter many times and, more often than not, the tips provided here have helped me bag mature bucks.

These are no-nonsense tips. They are not designed to sell you products or to try and impress you. They are all intended to have hard-core, sound advice on how to bag bigger, mature-antlered bucks. Some tips break the long-standing myths about deer and deer hunting. Others provide new and interesting break-throughs and you may find some controversial. In the end they will all aid your deer hunting strategies.

As I said in my first *Whitetail Strategies* book in 1995, consistently successful hunters, especially those who take mature bucks year-in and year-out believe in their hunting prowess. They are confident in their ability as hunters. Which leads me back to my original equation of C=PTxC=CS. Concentration + Positive Thinking x Confidence = Consistent Success! Nothing has changed my mind since I wrote that.

◀ These are antlers that dreams are made of and they would satisfy even a seasoned trophy hunter.
(credit: Ted Rose)

▲ This buck is putting the finishing touches on one of his scrapes. Bucks average 25 scrapes per year.
(credit: Ted Rose)

- If you want to identify a buck's scat from that of a doe's, all you need to remember is what many biologists have to say about the subject as well as many seasoned hunters. When a mature whitetail buck defecates, his pile of scat will have about 75 to 85 droppings littered about with each pellet measuring about 1 to 1½ inches in length. So when you come across a pile of deer scat as described above you can be pretty sure it was left by a mature buck–maybe even a trophy class buck.

- I have always recommended to hunters seeking their buck during the rut, to post near preferred food sources. Why? When you want to take a buck, especially during the rut, hunt the does. Inevitably, they will bring a love sick buck to the place they are feeding.

- Hunt the early-season rubs! Many older bucks start rubbing earlier than younger bucks in an attempt to display their rank in the pecking order. Sometimes they will begin making rubs at least two weeks before younger bucks. These signposts provide bucks sharing the same range with both visual and olfactory information about trophy's social ranking.

- Mature bucks make an average of 25 scrapes per year. Most of the time the scrape is made on level ground. They're always located beneath an over-hanging thin, pliable branch that the buck chews to deposit scent from his vomeronasal organ located on the roof of his mouth. He also deposits scent from his forehead-gland on the branch as well.

- Research has confirmed that the time of day when most mature buck's revisit their scrapes is between 12:30 pm and 2:00 pm Because mature bucks instinctively realize it is daylight when they visit their scrapes during this period, they do so more cautiously. Therefore, hunters should not expect a buck to directly approach their scrapes. Instead, bucks will scent-check them from 50 to 75 yards downwind while remaining hidden in the thickest cover available.

- Bucks are lazy by nature. When they are not running from danger, they prefer to walk across level terrain. It is rare for them to move straight up- or downhill. This is good to remember when you're scouting for deer trails.

- Because bucks in the 5–7 year age class have a much lower testosterone level than younger bucks they rarely fight with other males. The lower level of testosterone reduces their desire to breed, enabling the energetic and much more sexually active 3–4 year-olds to chase after hot does. These older bucks often have the largest antlers and are most likely the most reclusive animals–making them harder to hunt. To take one of these old monarchs, your plan should include hunting the thickest and most impenetrable cover you can find–especially thick cover close to prime food sources.

- Despite what you have heard about genetics being the most important element in producing trophy racks–it simply isn't true. The single most important factor to a buck's antler size is age. Once a buck reaches 3½ years old, his body and weight no longer require most of his nutrition. Now the rack gets most of the nutrition the buck eats and it begins to get larger with each passing year until the buck reaches about 6½ years old. At this point, his rack will start to decline in size or at least become more and more nontypical. A given buck produces his biggest antlers during his fourth through his sixth year of life. But, because of hunting pressure, fewer than four percent of all bucks ever live long enough to see their third year.

- A mature buck trail is hard to find because it is primarily used by animals traveling alone. If you locate a well-defined deer trail used by a large numbers of does, yearlings, and fawns, then scout the terrain within 50 yards or so on either side of that trail. It won't take long before you discover the less used and less visible trails of a mature buck. These trails are most often found parallel to and downwind of trails used by doe-family units.

- One of the most frequently asked question is "How can I take larger racked bucks?" My answer is very simple. You must first decide what size rack you–not anyone else–considers a trophy. Once you have done that, then you must let every buck with antlers smaller than that pass you by. Soon, you will raise your own personal bar on the size of antlers you consider good enough to take from year to year.

- Most young bucks are curious and learn from lessons–good or bad. Some are born with what I have termed the "nervous-wreck" factor ingrained in their genes and they turn out to be the mature bucks that are seldom fooled twice–because they are so frightened by everything around them. This makes them seem like they have the ability to think or reason. They can't. The nervous wreck factor just makes them more reclusive and less likely to make the same mistake twice. If one of these types of mature bucks sees you on stand, smells you or hears you go to your stand the same way two or three times in a row, you can forget about him hanging around. To get a shot at a buck like this, you'll have to relocate your stand at least 250 yards away from the original location.

◀ Deer will come to eat corn as soon as the temperatures begin to fall below 28 degrees F.
(credit: Ted Rose)

▲ Bucks will often seek small watering holes, not only to drink several times a day during the rut, but also to cool off after chasing does.
(credit: Ted Rose)

- Mature bucks frequently rub on the same trees year after year, and some of these areas are conducive to making primary scrapes beneath the same overhanging tree limbs from season to season. Mark where you find these rubs and scrapes on a map. That way you will save time scouting and create less pressure in the area, too. You can simply begin your hunt based on where last year's sign was and see if there is any new sign.

- Biologists tell us that a deer's three favorite crops are alfalfa, corn, and a real favorite–soybean. If you find a good alfalfa field or soybean patch, plan to hunt over them. With smaller soybean fields, deer sometimes don't give them a chance to mature and the soybean fields end up looking as if they've been mowed by a tractor. Larger fields of soybeans produce better sighting results.

- Often a buck will bed near other deer, but not too close to them. First, locate the beds of does and younger deer. They will be numerous, various-sized ovals in the snow or grass that are matted down. Then start looking carefully for nearby high ground–even a slight incline–downwind for a larger, single bed. Mature bucks like to bed relatively close to doe-family units (which make ideal sentries) and will almost always look for the slightest of high spots to bed in.

- I'm often told by hunters that bucks don't travel far from their home ranges even in the rut. Take this to the deer hunting bank–a mature breeding buck will travel as far as he has to in order to locate a hot doe. If the area he calls home has an excellent buck-to-doe population he will not travel too far. But if the doe population is off, then he'll put on a pair of traveling shoes and cover a scrape line out over seven to ten miles or more! On the other hand, where does number as many as 20 per square mile, a buck may travel no further than several hundred yards on a given day.

- In moderate to cold temperatures, deer of all ages require about a gallon of water each day. In hot weather, however, the water-intake requirement of smaller deer is about two gallons per day. Larger bodied deer, including mature bucks, require three or more gallons per day. That is why I have several small watering pot holes on my farm, along with a small pond. Watering sources, particularly man-made watering holes, tucked away in thick cover are hot spots for hunting trophy bucks–especially during the peak of the chase when bucks are chasing does hard. They become dehydrated fast during this time and will often take a quick break and go to a secluded pot hole to take a long, cool, drink of water before getting back to chasing does. Smaller deer, on the other hand, can generally get all the water they need from random streams, ponds, and even puddles.

- As many of you have heard me say at my seminars, the most reliable way to take a mature buck is to hunt "off-hours." In research studies, biologists have confirmed (time and time again) that mature bucks (and does) have three peak drinking times during a 24-hour period. These times are 7:00 am, 11:00 am, 6:00 pm and 1:00 am These drinking times have nothing to do with thirst, but are related to daily body metabolisms and related cud-chewing periods. The magic hour of catching a buck drinking or browsing over my many years of hunting has been between 11:30 am and 12:30 pm

- When a number of mature bucks share the same home range, they do not set the rules for who breeds first–the does often determine which bucks get to breed the most. When does visit scrapes made by various bucks, they also use their vomeronasal organ in the roof of the mouth to smell and chemically analyze each buck's urine. A buck that is metabolizing carbohydrates and excreting them in his urine is seen by a doe as a healthy and virile buck. Biologists believe a doe's vomeronasal organ can signal to her when a buck is metabolizing fat and protein and is beginning to decline in health and probably has a low sperm count.

- Deer eyes possess 1,000 times more motion-receptor rods than the eyes of humans. This is how a deer can detect your slightest movement–especially a mature buck when he is looking in your direction.

- As I mentioned above, bucks like to bed on higher ground–especially mature bucks. Unlike younger bucks and other deer, trophy-class whitetails seek out bedding areas that are on slightly higher ground. They will also reverse their line of travel for a short distance before lying down. This enables them to watch their back trails. When you follow tracks, always be alert to movements in the direction of higher ground. That's most likely from where your buck will jump up.

- Contrary to what you have heard, mature bucks often share rubs and scrapes. Biologists believe the behavior may play some kind of role in their social system. Common sense tells me it abso-

lutely does! If a hunting companion kills a trophy buck over a given rub or scrape, check back a few days later to see if that scrape or rub has been revisited and freshened. If is has, you can bet you have a good chance at bagging yourself a good buck!

- If all sign indicates the presence of a mature buck in an area but you don't see him after many outings of sitting on stand, don't become discouraged. Use some other type of tactic, change the times you go and leave the stand; hunt it every three days instead of every day; call, rattle, decoy, and use scent–in other words, don't be a passive hunter. Instead, be a pro-active and positive-thinking hunter. Make things happen and your trophy of a life-time might just step into view!

21. Rut Hunting

This tip chapter supplements the more detailed chapter in this book on the rut. To be frank, I could dedicate an entire book to all aspects of the rut biology, strategy and science. But until I get around to writing that book, this chapter and the more detailed chapter will give you a lot of straight information on a subject eliminating all the horse crap that is often spread about the rut.

What you read here and in the other chapter will be material you can rely on and not have to question. It is information that has taken me years to accumulate. I have tested it through trial and error and share with you the cream of information that rose to the top.

I'm very confident that between this tip chapter and the full chapter on the rut, you will gain insight to this often misunderstood and misspoken subject. It will hopefully shed some light on the inner workings of rut behavior, biology, and some new tactics you can try on the very next rut.

- Using a scent out of season, like estrus-urine before the breeding or the "chase phase" starts, won't attract bucks. They interpret the aroma as unnatural and will only shy away from it. Pay attention to the timing of scent use, and use such scents only when the rut is clearly under way. Use them sparingly and you will also get a more natural response.

- You have heard me say over and over again that it is hard to judge what size buck made a rub. As a rule, the larger the diameter of the rubbed tree, the larger the buck that made the rub. Big-antlered bucks do rub small saplings, however, and although young bucks don't usually rub large

▼ This buck is on the trail of a hot doe. By making an enticing estrus doe blat, you would get the buck's attention quickly. (credit: Ted Rose)

▲ The preorbital gland senses decreasing daylight stimulating the pineal gland which sends a chemical message to the pituitary glad to increase testosterone and the onset of the rut begins. (credit: Ted Rose)

trees–they do on occasion. Look for hook marks in the tree trunk or little indents or holes. These are made by the tips of antler tines. Usually, this is a good way to judge if the buck that rubbed the tree had at least a multi-pointed rack.

- Biologists say that the scrape of a mature buck averages 18 to 36 inches in diameter. Find one that is greater than 24 inches and you have a scrape to hunt over.

- Biologists don't have a definitive explanation why the quantity and quality of the acorn drop affects the number of rubs bucks make each fall. Basically, when there are fewer acorns, there will be fewer rubs, so finding only a few rubs doesn't necessarily mean that the buck count is down. There may be more bucks in an area with lower acorn drop than the lack of rub sign would lead you to believe!

- When you're setting up a stand so you can watch a scrape, don't get too close, or a returning buck is very likely to detect you. Since bucks commonly scent-check their scrapes from 30 to 40 yards downwind, the spot for your tree stand should be 50 to 60 yards downwind of the scrape if you're a bow hunter, and further still if you're a firearm hunter. Then the returning buck should pass right between you and the scrape with his attention focused in the opposite direction.

- Don't pay much attention to scrapes and rubs made around field perimeters bordering woodlands. Most of this rutting sign is made and revisited only after dark.

- When you're scouting, never touch a scrape, licking branch, or rubbed tree with your bare hands or clothing. Even the tiniest amount of human scent transferred to the sign will alert deer to your presence and cancel the sign's significance.

- The rut is triggered when a decreasing amount of daily sunlight passes through the eyes of deer. This reduction of light stimulates the pineal gland, which in turn sends messages to the pituitary gland to increase testosterone levels in bucks and progesterone levels in does.

- Bucks are capable of breeding whenever they have hard antlers, which lasts for a five-month time span. But does are capable of breeding only when in estrus–which runs a 26-hour time span. So in reality, it's the does that "go into rut," not the bucks.

- When does are in estrus, it's virtually impossible to call in a buck with a grunt call. Use a doe bleat or fawn call to call in does instead. Any responding does that are in heat will have bucks trailing behind them, right to your deer stand.

- When you rattle antlers, don't rattle too loudly at first. Just tick the tines to make "click-clicking" sounds that simulate the sparring of immature bucks. If you start off loud and aggressive, you may intimidate and scare away bucks.

- If a doe comes by your stand with her tail extended straight back, freeze! She's at the peak of her estrus and is signaling to a following buck that she's ready to breed.

- The most intense action during any region's well-defined rutting period occurs when there is a 10 to 20 degree drop in the temperature. Conversely, rutting action slows dramatically when the temperature suddenly rises above the norm. This is not to be confused with the rut-regulating influence of sunlight; it's a separate, year-round phenomenon. Deer are always more active in cool weather, becoming lethargic when the temperature rises above the norm.

- Biologists tell us that the types of places where bucks most frequently make scrapes are (in descending order of importance) field edges, ridge crests, terraced hillside benches, narrow bottomland flats adjacent to creeks, and old logging roads.

- During the rut, bucks can to travel as far as seven miles per day and as little as 300 yards per day. It all depends upon how many does are available to a buck in a given region.

- When you're rattling antlers, simulate the sounds of a genuine buck fight by stomping the ground with your boots and raking the antlers through brush. Since the buck will come in focused on your sounds, make sure you are well camouflaged.

- Many experts agree that hunting a scrape area is more likely to result in success if you use a portable, climbing stand that you carry in and out each time you visit. If you use either a fixed-position stand or a ladder stand and leave them in place, a buck visiting the area during your absence is likely to see or smell the stand and avoid it from then on.

- If you're hunting a scrape area and spook a mature buck or shoot at one and miss, it's unlikely that he'll give you a second chance in the days or week to come. Relocate your stand to another scrape area at least 300 yards away.

- If you see a buck approaching a scrape cautiously, in a timid manner, with his head held low and his tail tucked between his legs, you might want to pass him up. He's exhibiting subordinate behavior that indicates the scrape he's investigating was made by another higher-ranking buck.

- Bucks commonly scrape in the same locations year after year. They may even lay down scrapes beneath the exact tree branches and rub the very same saplings as the year before. When scouting, be sure to check the scrape and rub locations you hunted the previous years. You may even find yourself being able to use the same exact tree for a stand as you did last year.

- Ignore so-called estrus-response scrapes. These are small and are commonly found in open fields and meadows. They're simply places where an estrus doe has urinated and a buck (in his random travels) has detected the scent and briefly pawed the ground. The buck may never return to that spot again.

- If a scrape you're hunting begins to dry out and is slowly becoming covered by windblown leaves and forest duff, it's no longer being visited and freshened by the buck that originally made it. Scout somewhere else for a hot scrape that's being regularly tended.

- Severe weather ordinarily causes whitetails to lay up in cover, often for several days, until things blow over. The exception is the peak of the rut. This is the time when most of the does are in full estrus. They are very restless and continually on the move. Bucks, likewise, are traveling and searching for does, regardless of what the weather is doing. So don't stay home just because high winds or driving sleet are ravaging your favorite deep woods. Get out and be in the woods during this time of peak deer activity.

▲ Unless the weather is extremely bad during the rut, bucks and does will continue to search for mates.
(credit: Ted Rose)

22. Tree Stands

One of the most common mistakes about deer hunting is not having confidence in where you placed your stand. I have heard many times from hunters who email me (peter@fiduccia.com) about this one subject, "Please give me some sound advice on where I should place my stand."

In this tip chapter, I share with you my best advice on this subject. Whether you hunt a farm, remote ridge in big woods or on heavily hunted state lands there is something here for you to glean.

Remember while you are reading these tip that while they may seem basic, many hunters despite knowing of them–do not use them to the best of their ability. The truth is paying attention to the dozen tips I mention here will help improve you deer sightings and shooting opportunities dramatically.

• If you're hunting a farm, it may be better not to walk in with your portable stand–unless you have no other choice. Remember, that on every farm or

▼ This is one of my favorite deer blinds it is called a DeerBox and they come in all shapes and sizes.

ranch, the farmer or rancher doesn't walk around his land. Farmers constantly drive tractors, trucks, or four-wheelers on their property and deer soon become accustomed to the comings and goings of vehicles. They even get more familiar with the one vehicle that is used most often. So if you have the opportunity to ride a tractor or ATV set up your stand you may wind up arousing less suspicion by the deer than if you walked in.

- When you're trail watching, don't position your stand along a straightaway stretch. Instead, place it on the inside of the bend. Deer usually walk the trail looking toward the outside of the bend and therefore, they are less likely to notice you.

- When you're hunting a bedding area, position your portable climbing stand so you can hunt the downwind side of the cover. If the wind direction changes on a particular day, go to a different stand location.

- For the best concealment from every direction, hang your stand in a multi-trunk tree clump–I like three-trunk trees. You will be spotted much more often from a single-trunk tree standing alone. Single trees just don't hide your presence as well as multi-trunk trees do and when a deer approaches, it usually makes you out.

- Early in the season, it is wiser not to go too high in your stand. With leaves on the trees, your vision is obstructed and there is more in your way when trying to get a clear shot. Instead, stay below the heavy leaves and foliage to see and get more action. Plan to set up higher later in the season, after the leaves have dropped.

- Once your stand is mounted and secure, try it out for comfort and to see if there are any dead branches, twigs, or loose bark in your way. If so, rub away the loose bark and snap the branches and twigs from the trunk. That way, you will prevent any unexpected noise as well as getting your clothing caught and making noises as you climb or turn your body to get into shooting position. More

deer are spooked like this than you can image. Most deer are never seen because they hear your noise and avoid the spot–leaving you thinking you got skunked for the day.

- I know it is hard, but try to avoid taking the same route to your stand every day; you'll eventually alert the deer to your presence. With a mature buck it won't take but a few times, at best, for him to get the picture of what is taking place. Try not to hunt from the same stand every day either. I like giving my stands a rest of at least one day, and preferably two or three days, between hunts. Of course, this means having other stands set up and ready to go so you can play the shell game when the wind is wrong or so you can avoid over-hunting a certain stand.

- Even the most active big-buck stand can be ruined if you hunt it when the wind direction is not completely in your favor. It takes a lot of determination, but if you know the wind is coming from the wrong direction or swirling erratically, don't go to the stand. The best advantage for having multiple stands in place is that you can choose the best location to hunt each day as conditions dictate.

- I regularly set out markers to help me not under- or over-estimate distances when I am bowhunting. I place markers at various distances around my stand for quick reference that I have measured off with a digital rangefinder. In the woods, there are plenty of places to hang markers. In a stand at the edge of a field, I use markers that stick in the ground.

- Whenever you have a choice, hang your stand on the north side of a tree. You will be less visible to deer because most of the time you'll be in the shade of the trunk.

- On our farm, we have at least 24 tree stands in different locations. Now, I don't recommend setting up that many unless you also own at least 300 acres, but if you are hunting a 50–150-acre

▲ This stand gets its best action when the wind is blowing from the southwest. The savvy hunter sets lots of stands to take advantage of different wind directions.

parcel you should have at least a half dozen stands up so you can work the wind and avoid hunting the same stand twice in a day. That way you will always have a hot stand to hunt from as the season progresses and conditions change. There should be a stand overlooking a prime feeding area, one overlooking an escape trail, swamp, a thick patch of pines, a hot primary scrape or rub, as well as one in a funnel, near a water hole, and one near a stormy-weather bedding area.

- I look for new tree-stand locations in March or April, because vegetation has not yet grown up to hide last year's sign. I also look during turkey season, too.

23. Calling All Deer

My most successful tactic over the last 45 years is using deer calls to attract deer, hold others from leaving, and stop running deer or even to intentionally spook deer from heavy cover. No matter what circumstance comes up in deer hunting–using a deer call can benefit you.

These are tips that can complement all the other information I have provided on deer calling over the years. Some of the tips I have mentioned before in my calling DVD *Tactics for Talking to Deer* or in other books or on my television show. I mention them again here to demonstrate their importance. You can take what you read in this chapter to the deer hunting bank–used as recommended you will be dressing out your buck or doe this fall!

- As I have mentioned many times, never call to a deer when it is walking toward you and especially when it is looking straight in your direction. The odds of the deer seeing you are much greater if you do. It may also see you move the call to your lips and just that movement alone may be enough of a warning for the deer to leave the area. Always give deer an angle before calling to them or at least wait until the deer looks another way. If you excite their sense of curiosity and keep him guessing where the call is coming from, a buck or doe will eventually get close enough for a shot.

- As many of you have heard me preach in my seminars and on our television show, blowing a grunt call like you're the biggest, "baddest" buck in the woods will only work against you. A loud, aggressive grunt only serves to intimidate most bucks–even mature bucks–and will scare them away almost every time. If you keep your grunt tone low so you sound like a "beatable" buck, you'll draw greater response from bucks that think they can whip you.

- If you see a distant deer respond to your call and begin coming your way, stop calling! Let the deer's curiosity work for you. By continuing to call to the deer, you'll only increase the buck's chances of pinpointing your exact location. Also, most deer do not vocalize repeatedly. This does not sound natural to them.

- An adult estrus doe blat is the perfect call to use at the peak of the rut. When a doe is in heat, she seeks out a buck. Often, the doe periodically stops and makes several soft blats, then looks around and listens for a soft grunt response from a buck. The cadence of this particular sound by the doe sounds almost like a standard grunt call; the difference is that it isn't continuous but includes three-second pauses between each one-second blat.

◀ This buck is making a lip curl (flehmening). He would respond immediately to a doe estrus blat.
(credit: Ted Rose)

▲ Learning not to grunt too loudly or aggressively will enhance your success post-haste. You can take that to the deer hunting bank!

▲ These are the tools of a deer caller. They include a grunt, snort, two adult blats, and a fawn bleat.

hear the fawn bleating may just follow the doe to your stand as well!

- When you rattle with a partner–antler rattling is doubly effective. Place the shooter in a tree stand, ground blind, or in heavy cover, about 35 yards from the rattling hunter. If a deer responds, he'll usually walk right by the shooter to find the two "other bucks" that are sparring or fighting—many times offering the shooter an exciting shot.

- Deer don't continuously vocalize among themselves, so don't overdo your calling. The exception to this rule is during the rut, when both bucks and does use a variety of vocalizations far more frequently. During this time of the season, you can risk calling more often—say every 20 or 30 minutes throughout the course of the day.

- Calling when you actually do not see a deer can be effective, but calling to a deer you can see works best as you can watch to see if the deer is interested or not.

- When you're using any type of deer call, don't always expect a deer to immediately respond and head your way. Quite often, a deer will stare for a long period of time, trying to see the other deer before venturing closer. This is where my natural deer tail decoy works its magic. Full size decoys also work well to entice deer to come in as well.

- When you rattle, pay close attention to your immediate right, left, and behind you. A majority of bucks I have called in didn't come straight to me from the direction I expected. Instead, they often circled and tried to come in downwind of me. Keep that in mind when you are using pro-active tactics like calling, rattling, and decoying.

- I wish I had a dollar for every time I could not control the need to cough or sneeze while on stand. When it happens, I try to muffle my mouth against my jacket sleeve. Then, I immediately try to cover my sound and stimulate some other type of deer vocalization that will match the time of

- If you blow your call at a distant deer, he will react almost one hundred percent of the time. He may not always turn and immediately come your way, but you'll see some recognition of the call. He may flag his tail twice, raise his head slightly, either slow down or speed up its gait, look in your direction, or simply cup an ear toward you. If none of these body language signals takes place, the buck most likely did not hear your call. It is worth trying to call to this deer once more, slightly louder.

- More and more hunters, especially bowhunters, are using the alarm-distress fawn bleat to call in does. Why call does? Because a doe's maternal instinct causes her to respond to what she perceives is a fawn in trouble. And if you call her in, any buck that's with her or even near enough to

▲ It is as important to use your eyes and ears when calling as it is to use the right call under the right conditions.

▲ Generally, antlered game does not want to spill blood when they fight. On rare occasions, a serious injury or death may happen, most fights are nothing more than shoving and sparring matches.

season I'm hunting. A nearby deer that hears your throat-clearing noise and then a grunt, or blat, or some other deer vocalization won't be alarmed as he would've been if you'd just coughed. When I sneeze–I quickly make a soft, social snort to cover the noise made by the sneeze.

- In addition to my deer calls, I carry a small predator call that imitates a screaming rabbit. Many deer respond to predator calls based purely upon curiosity.

- Using your ears and eyes are critical to successful calling. It is said that 80 percent of the animals called in by hunters come in without being seen. Whitetails have an uncanny way of slipping in close without making a sound or exposing themselves in the open. Continually scrutinize the cover in all directions around you for the slightest glimpse of a wary buck putting the sneak on you. I have often heard a buck make very soft guttural grunts before I ever saw him. Other times, I heard and saw a sapling being rubbed or brush being attacked by a buck that responded to my call, but kept himself well hidden in cover. When this happens, sometimes a soft doe blat draws the wary buck closer to you.

- During the pre-rut, savvy callers combine what I term the "Big Four." Use a grunt call, mixed with an estrus doe-blat, rattling antlers, and a decoy. Note: During the firearm season I only do this on my farm in an area where no other hunters are present. For safety's sake, either do this on your own land or only during the bowhunting season. For goodness sake–don't do it on the opening day of firearm season anywhere!

- Throughout the year, does are far more vocal and social than bucks. Because of this, many deer you call in will be does. Young 1½ year old bucks also fall into this category.

- If you call in a buck and he hangs up just out of shooting range and won't come any closer, wait a few minutes before doing anything more. Allow him to turn and walk away until he's almost out of sight. Then, make a soft grunt quickly followed by a slightly louder estrus blat. Many times I have had a buck stop in his tracks, spin around, and come trotting in with his guard down. It creates the entire illusion for the buck.

- Take this to the deer hunting bank: There is no truth to the legend that large rattling antlers will call in the biggest bucks. Again, big bucks are frightened of their own shadows most of the time and when they are spurred on to be brave during the rut, they still avoid encounters with big or bigger bucks. Use an average set of antlers and you will have greater response. Yes, it's true that bleached or dried-out antlers don't yield the same authentic sounds as fresh ones–I guarantee that. And yes, I have used synthetic antlers for over 20 years when I rattle. You can find them at www. woodsnwater.tv .

- If hunting pressure is usually intense in your region, you'll have your best success calling deer during the off-hours and midweek, when fewer hunters are in the woods. Hunt the heaviest cover you can find during this time.

- Most buck fights are nothing more than sparring sessions. Only where there is a one-to-one buck-to-doe ratio do bucks get into more serious fights. So don't smash your antlers together hard especially during the early fall or you'll scare off even the big bucks. Many times this type of over-aggressive rattling will scare off a hot doe during the rut and then you might as well move your location. By just lightly tickling the antlers you will attract more bucks. The time to clash your antlers a little louder is later during the big chase, when bucks are fighting more aggressively, but still not getting into all-out fights.

- When calling or rattling, remember if you call in a small buck, you may want to let him pass. Or, at least wait a few minutes to see if he is being followed by a larger buck–which often happens. Don't expect the bigger buck to just walk in. When you spot the young deer, take a moment to scan the cover for the bigger buck.

- When you're rattling, this is the time to create the entire illusion. Add more realism by meshing and grinding the antlers together. If you're on the ground, kick dirt and rustle leaves with your boots and don't be afraid to break dry branches to simulate the various sounds that bucks make when fighting. If you're rattling from a tree stand, rake the tree's bark and break smaller branches. Don't get over aggressive but make sure to include all of the above. I know I have said in earlier books to be very aggressive when rattling. Well, we all continue to learn the more we hunt. After rattling for 40 years, I can now say being less aggressive pays more dividends than being overly aggressive.

- Don't expect deer to respond to your calling every day–it just won't happen. That's the reality of calling, rattling, and decoying. Sometimes deer will come to you one day, and they won't respond the next day. Don't be frustrated and give up calling. Instead stick with it–it will be worth your while.

▲ I often carry my deer calls during the spring and summer while I work on my farm. It gives me an opportunity to practice on any deer that I happen to come across. Practicing during the off-season is crucial to becoming a confident caller during the hunting season.

24. Hunting Farmlands

Several years ago, my cousin Leo Somma and I purchased over 300 acres of land in Otsego County, New York. Leo's 110 acres has about seven tillable acres and my property has 35 agricultural acres. Between both our farms we have not only learned how to become pretty good farmers, but we have also learned how to improve the soil, pH, and the mineral content of the soil.

We have gained invaluable experience on how to successfully grow many different types of crops that attract, hold, and help the overall health of the deer and other wildlife.

We regularly grow different types of vegetables, melons, clover, grains, legumes, brassicas, buckwheat, sugar beets, turnips, and millet. We also plant and grow specialty crops like white acorn trees, wild fruit trees, soybeans, sunflowers, a wide variety of shrubs, and even inedible cover crops.

By growing these crops (through trial and error), we have come a long way to understand what deer eat, when they eat it, what they prefer to eat and how they use the fields and other areas on our farms in their daily routines.

The day we bought our land we decided we would improve our soil minerals, create sanctuaries, and manage the crops, woods, water sources, and the game as the first step to begin our quest to start a genuine quality deer management program.

We have also learned that deer not only respond very well to having fields or food plots to feed in, but they also develop a predictable pattern regarding travel routes, feeding times and places, and other behavior that helps our hunting to be more successful.

Following are some suggestions for anyone who hunts on lands that include agricultural fields, small food plots, or other types of plants, shrubs, trees, or vegetation that deer eat.

- Biologists claim that the preferred domestic foods of deer are soybeans, corn, cabbage, sugar beets, carrots, navy beans, turnips, apples, pears, peaches, and legume grasses such as alfalfa and clover. You can take that to the deer hunting bank. On our farm, alfalfa is the number one favored crop followed closely by soybeans, corn, and carrots.

Next are apples and pears. I'll bet they are also favored in this order on most farms you hunt.

- We have noticed over the years that deer normally enter crop fields at the inside or outside corners, not along one of the side edges. When you're looking for a stand location, spend most of your time scouting for entrance and exit trails at these corner spots.

- Hunters don't often pay enough attention to harvested cornfields or other croplands when they are covered by snow. I promise you, deer can smell the food beneath the snow. I've seen them paw down through a foot of the fresh snow to get at the broken corn cobs, grasses or other food.

- As a rule of thumb, it is easier to get deer hunting permission on a farm where crops are grown than on a tract of land not used for agriculture. Too many deer can destroy certain crops (like soybeans) making most farmers welcome hunters in hopes of keeping their deer population in balance.

- I discovered that deer love all types of melons—which are like ice cream to deer (so are turnips). They stomp the melons apart with their hooves, and then eat the sweet inner fruit. A field littered with broken melon parts is a deer hunting hot spot you should never overlook. Pumpkin fields also produce the same attraction to deer.

- When fields of low-growing crops (grains, grasses, and large plantings of garden vegetables) are close to dense cover, woods, or stands of evergreen pines, deer feed on them most often during daylight. Other fields that place deer out in the open (especially mature bucks), aren't worth hunting after the hunting pressure gets going. Does and young bucks may eat there during the last 30 minutes of light, but mature bucks will not venture into the open fields until well after dark.

- I have seen deer on my farm walk right through my cornfields, without stopping to even nibble on the corn, to reach a small five-acre soybean field.

▲ This is a field of corn on my farm. I often spot deer leaving the woods and feeding during the midday on my corn.

Soybeans are so highly sought-after by deer that they eat the entire plant; first the beans, then the leaves, then the stems. That is why if you are going to plant soybeans plant at least five acres. Despite being warned by my cousin Ralph to "double or triple" the number of acres I was planting, I didn't. The deer never gave my soybeans the chance to grow. They ate them to the ground. Ralph regularly hunts huge soybean fields in Colts Neck, New Jersey, and knows well how fast deer will eat up a small field planted in soybeans. After the beans have been harvested, they'll revisit the field to paw the ground and get at the roots. If you have a choice of various types of cropland to hunt, always pick the soybean field–even over alfalfa when the

area around you has other alfalfa fields but no soybeans fields available!

• I have also discovered that when there's no heavy bedding cover adjacent to a cornfield, and sometimes even when there is, deer regularly bed in the standing corn–right through the firearm season! If hunting the perimeter edges doesn't produce, put on very small pushes. One hunter should slowly walk through the standing corn zigzagging back and forth. If there are deer bedded there, they will slowly move ahead of the hunter and when they get to the edge of the corn they will trot out into the surrounding woods or other cover surrounding the corn field! I also use standing corn to make

▲ I plant corn and sorghum for food, cover, and as a natural fence along my property's borders and roads. I leave the crops standing through deer season. As the hunting pressure increases deer quickly use them to bed and escape from hunters on nearby properties.

an alarm-distress snort. If deer are there, they will move from the corn offering you a shot.

- It didn't take me long to find out deer don't like to dig for their food. As soon as we cut a crop or harvest it, they'll eagerly head to the fields to eat the broken pieces of these vegetables that the harvester or other farm equipment leaves behind and are turned up to the top of the soil.

- The number one question I get when I give food plot seminars is, "What should I plant on my land?" My answer is from what I have learned through six years of farming experience, "Always try to plant what your neighbors are not planting!" By planting crops your neighboring hunting clubs or numerous farms don't plant, you will offer the deer something new and interesting to eat that

they can't find anywhere else! If everyone is growing clover, there is no reason that deer have to come to your land to eat clover. But if you offer chicory or sugar beets or anything else other than what is growing around you, deer will make a beeline to your place first. That means they will be there during shooting hours!

- If you don't have your own land to grow crops, always try to gain hunting permission on a farm where something different is grown than on other farms in the area. Deer are varietal feeders, meaning that their body metabolisms don't function properly on just one type of food. Therefore, if most of the farms are planted in corn and hay, the lone farm that has leafy vegetables will act as a magnet to the local deer population. If most of the farmers in the area raise apples and other fruits,

▲ To draw as many deer as you can from your land and your neighbors' properties, plant crops that are not planted by your surrounding neighbors or farmers.

the lone farm with grain (i.e. wheat or oats) will be high on the deer hit list.

- When hunting any cropland, stay on stand as long as possible each day. A good way to do this is to hunt one stand from dawn till around 9:00 am Then if you want, go back to camp and eat a quick breakfast (not bacon or other smelly foods). Then head back out to another stand–not the one you were in–and hunt there from 11:30 am to 2:30 pm Then, move to a third stand to hunt until legal light is over. This strategy doesn't take long before it produces more deer sightings for the average hunter. Deer living in farm areas are more accustomed to having close encounters with vehicles, farm equipment, and farm workers, so they're not nearly as nocturnal as in non-farm country where they will dart to the thickets to bed soon after sunup.

- Many farmers know that whitetails focus their attention on soybean and cornfield spillage and remaining orchard fruits during bitter-cold weather. As I have often mentioned, deer instinctively know these particular food types yield the highest conversion rate (conversion is the metabolic transformation of food into energy, body warmth, and accumulated fat store). Therefore, when the temperature suddenly drops below 27 degrees, head to corn or soybean fields to hunt.

- In my first book, I wrote that during the rut, find the does and you'll find the bucks. Nothing has changed about that plan over the years. When hunting on farms, you'll locate the does in the fields of whatever crop happens to be in its prime. The bucks will be skulking close by in any available cover.

- The very worst thing you can do during the firearm season is to hunt directly over a crop field. Instead, put your stand at least 100 yards from where you think the deer will be feeding. During bow season, put it on the entrance trail at least 50 yards back into the adjacent woodland cover. Does and small bucks may enter a cropland well before dusk, but mature bucks commonly stay back within the protection of cover until full dark.

- After you have permission to hunt on a farm that's raising crops, ask the landowner where he sees deer feeding, where they come out of surrounding woodlands, and how they travel back and forth across the property. He sees the activity day in and day out and knows best where the deer feed most every day. Following this advice can turn your scouting time into hunting time instead!

- If you have a stand that overlooks a crop like alfalfa or soybean, don't go to your stand in the pre-dawn darkness, by walking across the open field. It is more than likely you will spook deer that are feeding in the field and you will send them scurrying off to find cover. Instead, walk the edges or circle around to approach your stand by coming through adjacent woodland cover. During the evening post, reverse that practice. Don't walk through the woodlands to reach a stand that overlooks a field, because you'll probably spook deer from their beds or who are moving slowly toward the fields. Instead, take the shortest route across the open field to get to the stand unnoticed and unheard.

- Although grass legumes such as alfalfa and clover are deer magnets, their attraction is strongest in the early fall when they're still lush and green. Later in the fall and into early winter, after several hard frosts, the grasses go into dormancy, become dry and aren't as palatable or nutritious. This time of year, deer seek out crops like turnips and sugar beets as these plants become much sweeter after they have frozen. Turnips have 17 to 24 percent crude protein and their roots have 12 to 15 percent protein. Turnips are another "ice cream" plant for deer especially after heavy frosts when other crops are less attractive to deer.

- During periods of drought, the hot spot for deer hunting is in a field planted in legumes. The prime time to be on stand is early morning when deer eat the wet grass and lick the dew from it (as an added benefit). Soon after the sun burns off the dew, the deer will boogy for nearby shaded woodland cover.

▲ We set up a lot of our food plots in areas where our stands are at least 40 to 50 yards in the woods so the deer don't associate the food plots with danger. During bow season we will hunt the edges of our fields more, however.

▲ We never let a planting season go by without putting in turnips for the deer. After a heavy frost turnips are to deer as iron is to magnets.

25. Camo or Not?

When hunting in snow I try not to wear all white clothing. Often, it will make you stand out brighter than your surroundings in the woods. Even in full sunlight, snow has a muted dirty-white or grayish cast due to overhead clouds and tree shadows. The best camo for hunting in the snow is a snow-camo suit mixed with another color or two that look like branches, pines, brush or tree trunks.

- In a recent book that my cousin Leo Somma and I wrote, "*25 Projects for Outdoorsmen–Quick and Easy Plans for the Deer Camp, Home, Woods, and Backyard*," (available at www.woodsnwater.tv) we included several portable and permanent wooden tree stands. In each project, we made sure to emphasize to the reader the importance of making sure the bottoms of the platforms were painted with grey, black, brown, and green paint so if any deer was to glance up, the stand would be so well camouflaged they wouldn't be disturbed by it. We also paint the ladders, railings, and all the other wood camo, too.

- Despite what you may have heard from the hoards of experts who dress only in camo–green wool or green and black wool are also excellent camouflage clothing. No matter where you hunt–even in places where there is snow, or open fields, etc., it isn't unusual for deer to see a single evergreen tree. As long as it isn't moving. When hunting in swamps, pines, or even in alfalfa or other green fields, green wool or lighter green garments work as good as traditional camo clothing. Knowing that you can occasionally wear green, gives you the advantage of having more than one camo outfit, too!

- Over the years, we have learned to attach cedar branches with the greenery to our stands. It not only helps to break up the outline of your legs–the odor of the cedar helps to mask your human scent, too.

- If you use a fixed-position stand and either screw-in tree steps or hang-on tree steps, install them on the opposite side of the tree from the direction you expect deer to approach. To make using screw steps safer and easier, check out E-Z Kut at www.woodyhunting.com.

- When you use natural materials to make a deer ground blind, design it so you can shoot out of the middle or at least around one of the sides rather than over the top. Popping up over the top is sure to alert any deer you're trying to ambush.

- Learn to mix and match your camo hunting clothes. During the bow season, I often wear green

◀ We paint every inch of our tree stands including the bottoms of the platforms in order to help the stand be less visible to incoming deer.

▲ Green clothing is overlooked as an effective camouflage. This deer passed just 20 yards from me as I stood in front of the pine tree (over my left shoulder) in Filson wool clothing. As long as a hunter remains motionless, game see the object as a stationary green bush or pine tree—even in open terrain.

◄ To ensure your safety when using tree steps they should be sturdy and capable of holding into the tree under a lot of weight. (credit: E-Z Kut)

pants and an over-shirt that has a lot of red, gold, yellow, and orange in it. That way, I can hide my legs (especially if I'm hunting from a pine), and blend in with the fall leaves in all their splendid colors. It is a good idea to wear a different camo pattern on your upper torso than on the lower part of your body. A leaf pattern on your jacket and a tree-trunk or branch pattern on your trousers is also a good combo and can (in some instances) really help you blend into your surroundings.

• If your stand is hung in an area bathed in bright sunlight, even your slightest movement will be magnified out of proportion. Instead, hang your stand in a place where there will be shadows during the times you plan to be in it.

▲ Ralph Somma (right) took this buck as it was pushed from a patch of pines, across the road and into this field.

26. Deer Drives

I'm not big on driving deer especially in heavily hunted areas or in places where driving small acreage only sends deer to the neighbors. I'm also never too impressed by killing a deer that was driven to me. It seems to take something out of the hunt for me. But let me be clear that by no means am I being critical of anyone else who enjoys the strategy. I feel to each-his-own when it comes to how you like to hunt deer.

The way I drive deer isn't really a drive at all. It is more like a strategic low-key push. Small drives always seem to work better than large ones do–for me anyway. The real fact is that hunters seldom really drive, push or move deer in directions the deer really don't want to go!

Remember that all deer drives do include elements of strategies that to the best of our hunting skills try to get deer to move in a direction that makes it more vulnerable to moving past another hunter lying in ambush.

Any type of push or drive requires a lot of pre-planning not only to get the deer moving but also to get both the pusher and stander coordinated. All drives must include the utmost concern to safety. They must include a drive master whose is in charge of the push and whose instructions are followed in unwavering detail and are viewed as the final word by all other participants of the deer drive.

The tips in this chapter are only suggestions and should be adjusted to the type of drives or pushes you do. They are in no way meant to suggest that driving deer is inherently dangerous or any more unsafe than any other type of hunting. But with that said, they do require your utmost concern to safety and overall participant numbers. One final suggestion–it is wise not to include first time hunters on deer drives for the

▼ When you're a poster on a deer drive and you want to stop a running deer that is moving by your stand, make a loud alarm blat. The buck or doe will skid to a halt giving you a better opportunity for a safe and accurate shot. (credit: Ted Rose)

▲ In order to get the best results from his pushers and standers, the savvy deer drive captain uses a wind detector before making the plans for his drive.

obvious reason that they lack experience in this type of hunting.

- If you employ deer drives as one of your tactics remember this: Always appoint a drive master to be in charge of your drive group. His word is the last word on anything related to how the drive is to take place. No one overrides his instructions or decisions. The drive master should have the best knowledge of the terrain and the habits and whereabouts of the deer on the land including where deer bed. The drive master should also know where they usually move when pushed.

- I don't recommend pushing deer with a large group of hunters, because it is less effective than driving with smaller groups. Larger drives also take more time and effort to organize for maximum success. Smaller groups of three to six hunters are easier to organize and move around.

- Driving large tracts is usually a waste of time as it takes a lot of time and gives deer too many opportunities to take advantage of all the escape routes. The savvy driver understands that it is to everyone's advantage to drive a 50-acre piece versus a 100-acre tract. Smaller plots offer better results.

- Over the years, I have noticed that when driving thick cover, if there's a big buck in the cover and he has other deer with him, most often, he's either the first one to break out, or he is going to hold tight and won't come out at all.

- On my farm, we began planting over 100 six- to eight-foot pine trees in a five-acre pasture in order to provide future cover and a place for deer to seek refuge during heavy snow or extreme cold temperatures. Immature pine plantations, with individual trees no more than eight feet high and packed tightly together, can hold a surprising amount of bedded deer. Evergreen patches become prime places for two- or three-man drives in just a few short years. The thick groups of branches close to the ground limit visibility to only feet and give deer a feeling of great security. When I consult with landowners about deer management or what types of food plots to plant, I always strongly recommend that they including planting a patch of pines as part of their quality deer management program.

- When you're planning a drive and considering the wind direction, it's advantageous to allow the deer to get a nose full of human odor from the drivers. The best situation of all is driving in a crosswind, as the deer won't be able to directly catch the scent of either the standers or the drivers.

- An old tactic to get a wily buck out of a thick patch of cover is to drive it slowly the first time. If you're sure he is in the cover, but your first drive didn't push him out try the drive again. This time, however, make sure you drive the cover from a different direction.

- To prevent deer from circling back past the drivers, consider using what some call a fishhook drive. The drivers move through the thick cover in the usual manner. About half way through the drive, two drivers reverse their line of travel and slowly hunt back in the direction they came from. Often they'll get up-close shots at deer that are focusing their attention on the drivers moving away in the distance.

- Try a drop-drive to ambush any bucks that try to sneak through the driveline. A drop-drive has the drivers moving through the cover in the usual way, trying to push deer to other standers positioned ahead. But soon after the drive begins, a couple of stand hunters stop and take stands behind the drivers at the spot where the driveline initially enters the cover. These hunters often get action about halfway through the drive.

- Remember that mature bucks act a lot like rabbits. They take advantage of the smallest amount of cover. So don't overlook even the smallest pieces of isolated cover. After hunting pressure has been on for several days, a brushy culvert in the middle of a farm field, or thick patch of undergrowth only one acre in size may hold a your trophy buck.

TIPS THAT GET TO THE POINT

- One of the most effective drives is a two-hunter drive. One enters the cover and begins to slowly still-hunt. The other hunter waits at least 15 minutes and, from a higher or lower position, takes the same general route as his partner who, by now, is 500 or more yards ahead of him. Deer that detect the lead hunter will often make either a circle to get behind him or escape to his left or right and offer a shot to the trailing hunter.

- Ah, how often have I preached that windy days are excellent to post, still hunt and especially drive. Deer drives often have the most success on windy days, even with gusts exceeding 15 miles per hour. Bedded deer usually don't hear the approach of drivers or posters going to their stands. The sounds and effects of the wind and swirling air currents carry human odors in random directions often confusing the senses of driven deer, causing them to travel slowly and cautiously, presenting easier shots.

- If you drive a piece of cover one day and don't push a deer out, that doesn't mean you shouldn't give that patch of cover a second chance the next day. Deer may have moved into the area during the night.

- The designated drive master should always make it clear to a stander that once he has arrived at his assigned location, it is crucial that the stander not move from his stand even if he thinks he spots a better vantage point only 50 yards away. Always trust the drive master's knowledge of the terrain and how deer move through it.

- The one drive situation that's more successful than most other drives is made through a long, cover-choked ravine that, at some particular spot, bottlenecks down into a narrow passage or funnel that escaping deer naturally get pinched through to make their escape.

- Any savvy driver knows that it is not wise to walk by large brush piles or blown-downs. Remember what I said above, mature bucks act like rabbits. When making your way through cover like this, make sure to kick the brush and snap twigs on blow-downs. Often deer hide right in the middle, waiting for you to pass and then try to escape unnoticed. Shaking things up is likely to put a good buck on his feet.

- If you're a stander and see deer running toward you, but they're moving fast, make a loud adult alarm blat call. Guaranteed that the buck that's about to run by you will briefly slam on his brakes and skid to a halt to try to determine where the danger is, giving you precious seconds to get him in your sights.

▲ It is in blowdowns like this that you are likely to jump a buck. The deer are well-camouflaged and can observe their surroundings without being detected by hunters.

27. Bitter Cold Weather

*M*any years ago I hunted for whitetails in Lamar, Colorado. The area was choked with deer–some of which were monster bucks. I came away from that hunt with two thoughts. The first was that I was sure over the next ten years Lamar would produce a buck that would challenge my good friend Milo Hansen's world record. Second, I swore I would never again hunt in bitter cold conditions without "dressing to kill" and without having an arsenal of cold-weather hunting tactics to use to help me bag my buck.

Since then, I have developed a much better routine for staying warm and some key tactics for bagging deer in extremely cold weather. Here are some tips that will put a big buck in your sights in really cold conditions and also keep you warm, too!

- While hot coffee or tea will help keep you warm on stand, a thermos of beef or chicken broth will keep your body temperature higher and keep you more comfortable every time. The broth offers nutritional value and will kick-start your internal body temperature to generate body heat. Coffee and tea won't be as effective.

- If you have staghorn sumac on the land you hunt, plan to be there when the temperatures fall. This plant has a higher fat content than any other native forage. Deer instinctively (there's that word again) know that this plant generates high levels of body heat. Deer seek the plant out quickly, particularly when the temperatures fall into the single digits. Staghorn sumac is easily identified by its bright red

▼ Hunting deer in extremely cold weather requires wearing the right clothes, and keeping your head and feet warm. When you stay warm you will remain on stand longer and possibly get the opportunity to shoot a buck like this. (credit: Ted Rose)

▲ Here is a full leaf of staghorn sumac. Its fruit is a tall red hairy structure, present from June through September.
(credit: Brandeis University)

seed clusters and long branches. It stands two to six feet tall and grows in thick groves.

- When the temperature begins to drop like a rock it is time to plan to hunt near where deer seek food. Deer need extra energy in bitter-cold weather and will search for high-energy foods. This includes corn, acorns, winter wheat, and turnips. Find and hunt near these foods or the trails leading to them and it won't be long before you'll be sitting by the camp's fireplace recounting the hunt!

- Have you ever noticed while driving along a highway after a snow fall that one side of the road is bare of snow and the other isn't? Well that's because south-facing slopes may be as much as 15 degrees warmer than north-facing hillsides. When you're afield keep this in mind. South-facing slopes are where you will see the most deer activity and you'll be warmer hunting there too!

- When the temperature gets frigid, some gun oils and lubricants may slow your firearm's action down considerably. During the colder part of the season, use a solvent to remove the present oil and lube, then lightly lube them with a high-viscosity oil.

- On the coldest of days, I carry two heat seats to my stand; one thin one and one thicker one. I place the thinner Thermaseat inside the back of my jacket around my kidneys. I use the thicker seat to stand on. With my kidneys and feet warm, the rest of my body stays comfortably warm too.

- When the weather gets just too cold to bear, go to a backup ground blind that you can use instead of suffering in your tree stand, especially during snow, ice, or sleet-filled days. On our farm, we have over a dozen shooting houses to retreat to when the weather turns sour. The ground blinds also enable us to hunt in heavy rain as well.

- Biologists say that some of the deer's favorite foods in winter include white cedar, red maple, mountain maple, aspen, and sumac. Find out if you have any of these trees on your land and hunt them just before and after storms.

- On cold days it is wise not to bring your firearms, optics or other equipment into a warm house, cabin, or tent. Condensation, fogging, and other problems are sure to happen if you do. Leave your gear on the deck, in your vehicle, or on a free-standing gun rack (I even included instructions for you to build your own gun rack in this book).

- Ever have trouble starting your vehicle (or ATV) at deer camp after a cold night? Ever have it parked the wrong way when you need a jump at deer camp? Well here's an idea that will help you. When you park your vehicle after the day's hunt, make sure it is facing in the direction you want to leave the next morning. You may also want to keep the transmission in first gear and the transfer case engaged. This will enable the engine to kick over easily in the morning.

▲ We keep our firearms outdoors during the hunt. It is not only safer than bringing them into the house, but it also keeps the scopes from fogging up.

- As mid-winter approaches the circadian rhythm, or daily activity cycle, of deer shifts. During this time they don't move a lot between dawn and dusk. Instead, they move about during the midday, from 11:00 am to 3:00 pm If you ever heard one of my seminars, the best tip I share is to hunt these so called off-hours. Most times it is way too cold to stay on stand all day. So, sleeping in until 10:00 am is a welcome break. Head to your stand around 10:30 am and you'll get there during the peak deer activity period.

- In heavy rain or snow, I place a piece of tape over the muzzle of my rifle to prevent snow and sleet from going down the barrel. This is really handy in case I trip or fall while walking through the woods. You can shoot through the tape without worrying about any loss of accuracy.

- In driving winds, look for deer to bed on lee hill-sides or in the middle of thick cover.

- When the weather has been cold and a warming trend is predicted, you can bet you will see an increase in deer movement. Keep in mind a warming may be only a few degrees above what the current temperatures have been over the last few days. For instance, if it has been in the mid-teens and the temperature jumps only five degrees higher, that's a warming trend for the deer and they will be on the move.

- When the weather turns really cold on our farm, we look for deer in the swamps. Usually, swamps are located in lower elevations than the surrounding land and are protected from cold blasts of northerly winds that are blown off ridges or across open fields. Lowlands, swamps, and boggy areas can be as much as 10 degrees warmer than higher ground only a few hundred yards away.

- When harvested crop fields are covered in snow, don't think the deer will not feed in them. I have seen deer paw through several inches of snow (as long as it hasn't frozen on top) to get to old corn or other vegetable or legume spillage left in the field after it was harvested. Deer can easily smell the food under the snow.

- When you're still-hunting or staging drives, concentrate on thick groves of cedars. When the trees are packed tightly, cedars are a preferred bedding cover for whitetails. They're also a favorite cold-weather food and deer don't have to spend a lot of energy traveling long distances from bedding sites to feeding areas.

- In frigid weather, deer will move with the sun during the day. You'll find them bedded on east-facing slopes in the morning, south-facing slopes during the midday, and west-facing slopes in late afternoon. You won't find them on north-facing slopes.

- A dry, cold day does not stop deer from moving as much as a damp cold day will. If the relative humidity is higher than normal on a given day, don't expect much deer movement.

- There are many brands of portable heaters on the market that burn odorless gas (I use Mr. Heater). They can be used for waterfowl hunting and deer hunting. They work to warm your whole body when used in a ground blind or you can put them between your feet when you're in a tree stand to keep your feet warm during severe cold weather.

- When a storm is approaching, the barometer begins to drop rapidly. Deer will quickly head to thick cover to bed. A rising barometer signals the storm is over which causes the deer to leave their beds and head to feeding areas.

- An old but true adage is that if you want to stay warm, wear a warm hat, because the head and neck region is where most body heat escapes. Keep you ears and head covered and you can last at least two more hours on stand on a cold day

▲ This is the railing of one of our stands that overlooks a group of thick pines. We use the stand every time there is a heavy snow storm or bitter cold wind. We can count on the deer moving in and out of the pines in front.

Section VI

YOU CAN DO IT YOURSELF

YOU CAN DO IT YOURSELF

28. Scoring & Field-Judging Bucks

Whether you want to measure a set of antlers from a buck you shot or field judge what a buck's antlers will score on the hoof, learning exactly how to properly estimate or measure antlers should be part of your deer hunting skills.

Let me assure you measuring or estimating the score of a set of antlers on the wall or in the field isn't as hard as you may think it is–not as long as you keep in mind some very basic guidelines.

When it comes to officially scoring a set of antlers for a net measurement for possible entry into any organization's books, however, it should be noted that all such organizations require that after the official drying out period is over, the antlers must be measured by an official measurer.

There are several record-book organizations including national, regional, state, and some local clubs. They include the well-known organizations like Boone & Crockett, (the official scoring system for North American Big Game Trophies), Pope & Young (the official scoring system for Bowhunting North American Big Game), the Longhunter Society (National Muzzle Loading Rifle Association), Buckmaster's (Whitetail Trophy Records), and dozens of other groups across the nation and Canada as well.

The information in this chapter will give you the ability to learn how to rough score any set of deer antlers or how to quickly estimate a rack you see when you are hunting. Once you have learned the technique and have measured a few sets of antlers, you will probably become proficient enough to measure a set of antlers to within 10 points of its official score and be able to field judge a buck's antlers within 30 seconds or less to within 10 to 15 points!

Let's divide the two reasons for measuring antlers at this point. The first group is predominantly made up of trophy hunters who, before pulling the trigger on a buck, want to know if the antlers are large enough to make the record books or to judge if they are larger than bucks they have taken in the past.

For yet still others, a trophy can mean taking a buck with a 16-inch wide rack and four good tine points to a side. A buck like this will score between 110 and 120 points, providing the other

◄ This would be a difficult buck to score. No matter–his weird rack makes him more attractive. (credit: Ted Rose)

measurements, such as overall length and circumference of the main beams, are within certain parameters. A buck like this is not large enough to make most books, but it is good enough to make a lot of hunting companions envious. Keep that in mind when

▼ This buck's position makes it difficult to estimate the width of his rack where a lot of inches are gained. A true trophy hunter would have to let him pass. I wouldn't waste time trying to score him—I'd shoot and score later! (credit: Ted Rose)

you consider letting a 120-class buck go. If you have never taken a 120 that may be the buck to start with! Remember, no matter what size racked buck you are looking at, whether he's a 110- or a 170-inch class buck, you should know what to quickly look for in order to field judge him accurately.

Field-Judging White-Tailed Bucks

If you are a hunter who belongs to Group # 1 and your goal is to either take trophy-class bucks or larger antlered bucks you should learn to quickly and accurately field judge a buck's antlers on the hoof. To put a white-tailed buck in the record books, it only makes sense that you should be able to know if a rack will score high enough to qualify for entry in the books before you decided to shoot the buck.

Contrary to what you may think, field-judging a buck's antlers on the hoof isn't all that difficult. The tricky part is whether or not the buck will provide you with enough time to look at his antlers for at least 30 seconds. With practice, you will soon be able to add up the measurements in your mind quickly and accurately in the field.

The one downside to this is that it is not often when you're about to squeeze the trigger or release the arrow that a buck will hang around long enough to offer you an unobstructed view of his antlers. This means you will have to prevent the buck from scenting or spotting you as best you can. Most times, things happen way too quickly for that. So in order to become a hunter who commits to taking only trophy class bucks, you have to make a few sacrifices and let some go.

First, you must not shoot before you are quite confident of the rough

▲ You can get a lot of good practice by scoring mounted heads. After awhile you will get good enough to judge the overall score of a buck's rack in under a minute.

score of the rack. That's easier said than done. Second, you must also let smaller bucks–especially yearlings–walk by because many times they are followed by larger racked bucks.

▼ This buck offers a good view of all his tines and the length of his main beams but not much else is visible enough to score him quickly.

I can guarantee you there is rarely time to look over a buck's antlers and jot down the information on a score sheet! All of this must be done quickly in your head.

In order to score properly, however, you must first understand what you have to score to begin with. Most scoring organizations like Boone and Crockett and Pope & Young take measurements of the inside spread, the length of the two main beams, the height of each tine, and the circumference of the main beams in four different locations. Remember that in order to score high, a typical rack must have symmetry. The more symmetrical the antlers are the more likely it will score high.

To get good at measuring antlers you should practice on as many mounted heads as you can before you try to do it for real in the field. Look the mounts over carefully and estimate and record on paper (now is the time for that) all the information.

First, guess the width of the inside spread. Then guess the length of the two main beams. Then, I like to guess the length of all the tines at this point. From here, I usually can make my decision on if I'm going to shoot or not. In the field, if I'm looking at a buck that has tines that are pretty close to being the same size on each side I only add up one side to save valuable time.

The same goes for the overall length of the main beams. There are four points on the antlers where the "H" measurement (which is the circumference of the main beams) must be calculated in four places on each side! I have learned to look at the overall thickness of the main beams and the bases and make a quick analysis of the mass on the main beams rather than waste valuable time trying to add up 8 different measurements in the field which 99.9 percent of the time is not practical.

When you practice on mounted heads, however, don't skip this step. It will help develop your skill level to quickly judge the "H" measurements. I might be off an inch or two in the end–but in the field (when time is of the essence) this is often the only way to score the rack quickly.

In reality, when a buck steps into the open for a few seconds, your brain has to be properly trained to rapidly assess his antlers before he walks too far off or even disappears.

Think quickly in four terms: overall mass, inside spread, overall tine length, and overall main beam length. If the rack is substantially lacking in one of these areas, it probably won't score high enough. Even if it has a lot of points but they are all different sizes, it probably won't score well. If only one is lacking, however, do the other measurements have enough of an impact to make up for the one that doesn't score well?

Forget trying to look to see if the antlers extend past the buck's ears. I have news for you–it is the rare buck (even a mature buck)–whose antlers get much wider than 20 inches. Most are smaller. In cases where you are hunting in trophy areas like Wisconsin, Minnesota, Illinois, or Iowa, bucks may have slightly wider racks. But even they don't get much wider than 22 inches– most of the time. So, I don't let this interfere with my field judging. I concentrate on more important things like symmetry and mass. Mass can over come many short comings in a buck's antlers.

I always look carefully at the tine lengths and if the main beams are relatively straight. A good circumference of the beams will be three to four inches, but the most deceiving aspect to field judging antlers is circumference. If you're going to misjudge a rack it is usually in this area.

When I see a buck walking my way, I quickly start to calculate the mass, spread, and tine length in my head rather than get distracted by the whole buck. I'm not a certified scorer, but it is the rare rack that I can't score within 5 points in less than 30 seconds! Now before

you say he's full of it–remember this. I have made this a hobby of mine for over 45 years.

When I first started scoring bucks in the field it took me several minutes. After shooting some of the bucks I was surprised to see that most times (for the first couple of years) I was off by 15 to 20 points! It takes constant practice to get good at quickly field-judging a bucks' antlers. Again, luck must play a role here as you need the buck to present you with at least 30 to 60 seconds of opportunity to look over his rack. But after doing it over and over again you train your brain to see the rack even when partially obstructed by brush. You begin to calculate the score almost instinctively and without much effort after a few years.

After 45 years, I have trained my brain to quickly calculate what a buck will score as he passes me. These days it has become second nature for me to calculate a buck's antlers on the hoof. After all these years, when I measure a set of antlers from mounted skull plate, however, I can usually guess the score to within five inches and sometimes even closer every time.

Green Scoring Your Buck's Antlers

The second group is made up of hunters who want to simply want to know what a particular buck's antlers score for their own satisfaction or to know if it scores high enough to be officially scored for entry into any of the organizations mentioned above.

For this type of antler measuring, time is not crucial. You can take all the time necessary to accurately score a set of antlers. All you will need is a few tools and patience.

As you begin, you can choose one of two ways to keep track of your measurements. The less formal way (especially when you don't have access to a score sheet), is to enter the numbers on a piece of paper. If you use this method you must be able to memorize all the entries you need to measure.

The more organized way is to use a score sheet from one of the many organizations that maintain record books. The combined columns take into account the spread credit, overall length of left and right antlers, the overall length of the main beams, and the length measurements of each individual tine on both main beams. The individual tine length is commonly referred to as is assigned a "G" measurement. The "G" measurements

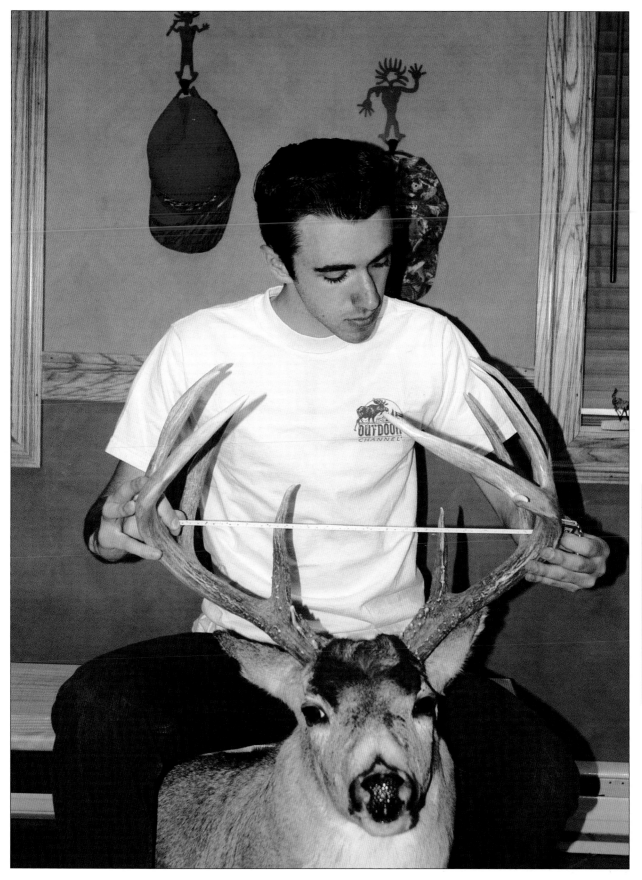

▲ When measuring the inside spread–it is from the widest point on one side to the widest point on the other side of the rack.

antlers are large enough to be scored by an official scorer, you can make some minor mistakes and still have the overall score within the ball park. Keep in mind that most organizations require a "drying-out" period of sixty days before they allow an official measuring to take place.

Basic Equipment Needed

The equipment needed to score a set of antlers is basic. A one-quarter-inch flexible steel measuring tape, which you will use to measure the antlers to the nearest one-eighth of an inch, a pencil, paper or a black score sheet, and, if you have trouble with fractions, a calculator.

The process begins with the eight (or so) basic measurements you must make.

Number of Points

This measurement is not calculated in the final score. First determine the number of points on the right antler, then the left. To be officially counted as a point, a point or tine must be at least one inch long. All points are measured from the tip of the point to the nearest point of the main beam.

Tip-to-Tip Spread

This measurement is also not calculated in the final score. Measure the width of the antlers from tip to tip. Simply stated, this means make a measurement between the tips of the main beams.

Greatest Spread

Again, although most organizations list this measurement it is also not calculated in the final score. Now, measure the greatest outside distance or spread of the rack. This is done by measuring the outside distance between the two tines that are the farthest apart.

Inside Spread

The inside spread of the main beams is measured at the widest point between the main beams. This number is used in the overall score. If the inside spread measurement is greater than the length of the longest main beam, than you have to use the longest main beam length as your measurement in this category.

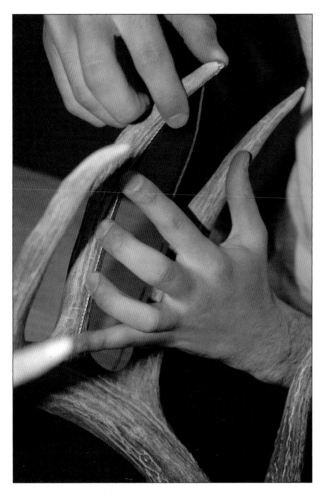

▲ When you really want an accurate measurement use a string not a steel tape ruler.

begin with the brow tines which are referred to as the G-1s. The next tines after the brow tines are called the G-2s, next are the G-3s, G-4s and so on.

The score sheet for each set of antlers will also include a deduction column with the exception of the Buckmasters Club. On this score sheet, the hunter gets credit for everything Mother Nature has given the buck's antlers.

There are three additional measurements that are recorded but that are not figured into the overall score. They are the number of points on each antler, the tip-to-tip spread and the greatest outside spread of the antlers.

To achieve the most accurate total score, you must know where to begin taking each measurement from the main beam. To begin the process, whether you are measuring for your own satisfaction or to see if the

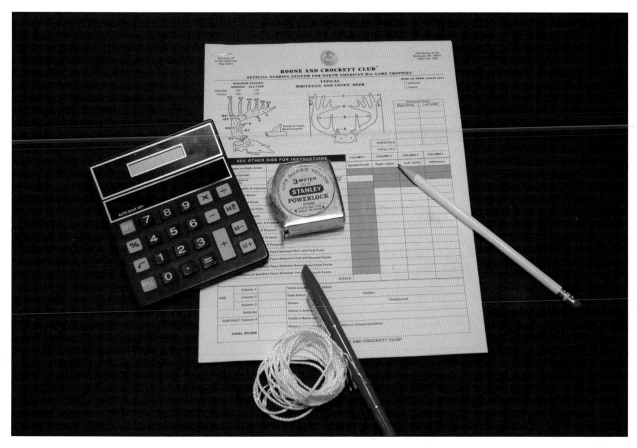

▲ These are all the tools you will need to measure the antlers of a buck.

Length of Abnormal Points

Abnormal points are those non-typical in location on the antlers or are also extra points beyond the normal pattern of points. They are often called kickers by hunters and are measured in the usual way.

Length of the Main Beam

Measure the overall length of the main beam from its lowest outside edge of the burr over the outside curve to the tip of the main beam. This measurement must be entered separately for both right and left antlers.

Length of Individual Points

Now measure each individual point on each main beam. Begin with the G-1s traditionally called brow tines or eye guard points. Every official organization refers to this point as the G-1. Each point up to the

main beam from G-1 is referred to as G-2, G-3, G-4 and so on. Remember, to be classified as a point, it must be at least one inch long. The old wives' tale that a point is anything you can hang a ring off of does not hold true officially when you score a set of antlers or when counting the overall number of points on a set of antlers. To properly measure a point, measure it from the nearest edge of the main beam over the outer curve to the tip of the point.

Now, measure the length of each remaining point on each beam and enter or write down the individual lengths. Do not measure the end of the main beam as a point—it is calculated in the overall length of the main beam.

Circumference of Main Beam

This measurement, referred on the score sheet as the "H" measurement is taken at four exact places along each main beam. What is important with these mea-

▲ This is what is referred to as an abnormal point.

surements is the location where they are made. The circumference measurement is made at the smallest place between two points. For example, the first measurement (H-1) is made at the smallest place between the burr of the antler and the first point.

The next "H" measurement is at the smallest place between the first and second points, and is called H-2. The remaining circumference measurements are H-3 and H-4. For the H-4 measurement, if there is no fourth point (or tine), then take the measurement halfway between the third point and the beam tip. There are no additional circumference measurements taken after H-4.

Totaling Your Score

This is where the suspense begins to peak. Now add and deduct all the measurements you have just taken. First, add the measurements of the column referred to as Spread Credit (the inside spread of the antlers) to the bottom of that column.

Next, add the left and right Antler columns to the bottom of the page. Then add the Difference column to the bottom of the page, too. Bring all the total figures from columns 1, 2 and 3 to the "Add Column" (found on the left-hand side of all official score sheets) and total them. Then bring the figure from column 4 over and subtract column 4 from the total you got by adding columns 1, 2 and 3.

▼ This do-it-yourself kit includes all 26 measuring methods as described on the SCI website (www.safariclub.org), instructions on how to use each method and step-by-step instructions on scoring any trophy. The suggested retail price for this kit is $44.95. This kit allows you to follow the SCI philosophy, "If God Grows It–We Score It."

This figure is now your subtotal green score sometimes also called the rough or unofficial score. Now deduct from the gross number the length of abnormal points and all the "difference" measurements. This number is your Net or Final Green score. The reason I say green or rough, is that until the rack dries out for sixty days and then is measured by an official scorer from Boone & Crockett or Pope & Young or any state record keeping organization, your score is not official and, therefore, only classified as a green or rough final tally.

By the way, before I begin to measure a rack on paper, I estimate what it will score and I write the number down on the page as "eye-ball score". When I am finished measuring the antlers with a tape or wire I compare it to my "eye-ball" measurement for fun. It adds some excitement into the process for me.

Knowing how to measure a set of antlers is really fun and important, especially if you want to be able to accurately tell your friends what your bucks or their trophies green score. You'll become the "go-to-guy" whenever anyone in your hunting circle shoots a buck. Everyone wants to know what his buck scored no matter how big or small his antlers are.

In the end, we all develop our own way of calculating and summarizing all the elements on a rack to get a good feel for the overall score. I know plenty of guys who after practicing a couple of years don't even have to add up scores anymore. They simply look at the buck's antlers and in less than a few minutes they can tell you if it scores 120, 130, 140 or whatever range it is.

So whether you call into group one or two or both, start practicing how to score racks right now. Begin with your own heads and then practice on heads that you see in stores like Cabela's, Bass Pro Shops, and Gander Mountain and in taxidermist shops. Before long, you will be a pro at estimating (notice I did not say guessing now), the overall gross score of a whitetail buck.

It's a lot of fun even if you're not planning on becoming the next Milo Hansen and bagging the next world record. Give it a shot (forgive the pun here), and I know it will not only be enjoyable, it will make you a more knowledgeable hunter as well as helping you to impress your hunting buddies.

SAFARI CLUB INTERNATIONAL
Method 17-T
Entry Form

For white-tailed deer with typical antlers. *Antlers that have one or more non-typical tines may be measured as typical at the owner's request, but only the typical tines will count in the score. Any non-typical tines are to be recorded as supplemental information.*

Hunter _____
How you want your name to appear in the Record Book

Membership No. _____

Address _____

City	State	Zip	Country

Ph. (____) _____ (____) _____ (____) _____
Home   Business   Fax

I certify that, to the best of my knowledge, I took this animal without violating the wildlife laws or ethical hunting practices of the country or province in which I hunted. I also certify that, to the best of my knowledge, the laws of my country have not been violated by my taking or importing this animal. Free-ranging ❏ Yes ❏ No

Signature _____

Submit to:
Safari Club International, 4800 W. Gates Pass Rd., Tucson, AZ 85745 USA.

Record Book fee   ❏ $30

Medallion Award fee   ❏ $40 USA, Canada, Mexico
(Walnut plaque)   ❏ $50 All other countries.

To enter Record Book and/or Medallion:
1) Add the appropriate entry fees together as necessary.
   (Medallion fee includes shipping & handling.)
2) All entries must be complete, signed by hunter and accompanied by fees and a photograph of the trophy.
3) Please clearly label back of photo with name of hunter, name and score of animal, and date taken.
❏ For simple horns and unbranched antlers:
   1 Photo included
❏ For animals with branched antlers:
   enough photos so that all tines can be clearly seen.

Checks on U.S. banks only. Credit cards preferred. Entry fees are valid for 12 months from date of form located in lower left hand corner.

We Accept: ❏ MC ❏ Visa ❏ AMX ❏ Discover ❏ Diners Club

Card number _____ Expiration Date _____

08/98

Animal _____

Remeasurement? ❏ Yes ❏ No   Former Score _____ Record No. _____

Date Taken _____
     Month   Day   Year

❏ Rifle ❏ Handgun ❏ Muzzleloader ❏ Bow ❏ Crossbow ❏ Picked Up

Place Taken _____
     Country   State or Province

Locality _____

Guide _____ Hunting Co. _____

I. Length of Main Beam		L _____	/8	R _____	/8
II. Length of Typical Tines	T-1	L _____	/8	R _____	/8
	T-2	L _____	/8	R _____	/8
(Use back of form for additional tines)	T-3	L _____	/8	R _____	/8
	T-4	L _____	/8	R _____	/8
	T-5	L _____	/8	R _____	/8
	T-6	L _____	/8	R _____	/8
	T-7	L _____	/8	R _____	/8
	Sub Total	L _____	/8	R _____	/8
III. Circumference of Main Beam	C-1	L _____	/8	R _____	/8
	C-2	L _____	/8	R _____	/8
	C-3	L _____	/8	R _____	/8
	C-4	L _____	/8	R _____	/8
	Sub Total	L _____	/8	R _____	/8
IV. Inside Span of Main Beams				_____	/8
V. Total Score				_____	/8

Supplemental Information

Length of non-typical tines, if any. (Not to be included in total score)	NT-1	L _____	/8	R _____	/8
	NT-2	L _____	/8	R _____	/8
	NT-3	L _____	/8	R _____	/8
	NT-4	L _____	/8	R _____	/8
Number of Typical Points (All typical tines plus beam tip)		L _____		R _____	
Number of Non-typical Points (All non-typical tines)		L _____		R _____	
Total Number of Points (All tines plus beam tip)		L _____		R _____	

Official Measurer _____

Measurer No. _____ MM No. _____

Day Measured _____
     Month   Day   Year

Signature of Measurer _____

Approved: Y   N

By: _____

Date: _____

COPYRIGHT © SAFARI CLUB INTERNATIONAL

▲ This is the score sheet for a whitetail deer with typical antlers for Safari Club International. Additional score sheets can be downloaded from their web site at www.safariclub.org or by writing to them at Safari Club International, 4800 W. Gates Pass Road, Tucson, Arizona, 85745.

POPE & YOUNG CLUB

Official Scoring System for Bowhunting North American Big Game

MINIMUM SCORE

whitetail   125
Coues'   65

TYPICAL
WHITETAIL AND COUES' DEER

KIND OF DEER (check one)

☐ whitetail
☐ Coues'

☐ **IN VELVET**

Detail of Point Measurement

Abnormal Points	
Right Antler	Left Antler

SUBTOTALS	
TOTAL TO E	

SEE OTHER SIDE FOR INSTRUCTIONS				COLUMN 1	COLUMN 2	COLUMN 3	COLUMN 4
A. No. Points on Right Antler		No. Points on Left Antler		Spread Credit	Right Antler	Left Antler	Difference
B. Tip to Tip Spread		C. Greatest Spread					
D. Inside Spread of Main Beams		SPREAD CREDIT MAY EQUAL BUT NOT EXCEED LONGER MAIN BEAM					
E. Total of Lengths of Abnormal Points							
F. Length of Main Beam							
G-1. Length of First Point							
G-2. Length of Second Point							
G-3. Length of Third Point							
G-4. Length of Fourth Point, If Present							
G-5. Length of Fifth Point, If Present							
G-6. Length of Sixth Point, If Present							
G-7. Length of Seventh Point, If Present							
H-1. Circumference at Smallest Place Between Burr and First Point							
H-2. Circumference at Smallest Place Between First and Second Points							
H-3. Circumference at Smallest Place Between Second and Third Points							
H-4. Circumference at Smallest Place Between Third and Fourth Points or half way between Third Point and Beam Tip if Fourth Point is missing.							
		TOTALS					

ADD	Column 1		Location of Kill:	(County)	(State/Prov)
	Column 2		Date Killed:	Hunter:	
	Column 3		Owner:	Telephone #: ( )	
	Subtotal		Owner's Address:		
SUBTRACT Column 4			Guide's Name and Address:		
FINAL SCORE			Remarks: (Mention Any Abnormalities or Unique Qualities)		

▲ This is the first page of the score sheet for a typical whitetail deer for entry into the Pope & Young Club record books. Please note there is a second page following this one. To download your own forms, go to www.pope-young.org or send them a written request at Boone and Crockett Club, 250 Station Drive, Missoula, Montana 59801.

I, _____ , certify that I have measured this trophy on _____
PRINT NAME   MM/DD/YYYYY

at _____
        STREET ADDRESS   CITY   STATE/PROVINCE   ZIP CODE

and that these measurements and data are, to the best of my knowledge and belief, made in accordance with the instructions given.

Witness: _____   Signature: _____
          TO MEASURER'S SIGNATURE   P&Y OFFICIAL MEASURER

                                                              _____
                                                                          ADDRESS

                                                              _____
                                                              CITY   STATE/PROVINCE   ZIP

BRIEF INSTRUCTIONS FOR MEASURING TYPICAL WHITETAIL AND COUES' DEER

Measurements must be made with a flexible steel tape or steel cable and recorded to the nearest one-eighth of an inch. To simplify addition, please enter fractional figures in eighths and in proper fractions. Refer to **P & Y Measurer's Manual** for a detailed description of measuring procedures.

A. **Number of Points on each antler**. To be counted a point, a projection must be at least one inch long AND, at some location at least one inch from the tip, the length of the projection must exceed its width. Beam tip is counted as a point but not measured as a point.

B. **Tip to Tip Spread** is measured between tips of main beams.

C. **Greatest Spread** is measured between perpendiculars at a right angle to the center line of the skull at widest part whether across main beams or points.

D. **Inside Spread of Main Beam** is measured at a right angle to the center line of the skull at widest point between main beams. Enter this measurement again in "Spread Credit" column if it is less than or equal to the length of longer main beam. If greater, enter longer main beam length for Spread Credit.

E. **Total of Length of Abnormal Points**. Abnormal points are generally considered to be those non-typical in location (such as points originating from a point or from bottom or sides of main beam). Sketch all abnormal points on antler illustration (front of form) showing location and length. Measure in usual manner and enter in appropriate blanks.

F. **Length of Main Beam** is measured from the center of the lowest outside edge of burr over outer curve to the most distant point of the main beam. Begin measuring at the location on the burr where the center line along the outer curve of the beam intersects the burr.

G-1-2-3-4-5-6-7. Length of Normal Points. Normal points project from the top of the main beam as shown in illustration. They are measured from the top edge of the main beam (baseline), over their outer curve, to their tip. To establish the appropriate baseline, lay a tape or (preferably) a cable on the top edge of the beam on each side of the point and draw a line under the cable to reflect the top edge of the beam as if the point was not present. Record point lengths in appropriate blanks.

H-1-2-3-4. Circumferences. Circumferences are taken at the smallest place between corresponding normal points, as illustrated. If first point is missing, take H-1 and H-2 at smallest place between burr and second point. If G-4 is missing, take H-4 halfway between the center of G-3 and tip of main beam. Circumference measurements must be taken with a steel tape (a cable cannot be used for these measurements).

ENTRY REQUIREMENTS

1. **Original scoring form** completed by an Official Measurer of the Pope & Young Club or the Boone & Crockett Club.
2. **Completed Fair Chase Affidavit.**
3. **Three photos of antlers, horns, or skull** (a view from the front side, a view from the left side and a view from the right side). A field photo is also requested, if possible.
4. **$25.00 recording fee** (made payable to the Pope and Young Club)

Drying Period: To be eligible for entry in the Pope & Young Records, a trophy must first have been stored under normal room temperature and humidity for at least 60 days after date of kill. No trophy will be considered which has been altered in any way from its natural state.

▲ This is the second page of the score sheet for a typical whitetail deer for entry into the Pope & Young Club record books.

250 Station Drive
Missoula, MT 59801
(406) 542-1888

BOONE AND CROCKETT CLUB®

OFFICIAL SCORING SYSTEM FOR NORTH AMERICAN BIG GAME TROPHIES

TYPICAL
WHITETAIL AND COUES' DEER

MINIMUM SCORES		
	AWARDS	ALL-TIME
whitetail	160	170
Coues'	100	110

KIND OF DEER (check one)
☐ whitetail
☐ Coues'

Detail of Point Measurement

Abnormal Points	
Right Antler	Left Antler
SUBTOTALS	
TOTAL TO E	

SEE OTHER SIDE FOR INSTRUCTIONS			COLUMN 1	COLUMN 2	COLUMN 3	COLUMN 4
			Spread Credit	Right Antler	Left Antler	Difference
A. No. Points on Right Antler		No. Points on Left Antler				
B. Tip to Tip Spread		C. Greatest Spread				
D. Inside Spread of Main Beams		SPREAD CREDIT MAY EQUAL BUT NOT EXCEED LONGER ANTLER				
E. Total of Lengths of Abnormal Points						
F. Length of Main Beam						
G-1. Length of First Point						
G-2. Length of Second Point						
G-3. Length of Third Point						
G-4. Length of Fourth Point, If Present						
G-5. Length of Fifth Point, If Present						
G-6. Length of Sixth Point, If Present						
G-7. Length of Seventh Point, If Present						
H-1. Circumference at Smallest Place Between Burr and First Point						
H-2. Circumference at Smallest Place Between First and Second Points						
H-3. Circumference at Smallest Place Between Second and Third Points						
H-4. Circumference at Smallest Place Between Third and Fourth Points						
		TOTALS				

ADD	Column 1		Exact Locality Where Killed:	
	Column 2		Date Killed:	Hunter:
	Column 3		Owner:	Telephone #:
	Subtotal		Owner's Address:	
SUBTRACT Column 4			Guide's Name and Address:	
FINAL SCORE			Remarks: (Mention Any Abnormalities or Unique Qualities)	

YOU CAN DO IT YOURSELF

▲ This is the first page of the score sheet for a typical whitetail deer for entry into the Boone and Crockett record books. Please note there is a second page following this one. To download your own forms, go to www.boone-crockett.org or send them a written request at Boone and Crockett Club, 250 Station Drive, Missoula, Montana 59801.

I, _____ , certify that I have measured this trophy on _____
PRINT NAME   MM/DD/YYYYY

at _____
STREET ADDRESS   CITY   STATE/PROVINCE

and that these measurements and data are, to the best of my knowledge and belief, made in accordance with the instructions given.

Witness: _____ Signature: _____ I.D. Number | | | | |
                                                        B&C OFFICIAL MEASURER

INSTRUCTIONS FOR MEASURING TYPICAL WHITETAIL AND COUES' DEER

All measurements must be made with a 1/4-inch wide flexible steel tape to the nearest one-eighth of an inch. (Note: A flexible steel cable can be used to measure points and main beams only.) Enter fractional figures in eighths, without reduction. Official measurements cannot be taken until the antlers have air dried for at least 60 days after the animal was killed.

A. Number of Points on Each Antler: To be counted a point, the projection must be at least one inch long, with the length exceeding width at one inch or more of length. All points are measured from tip of point to nearest edge of beam as illustrated. Beam tip is counted as a point but not measured as a point.

B. Tip to Tip Spread is measured between tips of main beams.

C. Greatest Spread is measured between perpendiculars at a right angle to the center line of the skull at widest part, whether across main beams or points.

D. Inside Spread of Main Beams is measured at a right angle to the center line of the skull at widest point between main beams. Enter this measurement again as the Spread Credit if it is less than or equal to the length of the longer antler; if greater, enter longer antler length for Spread Credit.

E. Total of Lengths of all Abnormal Points: Abnormal Points are those non-typical in location (such as points originating from a point or from bottom or sides of main beam) or extra points beyond the normal pattern of points. Measure in usual manner and enter in appropriate blanks.

F. Length of Main Beam is measured from the center of the lowest outside edge of burr over the outer side to the most distant point of the main beam. The point of beginning is that point on the burr where the center line along the outer side of the beam intersects the burr, then following generally the line of the illustration.

G-1-2-3-4-5-6-7. Length of Normal Points: Normal points project from the top of the main beam. They are measured from nearest edge of main beam over outer curve to tip. Lay the tape along the outer curve of the beam so that the top edge of the tape coincides with the top edge of the beam on both sides of the point to determine the baseline for point measurements. Record point lengths in appropriate blanks.

H-1-2-3-4. Circumferences are taken as detailed in illustration for each measurement. If brow point is missing, take H-1 and H-2 at smallest place between burr and G-2. If G-4 is missing, take H-4 halfway between G-3 and tip of main beam.

ENTRY AFFIDAVIT FOR ALL HUNTER-TAKEN TROPHIES

For the purpose of entry into the Boone and Crockett Club's® records, North American big game harvested by the use of the following methods or under the following conditions are ineligible:

    I.   Spotting or herding game from the air, followed by landing in its vicinity for the purpose of pursuit and shooting;
    II.   Herding or chasing with the aid of any motorized equipment;
    III.   Use of electronic communication devices, artificial lighting, or electronic light intensifying devices;
    IV.   Confined by artificial barriers, including escape-proof fenced enclosures;
    V.   Transplanted for the purpose of commercial shooting;
    VI.   By the use of traps or pharmaceuticals;
    VII.   While swimming, helpless in deep snow, or helpless in any other natural or artificial medium;
    VIII.   On another hunter's license;
    IX.   Not in full compliance with the game laws or regulations of the federal government or of any state, province, territory, or tribal council on reservations or tribal lands;

I certify that the trophy scored on this chart was not taken in violation of the conditions listed above. In signing this statement, I understand that if the information provided on this entry is found to be misrepresented or fraudulent in any respect, it will not be accepted into the Awards Program and 1) all of my prior entries are subject to deletion from future editions of **Records of North American Big Game** 2) future entries may not be accepted.

FAIR CHASE, as defined by the Boone and Crockett Club®, is the ethical, sportsmanlike and lawful pursuit and taking of any free-ranging wild, native North American big game animal in a manner that does not give the hunter an improper advantage over such game animals.

The Boone and Crockett Club® may exclude the entry of any animal that it deems to have been taken in an unethical manner or under conditions deemed inappropriate by the Club.

Date: _____ Signature of Hunter: _____
                                    (SIGNATURE MUST BE WITNESSED BY AN OFFICIAL MEASURER OR A NOTARY PUBLIC.)

Date: _____ Signature of Notary or Official Measurer: _____

▲ This is the second page of the score sheet for a typical whitetail deer for entry into the Boone and Crockett record books.

YOU CAN DO IT YOURSELF

OFFICIAL SCORESHEET

HARD ANTLER _____ **VELVET** _____

BUCKMASTERS WHITETAIL TROPHY RECORDS

FREE-ROAMING _____ HIGH FENCE _____

IRREGULAR POINTS

	RIGHT ANTLER		LEFT ANTLER
1		1	
2		2	
3		3	
4		4	
5		5	
6		6	
7		7	
8		8	
9		9	
10		10	
11		11	
12		12	
13		13	
14		14	
15		15	
16		16	
17		17	
18		18	
19		19	
20		20	
21		21	
22		22	
23		23	
24		24	
25		25	

SUPPLEMENTARY DATA

1. TOTAL NUMBER OF POINTS PER ANTLER	R.	L.
2. TIP TO TIP SPREAD		
3. GREATEST SPREAD		
4. INSIDE SPREAD BETWEEN MAIN BEAMS (CARRY FORWARD TO LINE 22)		
5. NUMBER OF IRREGULAR POINTS	R.	L.

6. TOTAL INCHES OF IRREGULAR POINTS (IRR)
7. LENGTH OF MAIN BEAM (MB)
8. LENGTH OF FIRST POINT (P1)
9. LENGTH OF SECOND POINT (P2)
10. LENGTH OF THIRD POINT (P3)
11. LENGTH OF FOURTH POINT (P4)
12. LENGTH OF FIFTH POINT (P5)
13. LENGTH OF SIXTH POINT (P6)
14. LENGTH OF SEVENTH POINT (P7)
15. LENGTH OF EIGHTH POINT (P8)
16. LENGTH OF NINTH POINT (P9)
17. LENGTH OF TENTH POINT (P10)
18. FIRST CIRCUMFERENCE MEASUREMENT (C1)
19. SECOND CIRCUMFERENCE MEASUREMENT (C2)
20. THIRD CIRCUMFERENCE MEASUREMENT (C3)
21. FOURTH CIRCUMFERENCE MEASUREMENT (C4)

SCORE PER SIDE →

TOTAL INCHES OF ANTLER* →

OFFICIAL SCORE

22. WITH INSIDE SPREAD ADDED →

COMPOSITE SCORE

HARVESTED BY _____

DATE OF HARVEST _____

LOCATION OF HARVEST (County) _____ (State) _____

GUIDED BY _____

OWNER _____

ADDRESS _____

CITY _____ STATE _____ ZIP _____

PHONE ( ) _____ DATE SCORED: _____

SCORER _____ SCORER NO. _____

COLLECTED BY:
LONG BOW _____
RECURVE _____
COMPOUND _____
CROSSBOW _____
MODERN RIFLE _____
SHOTGUN _____
PISTOL _____
BLK. POWDER _____
PICK-UPS _____
SHED ANTLERS _____

CATEGORY:
PERFECT _____
TYPICAL _____
SEMI IRREGULAR _____
IRREGULAR _____
% IRR. _____

MINIMUM OFFICIAL SCORES:
FIREARMS–140
BOW/CROSSBOW–105
PICK-UPS –140
SHED ANTLERS–75

OFFICIAL SCORE TO BE RECORDED INTO "BUCKMASTERS WHITETAIL TROPHY RECORDS"

▲ This is the score sheet for a typical whitetail deer for entry into the Buckmasters Whitetail Trophy Records. To download your own forms, go to www.buckmasters.com or send a written request to Buckmasters Whitetail Trophy Chairman, P.O. Box 244022, Montgomery, Alabama 36124.

29. How to Book a Quality Hunt

Since 1982, many of you who have watched my television show or came to my seminars have asked me where you can book a quality whitetail hunt. Booking a hunt that offers a quality experience overall is never easy to do but it is possible. The key is to do your homework before signing on the dotted line.

Your first decision is to decide on a budget. Once you do, you have to live within that budget and remain practical about what the money you are spending will actually buy you. Don't expect to book a top quality whitetail hunt at a high-end lodge for $2,500. It just won't happen. On the opposite side of the coin if you're spending $7,500 or more–don't settle for anything but the best hunting and services.

▼ Before booking a hunt, talk to other hunters who have had success in different areas of the country and then decide in what state you want to go hunting.

Next, decide on what part of the country you want to go to. When you have decided on a state, narrow it down to the best area in that state that offers good whitetail hunting. Now you can start your search for reliable, quality outfitters. When you locate a few, contact them and make sure to ask questions–lots of questions.

Actually, there are many ways to find and book the whitetail hunt of a life-time. Searching the web is an excellent way to start. Another way is word of mouth. This can be very reliable, especially if you know the person who is telling you about the hunt. Magazine and newspaper ads, booking agents and hunting consultants can also help you.

I always recommend going to a consumer sports show to book hunts. This option allows you to have a face-to-face, one-on-one conversation with the outfitter or one of his representatives. One piece of advice here. Keep your questions to the outfitter (in person or on the phone) entirely about the hunt. Don't bore him to death with your expertise, stories of past hunts, etc. If you do, he'll begin to lose interest and you will suffer for that in the end. Talk turkey. You want to know everything he offers from his success rate (which should be realistic), to how he hunts, to what he offers in lodging and other services.

The way you scout for an outfitter often resembles the real hunt in some ways. Being patient is very important. Recognizing a good deal when it comes along also helps. You can make your search for a hunt as complicated and stressful as you want it to be or what it should be–fun. You can be discriminatory and get what you are seeking, but you can do so without driving yourself crazy.

Outfitters are folks who conduct the hunt. Their guides are usually the people to actually take you on the hunt or at least that is the way it goes most times. So don't forget to ask who will be guiding you and if they are new to the outfitter or they have worked with him for a long time.

In Africa, they may be called Professional Hunters (PH). Most times the PH will be on the hunt along with his trackers and guides. Most outfitters, as they are called in North America, depend on their guides to take hunters afield. They hunt either land they own or they lease private land and sometimes a combina-

▲ My wife Kate poses with her Kudu taken during our South African hunt in 2008. Her PH, Willem Basson, spotted this Grey Ghost trophy hiding in the bush.

▲ This dandy warthog was taken by my son Cody in S. Africa while hunting at Zeekoepan Safaris owned and operated by Willem and Amanda Basson.

tion of both. Be careful about outfitters who operate on public lands. I have never had a good experience on these types of hunts–at least not for the money that was charged. Remember, it is the outfitter who owns the business, sets the prices, and provides the services.

Booking agents, who are nowadays more correctly referred to as hunting consultants, are just what the name implies. They book hunts. Their businesses have many outfitters in their stables so to speak. The booking agent handles all booking aspects for all types of outfitters. They know their outfitters personally, and most times, but not always, have been to their camps. The booking agents handle hunt deposits, contracts, license applications and so forth. As the so called middleman, the booking agent gets a percentage from the outfitter, not from you.

I always suggest (no matter who you use) to call them to discuss the hunt rather than talk over email or by letter. A conversation allows you to ask all the questions you have on your mind and receive immediate answers. Be sure to write everything down so you can refer back to it. Ask for a brochure and other printed literature including but not limited to the price lists. Be certain to ask for the current rates, because prices change from year to year.

After you boil it down to three or four potential outfitters you can move on to the next step which is checking his references. Have him give you at least three names of recent hunters. Remember here, he is not going to give you anybody who didn't have a good time. So, I always take what the references have to say with a grain of salt. The best way to get information from them is to congratulate them on taking a nice buck early on in the conversation. It is helpful to talk to the hunters who did not wind up getting their deer. Those are the folks who can give you the best informa-

▲ Today it is very easy to check what an outfitter offers by going online and visiting his site. It also makes it easier to check many more outfitters than you would be able to do at a sport show or over the phone.

tion. When you talk to a successful hunter, ask him if he went on the hunt with friends who didn't score on any deer or other game. Then ask for their phone numbers and call them.

You will also want to know if the deer herd is plentiful. Are conditions physically tough? Were the outfitter, guides, and cooks organized well and prepared for your arrival? Will they be picking you up and dropping you off at the airport? Do they offer the type of hunting you want to do (still-hunting, stands, drives, calling, rattling, decoying, etc.)? Is blaze orange a law and, if so, how many square inches must you wear? Ask if the guides are new or repeat employees? By the way, most guides have something negative to say about the outfitter. Take all of this with a grain of salt and don't get involved. All guides want to come off as more knowledgeable and skilled than the outfitter. The guides that are don't have to tell you they are. Their hunting skills will do the talking for them.

Once you have settled on an outfitter, make sure he is willing to put *everything* he told you in writing. Having a contract or agreement is good business for both parties. He should be as interested in providing you with an agreement as you are in getting one. If not, move on to the next outfitter. You have already encountered your first problem with this one and it will only get worse for there on in–I promise you that! Once you get the agreement read it carefully from start to finish making sure it includes everything you discussed with the outfitter and coincides with the notes you took during your talk with him. Most states require a contract between hunter and outfitter. Licensed and permitted outfitters are held accountable to many more regulatory agencies than you would think. If the outfitter you choose doesn't offer a contract, it may be due to the fact that he is either not a legal outfitter or one that has had problems. Check all outfitters with the state to be sure they have not had a lot of complaints filed against them.

Both the outfitters and guides are licensed by most states or provinces they work in. If you have any doubts, call the licensing agency and check up on them. Don't feel bad about doing it–it's your money and doing your homework is just good business.

If you take the above advice, it still doesn't assure you of a successful or fun hunt, but it does go a long way to help you have one. If you don't do your homework carefully, you're in store for a hunt destined to go bad. Remember you can always email me to ask any questions you have about booking a hunt, peter@fiduccia.com.

30. DIY Projects

Over the years the need to build permanent tree stands, gun racks, meat and game poles, and dozens of other useful projects has been the catalyst for this chapter. In this chapter I have included the plans and directions for you to build several of my favorite and most useful wood projects.

I took the projects from a book titled *25 Projects for Outdoorsmen: Quick and Easy Plans for the Deer Camp, Home, Woods, and Backyard*. My cousin Leo Somma, who is a master craftsman, and I worked together on that book. The projects include a free-standing gun rack to use at camp or home, a rustic picture frame to hold a map of your property or a favorite wildlife print, a sturdy shooting table and bench to sight in your firearms, a workbench to mount scopes, clean firearms, etc., and the plans for one of my favorite permanent tree stands used on our farm.

Each project will provide you with many years of reliable service and usefulness. They are all easy to make and the cost of the materials won't break the piggy bank. Each plan is included as a woodworking project meant for the whitetail deer hunter.

Leo and I both know you will find building these projects fun and satisfying. If after building them you care to build some of the others you can visit our website (www.woodsnwater.tv) and order *25 Projects for Outdoorsmen*.

Free-Standing Nine-Gun Rack

This is the gun rack Leo made from edge-glued and screwed pine. It makes a nice addition to any hunting camp, cabin, trophy room, den or home (if children are at home one need to have trigger locks for all guns kept in the rack). We have learned how convenient it is when everyone comes back from a hunt and has an orderly place to store their firearms. It can be made to hold any number of guns. This project includes instructions for making a nine-gun rack. You can change the size accordingly if you want the rack to hold more or less firearms. It can be stained, varnished, painted, or waxed depending on your desire.

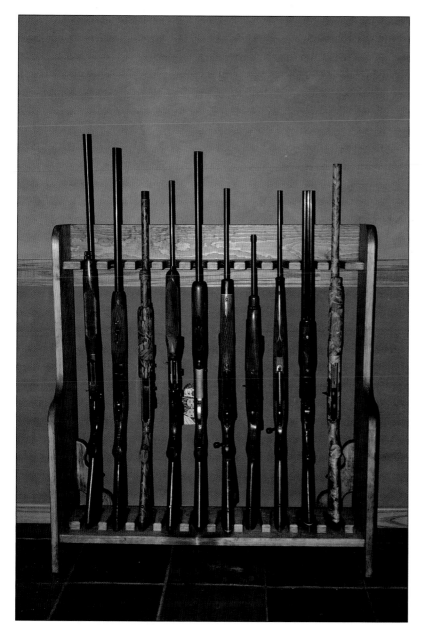

◀ This gun rack is a handsome project you can build for your own home or deer camp. It's a practical unit you'll be proud to work on.

Tools Used

Table saw or circular saw
Drill
Jigsaw
Belt sander
Hole saw
1 2-inch chisel
Block plane

Overall Size: 43″ high x 12″ deep x 36″ long

Cutting List

Key	Part	Dimensions	Pcs.	Material
A	Top back	11 2″ x 41 2″ x 331 2″	1	Pine
B	Top gun holder	11 2″ x 6″ x 331 2	1	Pine
C	Sides	11 2″ x 12″ x 43″	2	Pine
D	Bottom	11 2″ x 11 3/8″ x 331 2″	1	Pine
E	Lower butt holder	11 2″ x 9″ x 331 2″	1	Pine
F	Bottom corners	11 2″ x 41 2″ x 91 2″	2	Pine

Materials: Wood glue; 11 2″ wood screws; mushroom-style button plugs; finishing materials such as stain, lacquer, or varnish.

Note: Measurements reflect the actual thickness of dimension lumber.

Directions for the Free-Standing Nine-Gun Rack

1. Make the sides (C), top back (A), bottom (D), and bottom corners (E).

Cut the sides to length and overall width from 5/4″ by 14″ Pine using a table saw or circular saw as shown in the cutting list. If a circular saw is used, make sure that all the edges are smooth and square using a wood plane.

Transfer the side pattern to one side. Cut out the shape with a jig saw and smooth the cut with a drum sander, belt sander, or by hand. Repeat for the other side, and make the cutout.

Cut the top back (A) from 5/4 x 5″ pine and the bottom (D) from 5/4 x 12″ pine to length.

Transfer the bottom corner patterns on two pieces of 5/4 x 5 x 10″ pine. Cut with a jig saw and smooth with a sander.

Author's note: Using the patterns shown in figure 1, 2, 3 and 4, draw the actual shapes on pieces of oak-tag or brown paper based upon the scaled dimensions. Then, trace the patterns onto the appropriate pieces of wood.

2. Make the top gun holder (B) and lower butt holder (E).

Cut the overall length and width of the gun holder (B) and lower butt holder (E).

Measure and mark the nine (9) butt holder hole center-points (see figure 3). Drill the holes using a 21 2-inch hole saw.

Complete the butt holder cutouts using a backsaw or table saw to make straight cuts into the hole edges.

Repeat step 2 for the nine (9) top gun holder. (See figure 1.)

Sand all cut edges before assembling.

3. Mount the top gun holder and lower butt holder to (A) and (D) respectively.

Drill five 1¹⁄₆-inch pilot holes in the bottom part of the top gun holder (B) about ½-inch from the straight edge (opposite side of circle end). Using wood screws and wood glue, screw through these holes to mount top back (A) along the edge.

Place the lower butt holder (E) on top of the bottom (D), so that the front opening of the butt holder is 2 inches from the front edge of the bottom (D). Use wood glue and wood screws from the underneath of bottom piece to secure it to the lower butt holder.

**Part B and Part E
for the
Free-Standing Nine-Gun Rack**

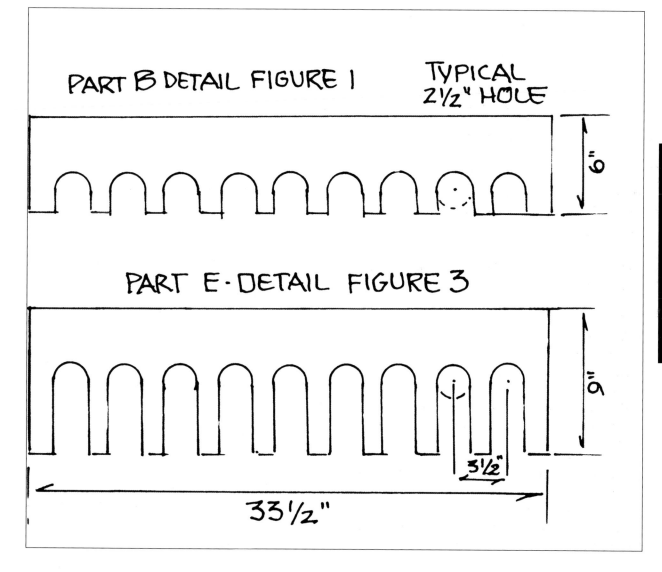

PART B DETAIL FIGURE 1

TYPICAL 2½" HOLE

6"

PART E · DETAIL FIGURE 3

9"

3½"

33½"

**Part F and Part C
for the
Free-Standing Nine-Gun Rack**

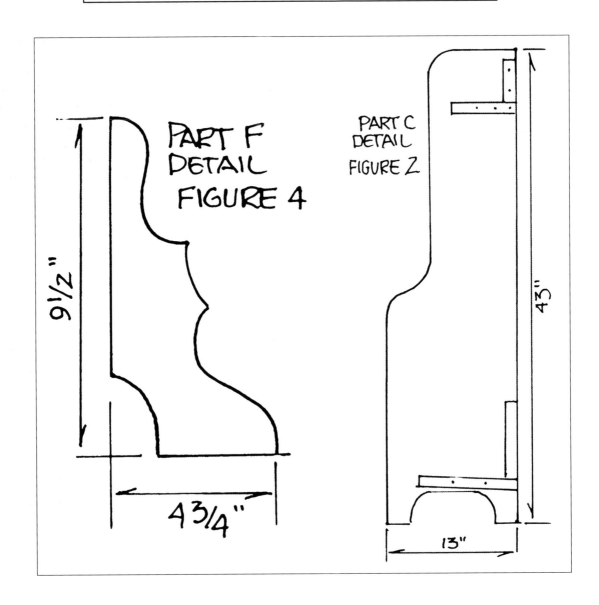

PART F
DETAIL
FIGURE 4

PART C
DETAIL
FIGURE 2

9½"

4¾"

43"

13"

Assemble the upper and lower assemblies as follows:

Drill 1$\frac{1}{6}$-inch pilot holes through the sides (C) at locations shown in diagram. Drill $\frac{3}{8}$-inch counterbored holes about $\frac{1}{2}$-inch deep into the same locations as shown on the outside of both side pieces. Use wood glue and mount the assemblies using the 11 2-inch wood screws.

Mount the bottom corners into place using wood screws.

Apply Finishing Touches

Scrape off any excess glue.

Sand smooth and apply your desired finish.

Install mushroom-style button plugs in all counterbores using a small amount of glue and tap them into place.

Outdoorsman's Picture Frame

This frame was built to hold a wildlife print in a mat that measures 18″ x 24″, which is a standard size. It's a simple matter to adjust the measurements if your print or original oil painting is smaller or larger. If the frame is made smaller, I would suggest adjusting the width of the actual frame pieces from 2½″ to 2″ or smaller.

This is one of our favorite projects because of its simplicity to build, the handsomeness it adds to any space, and the savings it provides when collecting wildlife prints. It also gets the most compliments from everyone who sees it. Build this frame as one of your first projects and the satisfaction you will get from it will motivate you to move on to another project in this book!

Tools Used
Hand saw and miter box or table saw
Hammer
Router
1 2″ round over router bit
1 2″ veining router bit
Wood file

Overall Size: 281 2″ long x 221 2″ wide

Cutting List				
Key	Part	Dimensions	Pcs.	Material
A	Frame rails	¾″ x 21 2″ x 24″	2	Red oak
B	Frame stiles	¾″ x 21 2″ x 221 2″	2	Red oak
C	Front rails	1 2″ x 1″ x 261 2″	2	Red oak
D	Front stiles	1 2″ x 1″ x 173 8″	2	Red oak
E	Backing	1 8″ x 18″ x 24″	1	Luan

Materials: Wood glue; 1-inch brads, $\frac{3}{8}$-inch corrugated joint fasteners; finishing materials: polyurethane; lacquer and/or stain; $\frac{1}{8}$-inch glass or Plexiglas 18″ x 24″; Framer's points; picture frame wire and eyelids.

Note: Measurements reflect the actual thickness of dimension lumber.

Directions for the Outdoorsman's Picture Frame

Measure and cut all the pieces (A), (B), (C), (D), and (E) as shown in cutting list. Use a hand saw and miter box or table saw to get square cuts.

Using a router with a ½-inch round over bit run it over the edges of the front rails (C) and stiles (D).

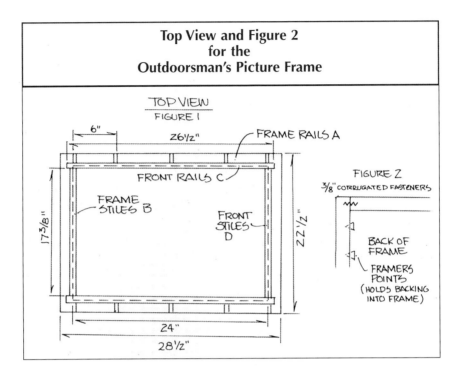

**Top View and Figure 2
for the
Outdoorsman's Picture Frame**

TOP VIEW
FIGURE 1

6" 26½" FRAME RAILS A

FRONT RAILS C

FRAME STILES B

FRONT STILES D

17⅜"

22½"

FIGURE 2

⅜" CORRUGATED FASTENERS

BACK OF FRAME

FRAMERS POINTS
(HOLDS BACKING INTO FRAME)

24"

28½"

Use a wood file and randomly file a grove approximately every 2 inches along the entire edges of the pieces. Set them aside for now.

Lay out the two frame stiles (B) on the front side against a flat work surface about 24 inches apart.

Lay the frame rails (A) in between the two frame stiles (B) as shown in figure 1.

Put a dab of wood glue at the four surfaces where the stiles meet the rails.

Make sure your frame corners are square using a square or by measuring the frame's diagonals (from corner to corner). When the frame is square the diagonals are equal.

Use wood clamps on the top and bottom of each stile and tighten them so that the stiles are snug against the rails. Using a hammer, nail a ⅜-inch corrugated joint fastener in each corner ensuring that the joint is tight (as shown in figure 2). Check again for square and allow the glue to dry for several hours.

When the glue is dry remove the clamps.

Using a router with a ½-inch round over bit, run it around the entire outside edge of the picture frame.

Use a wood file and randomly file a grove approximately every two inches along the entire outside edges of the frame.

Using the router with a ½-inch veining bit, cut four grooves in the top and bottom rails at the locations as shown in figure 1.

Lay one of the front rails (C) on the top rails (A) so that it overhangs ⅜-inch over the inside edge (this is what will hold the glass and photo/picture in the frame). Nail it to the rail using four 1-inch brads. Repeat this for the second front rail on the bottom.

Lay one of the front stiles (D) in between the top and bottom rails (C) so that it overhangs ⅜-inch over the side edge. Nail it to the stile using four 1-inch brads. Repeat this for the second front stile on the other side.

Sand smooth all surfaces using 120-grain sandpaper.

Apply Finishing Touches

Turn the frame over and place the front on a flat surface.

Install the hanging wire by securing an eyelid on each stile about 5" from the top of the frame. Simply twist the wire around each eyelid. The frame is now ready to be hung on the wall.

Finish-sand the shelf, apply the finish and allow drying. Apply at least two coats after priming first. Use smooth sand paper of steel wool on final coat.

The Stump-Sitter Tree Stand

This tree stand is one of our more desirable designs. Although it is mounted to a tree permanently, it does provide the option of easy relocation if need be by simply removing the mounting bolts used to secure it to the tree. This design requires you to find a single tree that provides a solid trunk that should be at least 14 to 16 inches in diameter, and does not have any large dead branches hanging above the platform. It should be placed in a group of trees or in an area that has additional cover to help conceal the stand.

Another great advantage to The Stump Sitter is that the entire construction of the stand can be done off-site in the barn or garage, and then brought to the desired location in pieces and erected. This allows you to build the stand at your leisure. In fact, it also allows you to build a few of them at once, and then plan a day to mount one or all of them in the field.

The height of the platform in this design is approximately 12 feet, but can be made higher by simply using 16-foot side rungs as opposed to the 14-foot rungs we used. The reason we used a lower height was to match the tree line in the particular location since placing it any higher would have cut out your view.

Once the stand is constructed, get it to the desired tree and begin the construction. You will need at least two people to place this stand against the tree and to secure it as well. We used this design to build several stands on our farm because of the convenience the stand offers in what type of tree to place it in and how fast it is to build it.

Tools Used
Chain saw, hand pruning saw, pole saw
Hand saw, circular saw
Drill and drill bit
Screw gun and bits
Air powered gun with 16d nails
Torpedo level
T-square
Socket wrench or open-end wrench set

Overall Size: 12' high x 24" wide x 30" long

Ladder steps- 24" wide

Key	Part	Dimensions	Pcs.	Material
A	Ladder Tree steps	1 1 2 x 3 1 2 x 24"	9-10	Pressure treated-ACQ
B	Ladder side rails	1 1 2 x 3 1 2 x 14'	2	Pressure treated-ACQ
C	Front/rear Platform supports	1 1 2 x 5 1 2x 27"	2	Pressure treated-ACQ
D	Side Platform	1 1 2 x 5 1 2 x 42"	2	Pressure treated-ACQ
E	Platform angle supports	1 1 2 x 3 1 2 x 6'	2	Pressure treated-ACQ
F	Platform decking plywood	1 2 x 30 x 42"	1	Pressure treated-ACQ-
G	Safety railing	1 1 2 x 3 1 2 x 30"	1	Pressure treated-ACQ
H	Seat brace	1 1 2 x 3 1 2 x 16"	1	Pressure treated-ACQ
I	Seat platform	1 2 x 15 x 15"	1	Exterior plywood
J	Seat support	1 1 2 x 3 1 2 x 17"	1	Pressure treated-ACQ
K	Platform tree support	1 1 2 x 3 1 2 x 14"	2	Pressure treated-ACQ
L	Ladder brace	1 1 2 x 3 1 2 x 52"	2	Pressure treated-ACQ

Materials: Hot-dipped galvanized nails- 16d, 10d; 1½", 2½", 3" wood deck screws; 20d nails and/or hooks; 20' nylon rope; ⅜" x 6" carriage bolts, nuts, and washers.

Note: Measurements reflect the actual thickness of dimension lumber.

Directions for the Stump-Sitter Tree Stand

Construct the ladder

Cut the ladder steps (A) to size as shown in the cutting list, using a handsaw or circular saw.

Lay out the two ladder rails (B) on edge on a flat surface. Measure the distance between each step and mark the edges of each side rail. The actual spread of the steps can be made to vary depending on your size and comfort level. You will find the older you get, the closer the spread of steps you will desire. For this particular design, using steps that are 3½-feet wide, the spread between each step was made at approximately 13 to 14 inches for a total of 9 steps.

Secure each step to the side rails by nailing one 16d nail in the center of the step to the rail on each side. If you have access to an air powered air gun, I highly recommend its use. It will save you lots of time and energy as you are nailing the pieces together and to the trees.

Provide additional support to the steps by using 3-inch wood screws. Screw two screws on each side of each step and repeat for both side rails.

Construct the platform

Cut the remaining pieces to size using a handsaw or circular saw as shown in the cutting list.

Lay out the two side platform supports (D) on edge on a flat surface approximately 27 inches apart. Place the front and rear platform supports (C) in between the side supports. Make sure that they are flush with the ends of the side supports.

Secure the plywood platform (F) to the platform frame using 1½-inch nails or screws into the platform frame edges.

Assemble the ladder to the platform

Layout the platform on end on a flat surface. Place the assembled ladder on the front platform support, so that the ladder extends past the top of the platform by approximately 24 inches. Temporarily support the other end so the ladder is perpendicular with the platform. Position it so that it sits evenly between the front platform board.

Drill two 3 8-inch holes through the side ladder rail through the front platform support about 2½ inches apart. Repeat for the other side.

Secure the ladder to the platform buy using two 3 8" x 6" carriage bolts, nuts and washers on each side. Tighten the nuts using a socket or open-end wrench.

Make sure that the ladder is perpendicular to the platform using a T-square.

Cut the ends of the platform angle supports (E) at 45-degree angles using a handsaw.

Place one of the supports up against the inside of the rear bottom of the platform and the other end so it just overlaps the ladder side railing. Secure it in place by using at least three 2½-inch wood screws at each location. Repeat for the other support.

Pre-drill three ⅜-inch pilot holes in the middle of the rear platform support. These holes will be used to secure the tree stand against your selected tree trunk.

Mount the tree stand and seat

Pick out the location and tree that you want to use for the tree stand.

You will need at least two people to erect it and secure it against the tree. Using the stronger of the two people have him/her pick up the platform end, with the bottom of the ladder on the ground, and start walking it up off the ground.

The other person should brace their feet on the bottom of the ladder to prevent it from slipping while grabbing and pulling up towards the tree by grabbing the steps.

Now that the platform back edge is against the tree, level off the platform by moving out the ladder away from the tree trunk. Have one person lean against the front of the ladder, putting pressure from the platform against the top tree trunk.

Carefully and slowly have the second person climb the ladder with a couple of 3-inch wood screws and a screw gun. Screw into the back of the rear platform support into the tree. For additional strength

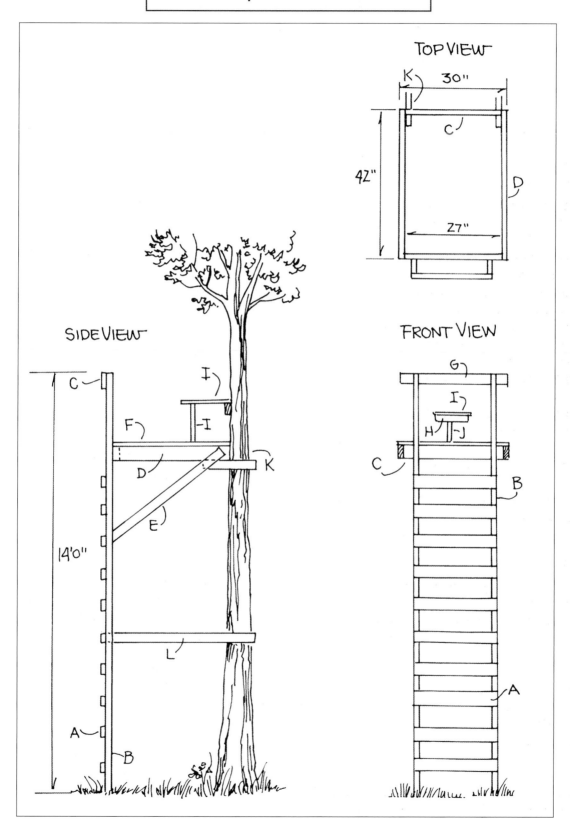

TOP VIEW

30"

K

C

42"

27"

D

SIDE VIEW

FRONT VIEW

C

I

F

I

D

K

E

14'0"

L

A

B

G

I

H

J

C

B

A

and support use three $\frac{3}{8}$-inch x 6-inch lag bolts and washers, tighten them into the tree using a socket or open-ended wrench.

For additional safety, secure two platform tree supports (K) to each side of the bottom of the platform angle supports and the tree limb. Use a screw gun and three 3-inch wood screws in each end of the supports and to the tree limbs.

Place the seat brace (H) against the side of the tree where you want the seat approximately 17 inches from the bottom of the platform. Secure it to the tree by using three 3-inch screws into the tree.

Position the seat platform (I) on top of the seat brace (H) and secure it by drilling four 1$\frac{1}{2}$-inch decking screws into the brace.

Place the seat support (J) in the middle of the front of the seat. Screw the seat bottom to the seat support by screwing two 2$\frac{1}{2}$-inch screws in the top end of the seat support. Secure the bottom of the seat support to the bottom platform by using a 2$\frac{1}{2}$-inch wood screw and toenail it into the platform.

Finishing touches

Using several different colors of exterior spray paint (brown, black, and green), paint the tree stand steps, platform, and railing so the tree stand blends in with the trees.

Use hooks or 20d nail and place several of them at heights above the platform to hang your bow, gun, and other accessories.

Measure and cut a piece of nylon cord and secure it to the top of the platform to be used to safely pull up your bow or gun.

Install camo netting to the top platform railing for additional concealment. Staple it to the rails and to the tree limbs.

Secure the ladder braces (L) on each ladder side rail. Secure using 3-inch wood screws into the side rails and into the tree limbs.

Using a chain saw, hand pruning saw or pole saw, trim any overhanging branches or limbs from around the tree stand location.

▲ To camouflage permanent treestands to blend into the environment, I spray paint them with green, black, and brown paint. This stand's platform was finished off with camo burlap to provide more concealment for the hunter.

31. Mouthwatering Venison

*I*n all of the *Whitetail Strategies* books I have written, I have always included a chapter with my favorite wild game recipes prepared by my wife and hunting partner Kate. As many of you know, Kate is not only an excellent big game hunter she is also a heck of a wild game chef.

Kate has written four wild game cookbooks and is finishing two more. The recipes I selected in this chapter have been quality-controlled by yours truly and have passed my venison palate with flying colors!

They are all quick and easy to prepare and will make you the hit of deer camp or at home when you make them for family or friends. Remember that you can visit our website at www.woodsnwater.tv to get more of Kate's free wild game recipes and her gourmet sauces to share with your family or friends. Good eating!

Tex-Mex Egg Rolls

Serves: 8 (2 egg rolls each)
Prep Time: 10 minutes

1 pound ground venison
1 medium onion, finely chopped
2 cloves garlic, minced
½ cup medium salsa (preferably a smoother type such as Pace Picante)
½ teaspoon chili powder
¼ teaspoon cumin
Salt and pepper
²⁄₃ cup shredded cheddar cheese
1 package egg-roll wraps
Vegetable oil
Sour cream and guacamole for serving, optional

In large skillet, cook venison, onion and garlic over medium heat until venison is no longer pink and onion has softened, stirring occasionally to break up meat. Drain grease. Add salsa, chili powder, cumin, and salt and pepper to taste. Simmer for about 5 minutes. Add cheese and stir until mixed thoroughly. Lay 1 egg-roll wrap on work surface; cover remaining wraps with plastic to keep them from drying out. Place a large spoonful of venison mixture on center of wrap and roll as directed on package. Place filled egg roll on platter and repeat with remaining ingredients.

Heat 2 inches oil to 375°F in deep fryer or large pot. Fry egg rolls, two at a time, until golden brown, about 2 minutes. Drain on paper towel–lined plate. Serve with sour cream and guacamole.

Venison Filet Wellington

Serves: 5 to 8
Prep Time: 45 minutes
Cooking Time: 10 to 15 minutes

Here's an elegant dish that will knock the socks off your deer-camp buddies. It may look complex, but it really is quite simple. From start to finish, Venison Filet Wellington will take about an hour. Read the directions at least once before preparing this dish, and you will see how quickly it comes together. Have all your ingredients ready, to make the assembly smooth and quick. Don't miss trying this recipe; it is well worth the effort.

2- to 3-pound venison loin, well trimmed
2 tablespoons clarified butter, room temperature
2 to 4 slices bacon
2 tablespoons butter
3 tablespoons olive oil
2 tablespoons chopped shallots
½ pound fresh white or straw mushrooms, finely chopped
1 egg, separated
2 tablespoons cold water
1 sheet (half of a 171 4-oz. pkg.) frozen puff pastry, thawed per
package directions
Flour for rolling out pastry
1 cup shredded fresh spinach leaves
½ cup shredded Swiss cheese
Hunter's Sauce

Heat oven to 325°F. Heat a large, heavy-bottomed skillet over medium-high heat. While skillet is heating, rub venison with clarified butter. Add loin to hot skillet and sear to a deep brown color on all sides. Transfer loin to dish and set aside to cool to room temperature. Meanwhile, add bacon to same skillet and fry until cooked but not crisp. Set aside on paper towel–lined plate.

While the loin is cooling, prepare the filling. In medium skillet, melt the 2 tablespoons butter in the oil over medium heat. Add shallots and sautî until golden, stirring constantly; don't let the shallots brown or they will become bitter. Add mushrooms and sautî until most of the liquid evaporates. Set mushroom mixture aside to cool.

Beat egg white lightly in small bowl. In another small bowl, lightly beat egg yolk and water. Set both bowls aside.

To prepare the shell, roll out pastry on lightly floured surface to a rectangle 1 to 2 inches larger on all sides than the loin. Spread cooled mushroom mixture over the pastry, leaving 1 inch clear around the edges. Layer the spinach, cheese and bacon in a thin strip over the center; the strip should be about as wide as the loin. Place loin on top of bacon. Brush edges of pastry with egg white; this will help hold the pastry shell together while it is baking. Wrap pastry around loin and crimp edges very well to seal. Turn pastry-wrapped loin over so the seam side is down. Place onto baking sheet. Brush pastry with egg yolk mixture; this will provide a beautiful glaze to the Wellington.

Bake for 10 to 15 minutes, or until pastry is golden brown. The loin should have reached an internal temperature of 130°F. Remove from oven. Slice into individual portions and serve immediately with Hunter's Sauce.

"Too Late" Venison Cutlet Gruyïre

Serves: 6
Prep Time: 10 minutes
Cooking Time: 10 to 15 minutes

One of the fun parts of hunting is naming deer stands. We have one we call "Torn Shirt" because Peter tore his shirt while putting it up. Another is named "Big View" because the stand overlooks several fields and has a . . . big view! The "Too Late" stand is near a pine-covered ridge and got its name because once the deer reach the peak of the ridge and come out from the cover to cross to the other side, it's too late. I first prepared the following tasty recipe with a buck taken from this stand.

¼ cup all-purpose flour
Salt and pepper
2 eggs
½ cup milk
3 cups seasoned bread crumbs
1 4 teaspoon garlic powder
12 venison cutlets (about 4 ounces each), pounded as needed to even thickness
½ cup olive oil (approx.)
1½ cups seasoned tomato sauce
2 large beefsteak-type tomatoes, thinly sliced
12 slices Gruyïre or Swiss cheese

Heat broiler. Place flour in large plastic food-storage bag; add salt and pepper to taste and shake well to mix. In medium bowl, beat together eggs and milk. Combine bread crumbs and garlic powder in wide, flat dish and stir to mix. Blot cutlets with paper towel.

Working with one cutlet at a time, add to bag of flour and shake to coat. Tap off excess flour, then dip floured cutlet into egg mixture. Dredge in bread crumb mixture; set aside on a plate. Repeat with remaining cutlets.

In large skillet, heat about ¼-inch of the oil over medium heat until it is hot but not smoking. Fry cutlets in batches, adding additional oil as necessary, until cutlets are golden brown on both sides and not quite done to taste; transfer cutlets to sheet pan as they are browned.

In small saucepan, heat tomato sauce over low heat; cover and keep warm. Place 1 or 2 tomato slices and 1 cheese slice on top of each cutlet. Place sheet pan under broiler just long enough to melt the cheese.

Ladle about ¼ cup warm tomato sauce on each of 6 plates and place 2 cutlets on top; or, place 2 cutlets on each plate and drizzle tomato sauce around the cutlets. Serve hot.

Venison Tamale Pie

Serves: 6
Prep Time: 20 minutes
Cooking Time: 40 minutes

Here's a dish that takes a little bit of extra time because of the cornmeal crust. But it's well worth the effort! It was during a whitetail hunting trip to south Texas that I first tasted true tamales. We were hunting at the Lazy Fork Ranch and the cook prepared many dishes native to her Mexican homeland. Although I wasn't able to get the exact recipe from her, this one comes close—and I haven't had any complaints on the receiving end when I serve it!

Filling
1 tablespoon canola oil
1 pound ground venison
4 scallions, chopped
1 can (8 ounce) tomato sauce
1 cup whole-kernel corn, drained
¼ cup chopped Anaheim peppers
¼ cup cornmeal
1 teaspoon chili powder
1 teaspoon salt
½ teaspoon pepper
½ teaspoon cumin
¼ teaspoon crumbled dried oregano leaves

Cornmeal Pie Crust
1 cup all-purpose flour, plus additional for rolling out crust
2 tablespoons cornmeal
⅓ cup vegetable shortening
3 to 4 tablespoons cold water

Topping
1 egg, lightly beaten
¼ cup evaporated milk
½ teaspoon dry mustard
1 cup shredded Monterey Jack cheese
1 cup shredded cheddar cheese
6 pitted black olives, sliced

Heat oven to 425°F.

To prepare filling: In large skillet, heat oil over medium heat. Add venison and cook until no longer pink, stirring to break up. Drain. Mix in remaining filling ingredients. Let simmer for 5 minutes, then remove from heat.

To prepare crust: In small bowl, blend together flour and cornmeal. Cut in shortening with pastry blender or two knives. When mixture resembles coarse meal

or very small peas, add water a little at a time, mixing with fork until dough is formed. Roll out pastry on floured surface until it forms a 15-inch circle. Fit pastry into deep-dish 9-inch pie pan and crimp edges.

Spoon filling into pie crust. Place pie pan on baking sheet and bake for 25 minutes. While it is baking, prepare the topping for the pie: Combine egg, milk and mustard in medium bowl; mix well. When pie has baked for 25 minutes, remove from oven, sprinkle cheeses over filling and pour milk mixture on top. Decorate with sliced olives. Return to oven and bake for an additional 5 minutes. Let stand for 10 minutes before serving. Serve with sour cream and chopped tomatoes.

Escarole Soup with Venison Meat-a-Balls

Serves: 6
Prep Time: 15 minutes
Cooking Time: 45 minutes

My mother, Lucy, introduced Kate to many different foodstuffs—escarole, broccoli rabe, scungilli and calamari, to name a few. She often reminded her about the way many Italian dishes are prepared: "Use garlic, garlic and more garlic." Both her escarole and broccoli rabe dishes started by sautîeing plenty of garlic; the greens were added as the garlic was cooking. After this, chicken broth was added to finish cooking the greens.

When Kate shared with her this venison version of her Meatball Escarole Soup, she was quite pleased, and Kate was happy that she had passed her test. Then she cautiously whispered in her ear, "But next time, use a little more garlic!"

½ cup bread crumbs
½ cup milk
1 pound ground venison
1 egg, beaten
2 tablespoons grated Parmesan cheese, plus additional for serving
1 tablespoon chopped fresh parsley
7 cloves garlic, minced, divided Salt and pepper
3 tablespoons olive oil
1 pound escarole, washed and chopped

4 cans (14½ ounces each) chicken broth
Italian bread for accompaniment, optional

In medium bowl, mix together bread crumbs and milk; let stand for about 5 minutes. Add venison, egg, Parmesan cheese, parsley, half of the garlic, and salt and pepper to taste. Mix well. Shape into small meatballs (small enough to fit on a spoon and pop into your mouth) and place on a plate. Cover and refrigerate while you prepare the rest of the soup mixture.

In large saucepot or Dutch oven, heat oil over medium-high heat. Add remaining garlic and sautî until golden; do not let it brown. Stir in escarole and continue sautîeing until escarole has wilted down.

Add chicken broth. Cover pot and simmer for about 30 minutes. Gently add meatballs to the simmering broth. Leave them untouched for a few minutes so they can set, then stir gently and continue simmering for 7 to 10 minutes longer, until the meatballs are cooked through. I always sample a meatball at about 7 minutes to see if it's done yet.

Serve hot, with grated Parmesan cheese and Italian bread.

Horseradish Cream Sauce

Yield: 1 cup
Prep Time: 10 minutes
Chilling Time: 1 hour or longer

▼ Kate takes a break in our kitchen where she often "Goes Wild" with her delicious cooking!

This makes a great dipping sauce for fondue, and also works well as a side for roasts or steaks.

1 cup heavy cream
2 scallions, minced
2 tablespoons fresh grated horseradish
¼ teaspoon paprika
$\frac{1}{8}$ teaspoon salt

In large bowl, whip cream until soft peaks form. Stir in scallions, horseradish, paprika and salt. Transfer to glass bowl and chill for 1 hour or longer to allow flavors to blend before serving.

Hunter's Sauce

Yield: 2 cups
Prep Time: 35 minutes

This classic sauce is delicious with venison roasts and pan-fried steaks.

3 tablespoons butter
1½ teaspoons vegetable oil
10 ounces fresh mushrooms, cut into quarters
3 shallots, minced
2 tablespoons all-purpose flour
1 tablespoon finely chopped scallion
2 tablespoons brandy
Salt and pepper to taste
½ cup dry white wine
1 cup brown sauce or canned beef gravy
2 tablespoons tomato sauce
1 teaspoon finely chopped fresh parsley

In small saucepan, melt butter in oil over medium heat. Add mushrooms and shallots and sautÎ until golden brown. Stir in the flour to absorb the juices. Add scallion, brandy, and salt and pepper to taste. Cook over low heat for 2 minutes. Add wine and simmer until liquid is reduced by half. Add brown sauce, tomato sauce and parsley. Heat until sauce starts to bubble, stirring occasionally. Pour into serving dish and serve hot.

Go Wild!
Kate Fiduccia